a Day's
Journey

365 Daily Meditations from the Word

Jon Courson

A Day's Journey

Published by Calvary Chapel Publishing (CCP),
a resource ministry of Calvary Chapel of Costa Mesa
3800 South Fairview Road
Santa Ana, CA 92704

Layout and Cover Design: Neil Godding

First printing, 2002

All Scripture quotations in this book, unless otherwise indicated, are taken from the KING JAMES VERSION.

ISBN: 1-931667-15-2

Printed in the United States of America.

INTRODUCTION

And there went forth a wind from the LORD, and brought quails from the sea, and let them fall by the camp...as it were a day's journey on the other side, round about the camp...

Numbers 11:31

But he himself went a day's journey into the wilderness...

I Kings 19:4

And Jonah began to enter into the city a day's journey...

Jonah 3:4

And when they had fulfilled the days, as they returned, the child Jesus tarried behind in Jerusalem; and Joseph and his mother knew not of it. But they, supposing him to have been in the company, went a day's journey...

Luke 2:43-44

Then returned they unto Jerusalem from the mount called Olivet, which is from Jerusalem a sabbath day's journey.

Acts 1:12

Whether the path before you leads 'round about the camp' of fellowship or into a solitary wilderness of testing, whether you travel to minister to the rebellious city of Nineveh or to the Holy City of Jerusalem to see Jesus and await His power, it is our prayer that these meditations from the Word will provide sustenance and light for your day's journey.

JANUARY 1

And when he had gathered all the chief priests and scribes of the people together, he demanded of them where Christ should be born. And they said unto him, In Bethlehem of Judaea...

Matthew 2:4

The results of a poll came out recently in the San Francisco Chronicle listing the ten biggest disappointments in the world of tourism...

Number one was the Polo Lounge in Hollywood where movie stars supposedly hung out. Tourists by the thousands would go into the Polo Lounge, but all they would see were other tourists. Number two was one of the casinos in Monte Carlo. Number three was Bethlehem.

Bethlehem is indeed a major disappointment for tourists because they go there expecting to see something special—but when they arrive, all they see is a somewhat dirty little city.

They go into the church of the Nativity, assuming it will be awesome. But as they walk in, they see the church itself divided into three sections: Catholic, Eastern, and Russian Orthodox because these three groups have been fighting for centuries over who should control the site. And there are objects hanging from the ceiling which look like Christmas tree ornaments in a garage sale. With church groups fighting and dusty relics hanging, no wonder Bethlehem appears to be disappointing.

But you know what? It's perfect!

You see, when Jesus was born in Bethlehem, He was born in a stable or a cave which was used as a stable. It wasn't the picturesque setting we often have in our minds. No doubt, it was dirty. There were cow pies on the ground and flies buzzing overhead. It had to be so. Jesus came to a real world as a real Man to help real people. And Bethlehem mirrors that reality.

Bethlehem—a very appropriate place for the Bread of Life to be born, for 'Bethlehem' means 'House of Bread.' Bethlehem was an unimpressive little city then and is an unimpressive little city still. But because Jesus was born there, more songs have been sung about, more poetry written about, more photographs taken of, more trips made to this insignificant little city than any other. Bethlehem is one of the best-known places in the world today for only one reason: Jesus was there.

And so too with you and me. Jesus comes into little people like us—people who are somewhat dusty and not at all that impressive—and He makes us great, not because of who we are, but because of whose we are. We are His.

JANUARY 2

And Jesus, when he was baptized, went up straightway out of the water: and lo, the heavens were opened unto him, and he saw the Spirit of God descending like a dove, and lighting upon him: And lo a voice from heaven, saying, This is my beloved Son, in whom I am well pleased.

Matthew 3:16-17

In this passage, we see a perfect picture of the Trinity—the Holy Spirit descending upon Jesus the Son as the voice of the Father is heard.

Why is the Trinity such an important concept? I struggled for many years with this question. 'Lord, why didn't You avoid this confusing Trinity concept altogether?' I asked. 'We are accused of being polytheistic. We're confused in our prayers. We get all tangled up. Why didn't You keep it simple—just You—just One?'

In recent years, however, I have come into this understanding of the Trinity, which, for me personally, has made all the difference:

God the Father, God the Son, and God the Spirit dwelt together in ages past—a billion years before years even began—perfectly content. The Father loved the Son. The Son honored the Father. The Spirit was for the Son and from the Father. The three of Them dwelt together in complete harmony, in total satisfaction. They are, and always will be, family—but They're only One.

This means God didn't need me. He went through billions and zillions of years without man, and you know what? He got along just fine.

God loves you immensely. He loves you so much that He gave His only Son to die and plunge into hell in order to redeem you. He's completely and totally in love with you—but He doesn't need you because He's absolutely fulfilled in and of Himself. And that takes all of the pressure off because when love is demanding, it isn't love.

When love is not a Trinitarian kind of love, it can become smothering and restrictive. It causes tension and anxiety. It causes one to feel caged in, cooped up, or put down; jealous or envious; used or abused.

Many of us erroneously picture God wringing His hands, pacing the clouds, worried about whether or not we're going to love Him in return. He's not. He's doing just fine. He's very happy, totally fulfilled, perfectly content. Yet He is so magnanimous and expansive that He has chosen to create us, love us, and say to us, 'Come unto Me and I will give you rest.' His request is neither a demand nor a need. It is an invitation.

Never forget that there is One who loves you who is not uptight about you or burdensome to you. And may the mystery of the Trinity give you rest in your relationship with Him.

January 3

And when the tempter came to him, he said, If thou be the Son of God, command that these stones be made bread.

Matthew 4:3

In the wilderness, there are multiplied millions of round, limestone rocks which look remarkably like little loaves of bread. No doubt, as Jesus fasted, those rocks must have taken on the appearance of bread. And Satan took advantage of this. 'If You're the Son of God, turn these stones into bread,' he hissed. 'If You're the Son of God, why are You hungry?'

Satan does the same to us when he whispers, 'If you are a child of God, where is your Father's provision? Why are those bills piling up? Why do you have need?'

'It's up to you to take care of this situation,' he insists. 'Exercise your faith. Make something happen.'

But God would have us be patient. We are His children. And He promises He will meet our needs as we pray for our daily bread. We need to wait.

I can recall when my son Peter John was just a few months old, he needed some supplemental meals. On one occasion, it was my turn to feed him his middle-of-the night bottle. But as I heated it, his cries grew louder. 'Hang on, buddy,' I said. 'The bottle's heating.'

Just then, the Lord whispered in my own heart in a way I'll never forget, 'Jon, the bottle's heating,' for that day I had been doing some screaming of my own.

Most of us want to reach the Promised Land without ever going through the wilderness. We want to get there immediately, but the Father says, 'No. There's a time of preparation. Wait. Don't panic. The bottle's heating. I will provide.'

'Lord, is it true that to You a million years is like a second?' asked the impatient man.

'Yes,' He answered.

'Wow. Is it also true that to You a million dollars is like a penny?'

'Yes,' He answered.

'Well, Father, could I have a penny?'

'Sure,' the Lord answered. 'Just a second.'

We need to realize that the Lord's timing is different from ours. Jesus knew that. He would not push or rush His Father by taking things into His own hands. He would wait. And soon—perhaps only hours later—angels would come to Him, bringing not dry little loaves of bread, but angel food cake!

How often I settle for bread because I try and do things in my own energy instead of waiting for the Father's perfect timing and the angel food cake.

JANUARY 4

But I say unto you, That ye resist not evil: but whosoever shall smite thee on thy right cheek, turn to him the other also.

Matthew 5:39

There have been those throughout history who have found that what Jesus said was potent and dynamic—that turning the other cheek actually puts one in control.

Mahatma Gandhi understood this. The entire sub-continent of India was freed from the powerful British rule because Gandhi read this verse and, although he was not a believer, he believed what Jesus said. He inspired an entire nation to turn the other cheek, and it blew the Brits away. After all, what could the British do? They could beat the people with clubs, fire guns into their midst—but not without destroying the morale of their own army in the process.

Martin Luther King Jr. found the same thing to be true. If the protestors had fought back, the US marshals would have felt justified in firing their guns indiscriminately—and the civil rights movement would have died. But peaceful resistance won out, and an entire people experienced liberation.

Jesus wasn't being a coward when He told us to turn the other cheek. On the contrary, He was sharing a very practical and potent principle: the one who controls the situation is the one who doesn't fight back.

In your family, at work, in your neighborhood, at school, take the words of Jesus literally. Don't fight back. You won't be a wimp. You'll be a winner.

JANUARY 5

Therefore I say unto you, Take no thought for your life, what ye shall eat, or what ye shall drink: nor yet for your body, what ye shall put on.

Matthew 6:25

Does this mean we should live recklessly? No. The word 'thought' implies anxious thought or worry. The word 'worry' literally means 'to strangle.' If you're worried about what you're wearing or eating—about what you have or don't have materially—your personality will be tied in knots and strangled.

It doesn't take much to strangle us. Even minor things worry us and sometimes destroy us. I read that it takes 60 trillion droplets of fog to cover 7 city blocks. Sixty trillion droplets or seven city blocks worth of fog can close down airports and tie up traffic. Yet if you condensed those 60 trillion fog droplets, you would end up with only half a glass of water.

That's a perfect picture of what worry is all about. You begin with something little—only half a glass of water—but you start thinking about it and wrestling with it, wondering, 'How is this going to work out? How am I going to do that?' And pretty soon, you can't see straight, and your airport is shut down. You're not hearing from the Lord, and you're not soaring with the Lord as you once did because you're all fogged in.

That is why Jesus said, 'Don't take any anxious thought whatsoever.' Don't let worry strangle you. Don't end up in a fog.

JANUARY 6

Therefore whosoever heareth these sayings of mine, and doeth them, I will liken him unto a wise man, which built his house upon a rock...

Matthew 7:24

Here is the familiar story of two men building houses. Both men used the same material. Both built in the same geographical location. But one man's house stood while the other man's house collapsed. The difference was in the foundations. One built on rock, the other on sand.

In Palestine, all land becomes parched in the summer, causing even the sandy and unstable areas to appear rock-solid. The true test doesn't come until the rain falls. Thus, Jesus is saying, 'Be careful where you build your house. Build on something tried and true. Don't take a chance. Build upon the Rock.'

Who is the one who builds his house upon the rock?
The one who hears the words of the Lord and does them.

Who is the one who builds his house upon the sand?
The one who hears His words but doesn't do them.

One of the great dangers for us who love the Scriptures is to think that hearing is equivalent to doing, to erroneously conclude that because we hear the truth and agree with the truth, we are automatically practicing the truth. But we are like the foolish man until we say, 'Your words are right, Lord, and I am purposing to obey You now. By Your grace, have mercy upon me, and help me to change my ways.'

The wise man not only hears Jesus' words but also puts them into practice. And his house stands when even the fiercest storm comes.

January 7

And, behold, a woman, which was diseased with an issue of blood twelve years, came behind him, and touched the hem of his garment: For she said within herself, If I may but touch his garment, I shall be whole.

Matthew 9:20-21

In Matthew's day, it was believed that there was certain power in the hem of a garment belonging to a rabbi or spiritual leader.

'If I could just touch the hem of his garment...'

This woman probably didn't have the strength to wrestle Him in faith or to grab hold of Him in unbelief. Yet she knew if she could even just lightly touch Jesus, she would be healed.

Perhaps you say, 'I would love to have Jesus touch me, but I don't feel His touch.'

Then be like this woman. If you're not feeling His hand upon your life, reach out and touch Him. Have you made the effort to press through the crowd of unbelief, of busyness, of entertainment, of activities—the crowd of all those things which are blocking you from Him? Press through and say, 'I just want to touch the hem of His garment. I know if I can touch Him, I'll be helped.'

This woman expended the energy to break through the crowd and touch Jesus.

Was her theology correct?
No.

Was her knowledge complete?
No.

She was most probably acting out of superstition. Yet the Lord didn't say, 'Since your theology is all messed up, I won't help you.' No, He's a Savior who heeds the cries of His children, even though their phrases are amiss or their theology's not right.

'Daughter,' Jesus said—a term He used for no other in Scripture—'be of good comfort; thy faith hath made thee whole.'

God never fails to honor the one who is desperate to touch Him.

JANUARY 8

Take my yoke upon you...
Matthew 11:29

Tekton, the word translated 'carpenter' in Matthew 13 to describe Joseph, is the word we use for a finish carpenter rather than a framer. Tradition has it that the carpenter shop where Jesus worked with His father, Joseph, specialized in making yokes.

Because there was always a lead ox yoked together with one who would follow, the yoke was designed in such a way that the lead ox would pull the greater weight. Thus, Jesus used an analogy illustrated daily in His trade and clearly understood by those who listened to Him when He said, 'Yoke with Me. Let Me be the Lead Ox. Don't try and figure out or change My direction. Let Me lead you.'

A story is told of a battleship cruising the Atlantic off the northern coast of Maine. One stormy evening, the Commander was notified.

'Sir, there's a light ahead. Oncoming vessel.'
'Signal the oncoming vessel to change his course ten degrees to the west,' ordered the Commander.

The message was sent.
But a light flashed back, 'Change *your* course ten degrees to the east.'

'Signal again. Change *your* course ten degrees to the west. I am an Admiral!' barked the Commander.

The light flashed back, 'Change *your* course ten degrees to the east. I am a Seaman Third Class.'

By this time, the Admiral was incensed as he thundered, 'Signal again. Change *your* course ten degrees to the west. I am a battleship.'

And the Seaman Third Class transmitted the message which would settle the altercation completely and decisively when he said, 'Change *your* course ten degrees to the east. I am a lighthouse.'

As we impudently and impetuously say to the Lord, 'Lord, let's go my way,' He answers:

'No, we're going My way.'

> I am the Lighthouse.
> I am the Light of the world,
> The Rock of your salvation,
> The Creator and Sustainer of your soul.
> I am the Alpha and the Omega,
> The One who knows the beginning from the end.
> Trust Me.

JANUARY 9

Again, the kingdom of heaven is like unto treasure hid in a field; the which when a man hath found, he hideth, and for joy thereof goeth and selleth all that he hath, and buyeth that field.

Matthew 13:44

In this parable, a man finds treasure and immediately buys the field in order to gain the treasure hidden therein.

You may have heard this parable taught like this: the treasure in the field is Jesus. The man is us. Therefore, like the man who found the treasure, when we discover Jesus, we should sell everything in order to follow Him.

I believe this is an improper interpretation. Instead, I believe we are the treasure and Jesus is the man.

After all, when you got saved, how many of you sold everything to follow Jesus? None of us did that.

> *But as many as received him, to them gave he power to become the sons of God, even to them that believe on his name: Which were born, not of blood, nor of the will of the flesh, nor of the will of man, but of God.*
>
> *John 1:12-13*

We were born again not by our will, not by our efforts, not even by our desire, but by God. God saved us; God elected us; God predestined us.

> *For God so loved the world, that He gave His only begotten Son, that whosoever believeth in Him should not perish, but have everlasting life.*
>
> *John 3:16*

We didn't sell anything to receive Him.
He gave His life to purchase us.

Why was the field—the world—purchased?
Did the Lord want another planet?
No.
He wanted the treasure which was buried in the world.
He wanted *you.*

JANUARY 10

> *But the ship was now in the midst of the sea, tossed with waves: for the wind was contrary.*
>
> *Matthew 14:24*

Why does God allow storms?

Scripture seems to indicate two reasons...

First, there are storms of correction. Ask Jonah about them. If we're out of the Lord's will, He will use a storm to get us back to where we need to be. Storms of correction discipline us.

Secondly, there are storms of perfection which develop us. In this passage, the disciples were obeying Jesus' command to go to the other side of the Sea of Galilee. This was not a storm to correct them, but to perfect them. In this storm, it was as if Jesus was saying, 'I want to test you now. I've been teaching you. I've been with you. And now I want you to exercise your faith to go through this storm.'

Faith is not believing in spite of the evidence. Faith is obeying in spite of the consequence. Faith is developed through struggle. Faith says, 'I will do what the Lord says even though it might mean a storm is headed my way. Even though there will be difficulties, obstacles, and challenges; even though it may be brutal and difficult; even though I must struggle, I will obey.'

Jesus was on the mountain praying for His boys (Matthew 14:23). And He's praying for you. When He sees the pressure get too great, He will come to you just as He came to them. In the meantime, allow the storm you may be facing to accomplish His loving work in your life.

January 11

And when his disciples were come to the other side, they had forgotten to take bread. Then Jesus said unto them, Take heed and beware of the leaven of the Pharisees and of the Sadducees. And they reasoned among themselves saying, It is because we have taken no bread.

Matthew 16:5-7

When Jesus talked about the leaven of the Pharisees and Sadducees, His disciples assumed He was speaking on a material level about something physical rather than something spiritual. This happened throughout the Gospels. Whenever Jesus spoke of a spiritual realm, people always confused it with the material world.

In John 3, Jesus said, 'You must be born again.'

'How does a man enter into his mother's womb the second time?' asked Nicodemus. Jesus was speaking spiritually, but Nicodemus was trying to figure it out physically.

In John 4, Jesus said, 'I have water to give you which if you drink you shall never thirst again.'

'Give me this water,' said the woman at the well, 'so I won't have to keep drawing water from the well.' She was thinking materially, but Jesus was speaking about the water of the Spirit internally.

In John 6, Jesus said, 'Unless you eat of My body and drink of My blood, you can have no part of Me.'

The crowds, thinking He was talking about cannibalism, began to turn away from Him. Again, He was speaking of the spiritual realm, but the people couldn't see past the material realm.

Jesus' desire is to free us from this material, physical world in which we're so caught up. He longs for us to gain an eternal, spiritual perspective. But, like the disciples, we so easily get hung up in the material realm. Even in our spiritual walk, we often count our blessings only in corporeal terms and recognize only those miracles we see physically.

But because only the spiritual realm is eternal, let us be those who look for Him spiritually as well as physically, to look for His work in our hearts as well as His provision for our needs.

JANUARY 12

And after six days Jesus taketh Peter, James, and John his brother, and bringeth them up into an high mountain apart.

Matthew 17:1

Scripture records three times that Jesus took Peter, James, and John apart from the others to minister to them in very definite and special ways. Interestingly, each of those occasions dealt with death.

The first time Jesus singled out Peter, James, and John, He took them into the house of Jairus, whose daughter had died. After moving out the mockers, Jesus brought the young girl back to life, and Peter, James, and John saw that He was victorious *over* death.

On a second occasion, Jesus would take them into a garden called Gethsemane. As He prayed, 'Father, if it be possible, let this cup pass from Me. Nevertheless, not My will but thine be done,' Peter, James, and John would understand that He was submitted *to* death.

And here in Matthew 17, Jesus takes the three up the mountain where they will see Him glorified *in* death.

I believe Peter, James, and John needed these special times of instruction concerning death because these three apostles would each have very unique encounters with death.

Peter would be the first disciple to be told of his death. In John 21, Jesus said, 'Peter, they're going to stretch out your hands and carry you where you don't want to go.' And that is exactly what happened when Peter was crucified upside down.

James was the first disciple put to death—sawed in half lengthwise by his persecutors.

John was the last of the disciples to die. Banished to the seemingly God-forsaken island of Patmos, it was a 90-year-old John who received the Book of Revelation.

The Lord uniquely prepared Peter, James, and John for what each of them would face. And He will do the same for you. He will prepare you through Bible studies, radio programs, friends, and books for what lies ahead for you personally. It's amazing to me how I'll study something or hear something only to discover a week later that a situation arises in which I need that exact information.

Remain sensitive to His voice and then see the Lord's faithfulness in lovingly preparing you for what lies ahead.

JANUARY 13

And the multitudes that went before, and that followed, cried, saying, Hosanna to the Son of David: Blessed is he that cometh in the name of the Lord; Hosanna in the highest.

Matthew 21:9

Because the word 'Hosanna' means 'Save now,' the crowd was essentially saying,

'Overthrow the Roman yoke politically. Save Now!'
'Help us economically. Save Now!'
'Lead us militarily. Save Now!'

No wonder that, as the week went on and they realized none of that was His intent, they turned against Jesus.

I see the same thing happen today. I listened as a young man sat in my office a few days ago and said, 'Since I became a Christian, my brother contracted a disease. I prayed for him, but nothing happened. My parents have been down on me ever since you baptized me a few summers ago. My friends no longer want to hang out with me. I don't sense God is using me. And so, even though I know Jesus is real, even though I know there's a heaven, I'm choosing not to walk with Him.'

I tried to reason with him, spent time talking with him, and cried for him. I know the Lord is not through with him. But I was reminded once again that the tendency is within the heart of each of us to cash it in when things don't work out. Once we were in church on Sunday singing, 'Hosanna. Bless the Lord, O my soul.' But then something—or a series of things—went wrong, and our songs turned to sighs.

If you are expecting Jesus to be a 'good luck charm' for you, if you expect Him to help you financially or physically, socially or vocationally, you will be disappointed when things don't go the way you thought they should or hoped they would.

We need to realize that Jesus Christ came to die for our sin and to pay the price for our iniquity. If He never does anything else in this life presently, that is more than enough to merit our loyalty, our affection, our devotion. If He never does another thing for me, if He never gives another blessing to me, I owe Him my life because of what He did on Calvary.

JANUARY 14

Jesus said unto him, Thou shalt love the Lord thy God with all thy heart, and with all thy soul, and with all thy mind. This is the first and great commandment. And the second is like unto it, Thou shalt love thy neighbor as thyself.

Matthew 22:37-39

The phrase 'like unto it' means 'linked to it.' In other words, the first and second commandments are inextricably linked together. The problem is, most of us separate the two because we have a 'TV Dinner spirituality.'

TV dinners have the entrée, peas, mashed potatoes, and the cherry dessert all in separate compartments. And that's just what we do spiritually.

'Oh, yes, I love God,' we say. 'I'm going to worship Sunday night.' But on Monday, we call our boss an idiot behind his back, and on Wednesday, we complain about how our neighbor idles his car too early in the morning. Yet Sunday finds us worshipping the Lord once again. We compartmentalize our lives, thinking that how we treat people has nothing to do with our relationship with God.

Jesus says our walk with God is not a TV Dinner. Rather, if we really love God, we will inevitably love people, and our walk will resemble not a TV Dinner, but a Chicken Pot Pie. No longer compartmentalized, the peas, potatoes, and chicken will all be mixed together.

Truly, if our love for God is genuine, it cannot help but flow into a love for people.

JANUARY 15

Now when Jesus was in Bethany, in the house of Simon the leper, there came unto him a woman having an alabaster box of very precious ointment, and poured it on his head, as he sat at meat.

Matthew 26:6-7

We know from John's Gospel that this woman was none other than Mary, the sister of Martha. She is seen three times in Scripture— each time at the feet of Jesus, for Mary was a worshipper. And her example speaks volumes.

When do you really become a worshipper? When you're broken. When you're finally at wits' end, when suddenly things aren't going smoothly, you humble yourself before the Lord and worship Him.

Worship not only comes from brokenness, but true worship is often costly. According to John's record, it cost Mary 300 pence, or one year's salary. What does worship cost you and me? Our image. Just as Judas would question Mary's act of worship, there will be those who say to us, 'Quit trying to be so holy. Do something more practical.'

However, although worship can be costly and misunderstood, worship is always beneficial. After Mary wiped the feet of Jesus with her hair, guess what happened? Her hair took on the same fragrance as Jesus' feet. That's what worship does. When you worship the Lord, you take on the fragrance of the Lord. Not only that, but John tells us that after Mary broke the alabaster box, the entire house was filled with the aroma of the ointment.

Mom and dad—does your house stink? Is there tension in the air? Is your marriage on the rocks? Are your kids falling apart? Take Mary's mindset. Gather your family together and say, 'Let's stop and seek the Lord's blessing for a few minutes.' The key isn't always counseling or child-rearing classes. As helpful as those things might be, the real power lies at Jesus' feet.

JANUARY 16

When Jesus understood it, he said unto them, Why trouble ye the woman? for she hath wrought a good work upon me. For ye have the poor always with you; but me ye have not always. For in that she hath poured this ointment on my body, she did it for my burial.

Matthew 26:10-12

In Jesus' time, bodies were anointed after burial in order to reduce the stench of putrefaction. However, Mary anointed His body *before* He died because, just as David prophesied, she knew He would not see corruption, or putrefaction (Psalm 49:9). She knew He would rise again.

How did Mary know this? Peter didn't understand it. John didn't get it. Thomas, Andrew, and Nathanael—they all missed it. Why did Mary understand what Jesus was saying? She didn't spend nearly as much time in His physical presence as the disciples. She didn't hear all of His teaching as they had. She hadn't climbed the Mount of Transfiguration with them. Yet she had an understanding of what was really going on.

How? Revelation and adoration are intricately linked together. When you're at the feet of Jesus Christ in worship, you see things that others don't. You understand things others miss.

The most beautiful statue I've ever seen is a life-size granite carving of Jesus by Danish sculptor Thors Walden. Walden sculpted the body of Christ in such a way that you can't see His face from a standing position. A sign next to the statue reads:

> If you want to see the face of Jesus,
> You must sit at His feet.

And sure enough, when you sit at the foot of the statue and look up, you can see His face perfectly.

To you who feel like you don't see the Lord in your home, at your school, in your situation, my question is: how long has it been since you've sat at His feet?

JANUARY 17

And the chief priests took the silver pieces, and said, It is not lawful for to put them into the treasury, because it is the price of blood. And they took counsel, and bought with them the potter's field, to bury strangers in.

Matthew 27:6-7

What was a potter's field?

In Bible times, if a potter discovered cracks or chips in something he had made, he would throw the marred vessel outside of his shop.

Over time, this area would become full of broken pottery. Because nothing could grow there, it was good for nothing except to use as a cemetery for strangers and travelers who had no other place to be buried.

Think with me for a moment...

The blood money of Jesus Christ was used to buy the place where broken pottery and dead bodies were. That's just what we are: shattered, dead, and good for nothing.

What hope is there for broken pottery?

Only this: if it can be heated hot enough and placed back in water once again, it will again become usable and redeemable.

So too if we as broken pieces of pottery become,

 Heated by the trials the Lord allows *in* us,
  Warmed by the love He has *for* us, and
   Washed by the water of the Word He gives *to* us,

we begin to be re-shaped and used for His glory.

JANUARY 18

When the even was come, there came a rich man of Arimathaea, named Joseph, who also himself was Jesus' disciple: He went to Pilate, and begged the body of Jesus.

          Matthew 27:57-58

John tells us that Nicodemus accompanied Joseph of Arimathaea. Both Nicodemus and Joseph were secret disciples of Jesus. What were they risking by burying the body of Jesus? Everything. They could easily have been sentenced to death for siding with this One who was crucified. They surely would have lost their prominent positions in the temple and in society.

We often hear Nicodemus and Joseph of Arimathaea criticized for being secret disciples. But I submit this for your consideration: the prominent boys who walked on water and did miracles—Peter, James, and John—where were they? They were hiding. They had split. It was the secret disciples—Nicodemus and Joseph—who were at the Cross, ministering to the body of their Lord.

Perhaps you feel like you don't do much. You don't walk on water very often. You haven't healed a whole lot of lepers lately. You're not on a worship team. You're not real vocal on the job about your belief in Christ. Listen—like Joseph and Nicodemus, you'll have your opportunity. Quite frankly, I think that sometimes the secret disciples are the ones who really shine when the way gets dark. The quiet ones, the unknown ones, are often the strongest and the toughest.

So it was with Joseph and Nicodemus. Their moment had arrived. Yours will too.

JANUARY 19

And as they went to tell his disciples, behold, Jesus met them, saying, All hail.

Matthew 28:9

'All hail' was a very common expression. Slang of the day, it simply meant, 'Hi.'

I like that! When the women came to the tomb, their doctrine was all wrong. They thought Jesus was dead. But guess who came to them? Jesus Christ Himself because, although they were doctrinally wrong, they were devotionally right.

I am convinced that a lot of us take pride in our doctrine when the Lord is saying, 'What I desire is your affection.' We are committed to precepts *about* Christ, but are we committed to the Person *of* Christ? Many believers are doctrinally right—but they're dead right because their doctrine is devoid of devotion.

And so I say to you today, that even if your knowledge is limited or if your doctrine is not perfectly accurate—if your affection for Him is real, Jesus will appear to you time and time again, saying, 'All hail...Hi!'

JANUARY 20

And Judas Iscariot, which also betrayed him: and they went into an house.

Mark 3:19

Would you have chosen Judas? More importantly, would you have called him 'Friend' even as he betrayed you? (Matthew 26:50).

Yet, with the exception of Judas, Jesus' disciples became men who did indeed turn the world upside down because of His Spirit within them. This means that when Jesus chose you and me, He knew we would also be changed and eventually impact the world both now and eternally. He chose us not because of who we are, but because of who He sees we can be.

When I make choices, sometimes they're good; sometimes they're bad. Why? Because my knowledge is limited. God, however, has no limitations on what He knows. If my knowledge was limitless like God's, I would buy a lottery ticket. Because I would know exactly which numbers to choose, it wouldn't be gambling, but a wise investment. So too, God picks winners.

You might feel like a loser. You might even be called a loser by those around you. But the fact that you were chosen by God, who sees the big picture, means you are a winner.

We need to realize that everyone who names the name of Jesus—regardless of her personality, or of the doctrines he may embrace—is a winner because they have been chosen by Him. And we need to treat each other accordingly.

JANUARY 21

And he was in the hinder part of the ship, asleep on a pillow: and they awake him, and say unto him, Master, carest thou not that we perish?

Mark 4:38

If Jesus is in your boat, it can't sink. If He's in your life, you won't go down. He has promised to complete the good work He has done in you (Philippians 1:6). And though the storm might rage, causing you to say, 'Master, don't You care that I'm perishing?' He's not worried. He's sleeping—not in apathy, but with great security.

'The Lord thy God in the midst of thee is mighty,' Zephaniah tells us. 'He will rest in His love' (Zephaniah 3:17). Thus, concerning the storm you may be going through even now or perhaps will face tomorrow, the Lord is not wondering if you're going to make it. He's resting in His love. He knows He's going to see you through. Therefore, if Jesus is at rest, you can rest as well.

JANUARY 22

And he departed, and began to publish in Decapolis how great things Jesus had done for him: and all men did marvel.

Mark 5:20

There are three prayers offered in the first half of Mark 5.

'Let us go into the pigs,' the demons cried.
And Jesus said, 'Go.'

'Leave our region,' said the Gadarenes.
And Jesus left.

'I want to follow You,' said the previously-demonized man.
'No,' Jesus said.

When you and I wage war spiritually, when you and I petition and pray perhaps reverently, we must remember, even as this story illustrates so dramatically, that Jesus can say, 'No,' and 'No' is just as much an answer as 'Yes.' In fact, 'No' is sometimes what God reserves especially for those He loves.

Why?

In the case before us, Jesus answered the prayers of the demons and of an unbelieving, cynical, hostile society. But He answered the prayer of a believer not in the way which affirmed his request, but rather changed his course. No doubt, this once-demonized man was disappointed initially, but he realized he must keep the directive of his Deliverer and thus returned to speak to his community. And church history records the group of believers which began to surface in the region. The Church had a powerful expression in the area—most likely birthed by the man Jesus sent home.

Take hope, dear friend. Your prayers not being answered in the way you desire are not indicative of God not hearing or not caring—for He only said 'No' to the one who loved Him.

JANUARY 23

And when Jesus was passed over again by ship unto the other side, much people gathered unto him...

Mark 5:21

Of the crowd gathered around Jesus, Mark will draw attention to two...

The most visible member of the community, Jairus, was famous.
The woman was anonymous.

Jairus was wealthy.
The woman lived in poverty.

Jairus was the leader of the synagogue.
Because of her physical condition, the woman was forbidden from entering the synagogue.

For 12 years, as his daughter grew, the house of Jairus was filled with laughter and joy.
For 12 years, the house of the woman was filled with despair and misery.

And so these two people—at opposite ends of life's spectrum—waited for Jesus.

Like Jairus, you might be riding high. Your business might be booming. Your marriage might be blessed. Your family might be growing. Your body might be healthy. But you don't know what the next moment holds. Before the clock strikes midnight tonight, you might find yourself totally, unexpectedly in the middle of a major tragedy. You and I do not know what the next moment holds. You who are Jairuses here tonight, realize this: like this man, the next moment might bring tragedy into your world.

Conversely, you who, like the woman, have either been going through an endless stream of setbacks or one persistent problem, don't know what the next hour holds. The next moment might bring you a miracle of astounding proportion.

Pondering this keeps me from complacency when I feel like I'm in Jairus' sandals, and from despairing when it seems like I'm standing in the woman's shoes. Both of their stories remind me that the Lord is my Shield and my Protector. And if He allows difficulty, setback, or tragedy to come into my life, He will also be my Glory and the Lifter of my head (Psalm 3:3).

JANUARY 24

And when he was come into the house, his disciples asked him privately, Why could not we cast him out? And he said unto them, This kind can come forth by nothing, but by prayer and fasting.

Mark 9:28-29

'This kind of problem will not be solved by sharing pearls of wisdom, trying to be a better dad, or following some family program,' Jesus told them. 'This kind of spiritual warfare is won only through fasting and prayer.'

'How did we have time to fast and pray?' the disciples might have wondered. After all, they certainly didn't know this problem would be laid at their feet that day. But that's the point. We never know when the moment for miraculous ministry will come our way or be needed in our families. Therefore, we must maintain a life of prayer and fasting because when the demonized boy is before you, it's too late to start.

Why were the disciples not maintaining a habit of prayer and fasting? I wonder if it wasn't due in part to the fact that they might have been feeling sorry for themselves. 'Thanks a lot, Lord,' they could have thought. 'You take Peter, James, and John—your favorites—up on the mountain. They see You shine. They hear the voice from heaven. They get to see Elijah and Moses. Us? We're down here at the bottom, forsaken and forgotten.' If so, how like us they would have been.

So often we think, 'I never am called to sing or to teach Bible studies. So why should I fast or pray?' And because we feel we're not important or useful, we give up. But once a year, once every five years, once in a lifetime an opportunity comes our way which is essential, important—an opportunity to move in the miraculous, to see salvation. Something exceedingly important could take place—but we're impotent and powerless because we haven't been praying, fasting, reading the Word, or seeking the Lord.

As a father, I have no other recourse than to maintain a life of prayer and fasting because I never know when the enemy will strike one of my kids. He has; he does; he will. And as a believer, I have no other recourse than to maintain a close walk with God because I never know the next conversation which will open up with a neighbor at the grocery store or in the park which will impact them for eternity.

'But I've never been used,' you say. Ah, but you might have the greatest opportunity for earth-shaking, life-changing ministry in the next moment or the next day. Therefore, be ready.

January 25

But many that are first shall be last; and the last first.

Mark 10:31

This statement runs crosscurrent to that which our culture propagates. Our society is becoming increasingly competitive in its orientation. And yet those who win society's competition seem to be increasingly disillusioned with the prize. That is, people who get to the top often find the top isn't what they thought it would be. This explains why top athletes, for example, often find themselves being sucked into the drug scene. They got the prize—but the prize was too small.

Jesus comes on the scene and calls us away from competition. How does this work out practically? In your mind's eye, travel back 2,000 years ago to a place called Bethesda where you see hundreds of people with all sorts of physical ailments positioned around a pool of water. Why are they there? The understanding of the day was that the first one in the water after an angel supposedly stirred it would be healed. Consequently, these blind, lame, hurting people jockeyed for position in order that they might be first in the pool.

But what does Jesus do when He arrives at Bethesda?

He finds a lame man seemingly at the back of the pack and says, 'Do you want to be made whole?'

'I have no man to help me into the water,' the man answers. 'I don't have a network. I don't have the skills. My college education is outdated. I don't have connections. How can I compete in this culture? I have no one to help me.'

This man had no stock options. He wasn't a member of the health club, not on the city softball team. He wasn't competitive. Yet, he and he alone captured Jesus' attention that day.

'Arise,' Jesus said. 'Take up your bed. I'm freeing you from this pool of competition.' And the man was healed (John 5:8).

I believe Jesus says the same thing to us today.

Maybe you've been jockeying, struggling, planning, conniving, attempting to get the edge, to make it happen, to get ahead financially, relationally, or even ministerially. If so, I encourage you to take a mental trip to Bethesda and be reminded again that the paradox of the Kingdom is that the first shall be last and the last first.

JANUARY 26

And whosoever of you will be the chiefest, shall be servant of all. For even the Son of man came not to be ministered unto, but to minister, and to give his life a ransom for many.

Mark 10:44-45

The easiest way to know if you're a servant is by how you react when people treat you like one.

All too often, I'm afraid, my heart is, 'Yes, Lord; I want to be a servant as long as people realize I'm serving. I want to be a slave as long as I become Slave of the Year.' If you're gladly slaving in the nursery, in the kitchen, or in the Sunday school class without being noticed, appreciated, or thanked—yours is the heart of a true servant.

Does the Lord want us to be slaves because He likes to see us grovel? No, it's because He's preparing us for the Kingdom—for the next billion years—and He knows that the best exercise for strengthening your heart is stooping down to pick up someone else.

The best workout you'll ever have is to serve others, because in serving, your heart is strengthened. Others might not acknowledge you. You might not be rewarded presently. But when you move into the Kingdom, when the Lord says, 'Well done, good and faithful servant. Enter into the joy of the Father,'—you'll do so with a large heart and a huge capacity to enjoy eternity.

If you want to rule, become a slave. It's a paradox indeed—but it's true.

JANUARY 27

For verily I say unto you, That whosoever shall say unto this mountain, Be thou removed, and be thou cast into the sea; and shall not doubt in his heart, but shall believe that those things which he saith shall come to pass; he shall have whatsoever he saith.

Mark 11:22

Did Jesus tell us to *pray* that the problem, obstacle, or mountain which looms menacingly before us might be removed? No. Did He tell us to *study* the Word that it might be removed? No. He said, '*Say* to the mountain be thou removed, and it will be cast into the sea.'

We often hear that prayer changes things. But that's not entirely true. *Faith* changes things. Prayer changes *us*. Jesus didn't say, 'If you encounter a mountain, pray that it might be gone.' No, He said, 'Have faith in God and then verbally, audibly tell the mountain to be removed. Speak faith.'

Why is verbalization so important? Why did Jesus tell us to speak aloud to the mountain? Why does Paul tell us to confess with our mouth that Jesus is Lord (Romans 10:9-10)? Why does the writer of

Hebrews tell us that when a promise is given to us, we are to boldly speak it out (Hebrews 13:6)? Because that's when faith kicks in. It's easy for me to think quietly or pray inwardly for the mountain to be moved, because then if it doesn't move, no one will know I prayed otherwise. There's no step of faith, no risk involved if I don't speak.

What mountain is it which intimidates you? Fear concerning an unsaved child? Depression over a business about to go under? Worry about a diseased body or a broken heart?

Jesus tells you and me to go on record in the ears of our kids, our parents, our peers, and our co-workers and to say, 'Be gone.' After all, it was as Jesus did so Himself in the ears of His disciples that the stage was set for them to believe (Mark 11:14).

Maybe you're praying intensely and hoping passionately that a certain problem or a certain situation will somehow be solved. But the fact is, Jesus said it's not enough to simply hope or even to pray. Rather, to whatever mountain intimidates or discourages you, you must say in faith verbally, 'Be gone. Be removed. Be cast into the sea.' And then watch what happens.

JANUARY 28

And as they sat and did eat, Jesus said, Verily I say unto you, One of you which eateth with me shall betray me. And they began to be sorrowful, and to say unto him one by one, Is it I? and another said, Is it I?
Mark 14:18-19

Only a few days previously, the disciples had argued over who was the greatest (Mark 9:34). At that time, Jesus was not in their midst. Like the disciples, whenever Jesus is not in our midst, we start arguing over our position, our importance, and our greatness.

But now, in the presence of Jesus, their attitude changes radically. They're not asking 'Who's the greatest?' They're asking, 'Will I be the one to deny You?'

True humility is always the result of true intimacy with Jesus Christ. If I am close to the Lord at any given moment, rather than boasting of my greatness, I'll be aware of my weakness and His graciousness.

'Woe unto you,' said Isaiah the prophet to all of the nations round about Israel in Chapters 1-5 of the book which bears his name. But when he saw the Lord high and lifted up, he said, 'Woe is *me*' (Isaiah 6:5, emphasis mine).

If we are those who are either overtly or secretly saying, 'Woe to you; woe to you; woe to you,' it's probably because we haven't seen the Lord as clearly as we should, for once we see Him, we see how sinful and unworthy we are ourselves and find ourselves joining the disciples in asking, 'Is it I, Lord? Could I be the one who sells You out? Could I be the one who turns my back? Could I be the one who walks away?'

JANUARY 29

And the veil of the temple was rent in twain from the top to the bottom.

Mark 15:38

In rending the massive veil in the temple which kept everyone but the high priest from going into the Holy of Holies where the Shekinah—the visible presence of God—dwelt, the Father declared, 'Open House! You can come boldly into My presence anytime you want because the price has been paid once and for all.'

This grace is free, but it's not cheap. It cost Jesus everything to open the way to the Father. Therefore, don't sew the veil back up, gang, with legalism, rules, regulations, or expectations. Don't feel as though you must prove something to God before you can come into His presence to present your petitions or to enjoy His fellowship.

Believers do this in subtle ways, like saying, 'Before we can enter into the glory of God, we must spend time praising Him.' Not true. The way is open. Nothing else remains to be done. Am I discounting the importance of praise? Of course not. Praise allows us to be refreshed in our knowledge of who the Lord is and what He's done. While the Lord is indeed enthroned upon the praises of His people, praise is not a prerequisite to fellowship. Neither is confession.

As valid as both of these elements are, we can come boldly into the presence of God not because of our ability to articulate confession or express praise, but solely because of what Jesus did on Calvary.

JANUARY 30

And when the centurion, which stood over against him, saw that he so cried out, and gave up the ghost, he said, Truly this man was the Son of God.

Mark 15:39

It was in the Lord's death that the centurion found life.
It was in the time of darkness that he saw the light.

'Lord,' we cry, 'if you loved Me enough to die for me, if the veil was rent to open the way for me, then why am I going through this difficulty, this tragedy?'

'Because there are centurions watching,' He declares. 'And they will see My light in your dark days.'

Dear saint, if you want to be used by God, there is no other way than to go through disappointment, difficulty, and pain in order that people might relate to you, observe you, and see by the reality of Jesus in your life that He truly is the Son of God.

People are not convinced of His reality when they see us sailing through easy times and prosperous days. Such times cause only envy and cynicism. When people are truly touched is when they see us navigating adversity and difficulty all the while trusting the Lord (II Corinthians 1:4).

This centurion was won, saved, and converted not because he was one of the 5,000 eating bread and fish in the sunlight, but because he saw Jesus in the darkness.

JANUARY 31

Now when Jesus was risen early the first day of the week, he appeared first to Mary Magdalene, out of whom he had cast seven devils. And she went and told them that had been with him, as they mourned and wept. And they, when they had heard that he was alive, and had been seen of her, believed not.

Mark 16:9

So deeply had they loved Jesus that, after three days, these rugged fishermen were still weeping with convulsive sobs. But when Mary Magdalene reported that He was alive, what did they do? They went right back to weeping. Why? Because of the thief of unbelief.

Maybe you're weeping tonight because your body is hurting, your business is collapsing, or your relationships are eroding. In reality, however, none of those are the source of your tears. Because the living Lord has said to you everything is working together for good, because He has said we are to give thanks in all things, because He has given us promise after promise that He is with us and will never forsake us, it is neither your job, marriage, family, finances, or health which cause your tears. It is unbelief. Period.

If the disciples had believed at that moment, like Mary, they would have moved into ecstasy. But they chose not to believe and remained in their sorrow longer than they had to, allowing the thief of unbelief to rob them of their joy.

It has been rightly said that a little faith will get you to heaven, but a larger faith will bring heaven to you. Indeed, you will experience heaven in your heart to the degree that you have faith that the Lord is alive, that He's faithful, and that everything is working out exactly as He promised.

FEBRUARY 1

Glory to God in the highest, and on earth peace, good will toward men.

Luke 2:14

Linguistically, the meaning of this first Christmas carol is, 'Peace on earth towards men of good will, towards men who are in God's will.'

'This is the will of God,' Jesus said, 'that you believe on Him whom the Father hath sent' (John 6). If you believe on Him whom the Father hath sent, if you believe on Jesus, you will indeed be one who, regardless of what's happening around you externally, will experience a peace in your heart internally.

Don't let anyone take that peace from you by implying that you should be doing more or trying harder. Instead say, 'Thank You, Lord, for the good news of great joy that unto me is born a Savior. I embrace this and I thank You for the peace I experience not because of what I've done, but because of what You did in coming to earth to die for me.'

I never tire of talking about the simplicity of the Gospel because I have discovered that it is constantly being challenged. Perhaps even subconsciously, we find ourselves saying, 'It can't be that simple. Surely I am supposed to do something, to earn something, to prove something.' But such is not the case.

'It is *finished*,' Jesus declared on the Cross (John 19:30). Therefore, all that remains for you to do is to love Him with all your heart, soul, mind, and strength in response to the goodness, grace, and lovingkindness He pours out upon you.

February 2

...And saw two ships standing by the lake: but the fishermen were gone out of them, and were washing their nets.

Luke 5:2

As we will see, one of these fishermen was Peter. If I were Peter, I would have been tempted not to wash my nets but to sell them because, after spending the entire night fishing, he had caught nothing. But Peter is an example for me that just because I may come up empty in ministry, empty in what I put my hand to do, I'm not to sell my nets; I'm not to turn back; I'm not to give up because, like him, I don't know what will happen right around the corner.

Peter was washing his nets because if a net wasn't washed and then stretched, it would rot. Each and every time it was used, a net would have to be washed with fresh water and stretched if it was to remain useful. So too, as fishers of men, we are nets which must be continually washed with the water of the Word and stretched by the Spirit if we are to remain useful.

You may be thinking, 'Why must I be washed and stretched? The Lord isn't using me. Why bother?' But, like Peter, you don't know what's going to happen tomorrow. When the Lord wants to use someone, He doesn't find the one who's rotten and brittle. No, He uses the one who's been washed in the water of the Word, the one who's been stretched and disciplined. Soak in the Word today, dear saint, for tomorrow might be the day He plans to use you.

FEBRUARY 3

And he said unto them, Can ye make the children of the bridechamber fast, while the bridegroom is with them?

Luke 5:34

The one who truly senses the presence of Jesus in his life will celebrate life like Jesus did.

What about us? Have we lost sight of the fact that Jesus Christ came to bring us life and life abundantly, to let us experience real celebration? Would we be invited to a neighborhood function readily? Do our co-workers include us when they get together—or is there something about us so Pharisaical that they conveniently forget to invite us?

Jesus was included in all kinds of parties. The common people embraced Him easily and loved to be around Him constantly. Why? Because He brought a higher degree of joy wherever He went.

I pray not only that we might be able to penetrate the parties of our society, that people would feel free to include us in their celebrations, but that we might do what Jesus did—for, although He came to people as they were, He left them different than He found them.

If you find the party or the people affecting you rather than you affecting them—watch out. But if, like Jesus, you can go into a place and make a difference by your joy and the unmistakable reality of God's work in your life, then go with God's blessing.

Acts 8 tells us that the early Church was so full of joy that they caused the entire city of Samaria—comparable in size to present-day Dallas—to be full of joy as well. Celebrate your salvation, gang, as you infiltrate your situation. Realize that Jesus can handle your humanity, that He would rather see you a friend of sinners than a self-righteous Pharisee. Then go on to make a difference in your community.

February 4

And no man putteth new wine into old bottles; else the
new wine will burst the bottles, and be spilled, and
the bottles shall perish. But new wine must be put into
new bottles; and both are preserved.

Luke 5:37-38

New wine cannot be put in old wineskins because when the new wine begins to ferment, the old hardened structure can't flex with it, causing the wineskin to burst and the new wine to be lost. So too, when people try and put something of a new moving of the Lord into an old structure, they end up not only quenching the wine of the Spirit, but blowing apart the structure in the process.

Does this mean that we who have known the Lord for awhile are doomed to become hardened old wineskins which cannot contain the new work of the Lord at any given time? I don't think so. You see, the Greek word translated 'new' in relation to wine is *neos*. But the word translated 'new' in relation to wineskins is *kainos* and literally means 'renewed.'

In Bible days, wineskins were relatively expensive, so when they began to get hard, those who didn't have money for a new one would soak the old one in water until the elasticity and the flexibility returned. I find the analogy interesting because throughout the Word, the Scriptures are likened unto water (Psalm 119:9, John 15:3, Ephesians 5:26).

How do you stay flexible, usable, and contemporary in whatever the Lord might want to do both corporately and personally? Soak not in traditionalism or denominationalism, but in the Word.

When the Bible no longer has predominance or priority in the life of a church or an individual and is instead replaced by programs, traditions, or denominational expectations, rigidity is sure to follow. If, on the other hand, you make the Word the priority of your life and the emphasis of your ministry, it will have a softening, renewing effect upon you.

If you are determined to soak in the Word, you will experience a continuing renewing—new discoveries, new understanding, constant softening. And the Lord will be able to continually pour a fresh supply of the wine of His Spirit into your life.

FEBRUARY 5

And when the Lord saw her, he had compassion on her, and said unto her, Weep not.

Luke 7:13

Compassion is your pain in my heart. It's a quality sadly lacking in our society, but one which Jesus exemplified constantly. He is called the Man of Sorrows because He took the pain of people into His own heart. And yet the irony is that the Book of Hebrews tells us He was anointed with the oil of gladness above His fellows (1:9).

How could He be the Man of Sorrows and yet anointed with the oil of gladness above any other human being who has ever lived—radiating such joy that multitudes would be drawn to Him? These are two qualities which seem contradictory—until we remember the words He taught us when He said, 'Blessed,' or happy, 'are they who mourn, for they shall be comforted' (Matthew 5:4).

One of the keys to happiness is to allow sorrow to penetrate your heart.

Eastern mysticism totally rejects this viewpoint. A foundational principle of Buddha's teaching was to avoid pain and sorrow, for if mankind would enter into the state of detached feeling, of nirvana, there would be no more jealousy or envy, no more wars and fighting.

This thinking has affected us more than we know. Having permeated the 60s culture, it was Eastern thought which caused us to say, 'I am a rock. I am an island,' as we sang along with Simon and Garfunkel.

Jesus, however, came on the scene and annihilated that mentality by saying, 'Happy is the man not who detaches himself, but who mourns, who is heartbroken—for he is the one who will be comforted.'

'Comfort' is an old English word containing the same root as that of the word 'fortify.' In other words, Jesus said that the one who is mourning will also be the one who is fortified. In the Garden of Gethsemane so deeply was Jesus mourning that blood burst from His forehead. And yet Luke tells us that even as He was agonizing in prayer, an angel came and comforted, sustained, and fortified Him (Luke 22:43).

When is the last time I have been at the place of being pained in prayer for someone else's problem, someone else's sin? Could it be that I am not comforted by the Comforter or the angelic presence because I am not doing what Jesus did? Blessed are they who mourn, who plunge into life and feel the pain of life. They shall be comforted.

Are you unhappy? Do you feel comfortless? Take seriously what Jesus said. It's an irony. It's a mystery. It runs crosscurrent to the thinking of our society. And yet the key to happiness is to mourn for others, to carry someone else's pain in your heart.

FEBRUARY 6

And on the morrow when he departed, he took out two pence, and gave them to the host, and said unto him, Take care of him; and whatsoever thou spendest more, when I come again, I will repay thee.

Luke 10:35

After carrying the beat-up traveler into the inn, the Samaritan said to the innkeeper, 'Here's money to take care of this man. If you need more, I'll repay you when I return.'

This puts the innkeeper in an interesting place. Two pieces of silver being a significant amount of money in that day, if he figured the Samaritan was not likely to return, he could dump the traveler on the street and use the silver to remodel his inn. That's what a lot of us do. We've been blessed by the Lord with money, jobs, resources, abilities, and talents. And what do we do with them? Use them for our own gain.

Or the innkeeper could have said, 'I'll take care of him until the two pence run out. Then, whether he's healed or not, he's out of here.'

A lot of us do this as well. 'We'll use what You give us, Lord,' we say, 'but don't ask us to extend ourselves in faith. We're not going to take on any new challenge or step into any new opportunity. We'll give what You require, but once that's given, that's it because we're not completely sure You're coming back or that we'll be repaid.'

I have news for you: Jesus *is* coming back. And, based upon the Word of God, I promise you that anything you have spent above and beyond the two pence you have been given will be rewarded *greatly.*

Not once in the next billion years to come will you regret that which you did not do for yourself because you cared for someone who was beat up, someone who was in need, someone who needed to grow in the ways of the Lord. What we will regret is that which we did not spend because we weren't living as though the Samaritan was really coming back.

The Lord has entrusted to you more than enough to take care of the half-dead people who come our way. The question is, will you release what He's given you?

Will you let it go?
Will you make the time?
Will you expend the energy?

Fellow innkeepers, I trust you will say to our Good Samaritan, 'You've already given me the gifts and the goods to care for whoever You send my way. Therefore, I will do whatever it takes, knowing You are repaying even now.'

FEBRUARY 7

And he said unto them, Which of you shall have a friend, and shall go unto him at midnight, and say unto him, Friend, lend me three loaves; For a friend of mine in his journey is come to me, and I have nothing to set before him? And he from within shall answer and say, Trouble me not: the door is now shut, and my children are with me in bed; I cannot rise and give thee. I say unto you, Though he will not rise and give him, because he is his friend, yet because of his importunity he will rise and give him as many as he needeth. And I say unto you, Ask, and it shall be given you; seek, and ye shall find; knock, and it shall be opened unto you. For every one that asketh receiveth; and he that seeketh findeth; and to him that knocketh it shall be opened.

Luke 11:5-10

In Jesus' day, the middle and lower-class houses consisted of a single room. One-third of the room's floor third was elevated about eight inches above the rest and contained a small fire ring around which the family would sleep. The remaining two-thirds of the room housed the animals. Thus, it is easy to see why this man was reluctant to crawl over the kids and stumble over the animals to answer his door. Yet he did so nonetheless. Jesus uses this analogy to say that because our Father never sleeps (Psalm 121:3), because our Father never says, 'Don't bother Me,' how much more would He be willing to respond to the one who keeps asking, keeps seeking, keeps knocking.

Many people have a huge problem at this point. 'Why must I *keep* asking, *keep* seeking, *keep* knocking?' they wonder. There's a reason. God is not trying to play hard to get. Nor is He treating us like puppies, trying to teach us to beg—and if we stand up on our hind legs and yap loud enough, He'll drop a biscuit in our mouth. No, no, no. We need to persist in prayer because it helps us determine that which is important to us.

The closer Christmas got, the more Benjamin and Mary, my 3 and 4-year-olds, changed their minds about what they really wanted—until finally a pattern began to develop based upon a few things to which they kept coming back.

So too with you and me. We're like kids. We want this to happen or that to work out. And then three days later, we want something else entirely. Consequently, I believe the Lord teaches us to persist in prayer to help us sort through what really is important to us.

But even more fundamentally, I think we are to persist in prayer simply because the Father enjoys being with us. And if He gave us what we asked for the first time every time, He knows us well enough to know we would just grab the goods and run. The fact that we must come to Him repeatedly helps us see that, in the end, it was His fellowship we craved all along.

FEBRUARY 8

And the Lord said, If ye had faith as a grain of
mustard seed, ye might say unto this sycamine tree,
Be thou plucked up by the root, and be thou planted in
the sea; and it should obey you.

Luke 17:6

Why were the disciples told to speak? Because while faith is implanted by the Word, it is unleashed through the lips (Romans 10:8-10).

How did God make the world? He spoke it into existence (Psalm 33: 6,9). So too, Jesus altered the course of the world and eternity when He said,

'Waves, be still.'
  'Lazarus, come forth.'
    'It is Finished.'

Made in the image of God, we also speak our individual worlds into existence and alter their course by our words.

This book of the law shall not depart out of thy mouth;
but thou shalt meditate therein day and night, that
thou mayest observe to do according to all that is
written therein: for then thou shalt make thy way
prosperous, and then thou shalt have good success.

Joshua 1:8

The Hebrew word translated 'meditate' means 'to mutter over and over again.' If you want to be prosperous and successful in that which the Lord has laid before you to do, mutter the Word day and night. The promises of God will be of no effect if they're simply written in your journal or underlined in your Bible. They only take effect when they're in your *mouth*.

With his back to the Red Sea and the armies of Egypt barreling down upon him, Moses cried to the Lord.

'Wherefore criest thou unto me? Speak unto the children of Israel, that they go forward' (Exodus 14:15).

You might be a great student of Scripture. You might even be a prayer warrior. But if you wonder why the Sea isn't parting, could it be that the Lord is whispering to you, 'Why are you asking Me? Speak to the sea, the tree, the mountain which looms large before you'?

It was when Joshua *spoke* to the sun that it stood still, when Elisha *spoke* to Ahab that there was no rain, and when Zerubbabel *spoke* to the cornerstone of the temple that the project came to completion.

So too, tomorrow morning when the alarm goes off, you will either say, 'Oh, no, it's Monday morning,' or you will say, 'This is the day the Lord has made. I will rejoice and be glad in it,'—and the choice you make will alter the course of your day.

Of God, the writer of the Book of Hebrews says, '...for he hath said, I will never leave thee, nor forsake thee. So that we may boldly say The Lord is my helper, and I will not fear what man shall do unto me' (13:5-6). God hath said that we may say—not that we may know, not that we may write, not even that we may pray—but that we may *say*.

Happy is the people whose God is the Lord (Psalm 144:15).

The Lord is my shepherd; I shall not want (Psalm 23:1).

The Lord is my light and my salvation; whom shall I fear? (Psalm 27:1).

The Lord is good unto them that wait for Him (Lamentations 3:25).

I challenge you to write down four or five such promises from the Word on 3x5 cards, put them on your dashboard or on your desk, and mutter them over and over again. Frame your world and your day with the Word as you speak it forth—and watch what happens.

February 9

So likewise ye, when ye shall have done all those things which are commanded you, say, We are unprofitable servants: we have done that which was our duty to do.

Luke 17:10

After encouraging His disciples to speak words of faith, Jesus comes right back and reminds them that they are servants. I believe this is precisely where the radical Name It/Claim It Confession Movement greatly misses the mark. They've lost the understanding that, while there is indeed power in the spoken word, it is always connected with servanthood.

So much of the Name It/Claim It teaching is based upon a 'Give me the goods' mentality (Luke 15:12), whereas a correct appropriation of faith and authority is only embedded in a 'Make me a servant' mindset (Luke 15:19).

The uprooted tree and moved mountain are always in the context of serving the King and seeing His will done—not in the context of personal luxury or prosperity.

If you miss this point, you will find yourself erring in your understanding of what faith is all about, for Jesus gave His teaching on faith not in light of getting a bigger house, but in light of forgiving others.

FEBRUARY 10

Nevertheless when the Son of man cometh, shall he find faith on the earth?

Luke 18:8

If God is a Father who loves us, Jesus is an Advocate standing beside us, and we are a Bride invited to come to a throne of grace, why don't we pray? Why is it that Jesus must ask, 'Will I find praying faith when I come back again?'

People stop praying whenever they go to the Lord with a problem, a need, and He doesn't answer them speedily. 'I've come to You, Lord, for weeks and months about this problem, and there seems to be no solution,' they say. 'I've come for years, but there seems to be no provision. Why pray?' they finally say. And they stop praying altogether, failing to understand that, because he is made in the image of God, he is composed of three parts—body, soul, and spirit— and it is the spirit which is most powerfully impacted by prayer.

You see, the body is that which relates to the physical world through the senses of sight and smell, touch, taste, and hearing. The soul, comprised of mind and emotions, is that which relates to people through one's personality. But because it is the spirit—the deepest part of man—which relates to God and will live forever with Him, it is most often through the spirit that prayers are answered.

The problem is that we limit our prayers to the realms of only the body or soul. Either we want a physical, tangible answer to our prayers, or we want to feel better after we pray. But God knows that what we are truly craving can only be fulfilled in the realm of the spirit.

'Father,' we say, 'my finances are low. I need bread.' And although He is a Father who will indeed provide our daily bread, He also knows bread will not satisfy us ultimately. So He sent His Son to *be* Bread for us (John 6:35).

'I need direction,' we pray.
'*I* am the Way,' Jesus says (John 14:6).

'I need peace,' we cry.
'In *Me* you have peace,' Jesus answers (John 16:33).

What we think we need is rarely that for which we pray. What we need is the Lord Himself.

I pray about making the basketball team, and the Lord says, 'That's not what you're really longing for, so keep coming. Keep asking. Keep knocking. Keep seeking. And as you do, you will find such fulfillment in Me that making the team will no longer be important.' And therein is the mystery of prayer.

Prayer is not to get the goods.
It is to enjoy the One who is good.

Prayer is not to get the gifts.
It is to have fellowship with the Giver of all gifts.

Prayer is not to claim the promises.
It is to embrace the Person.

Everything you crave is found in the Person of Jesus Christ—and you will discover that to be true if you pray and don't faint.

February 11

And if any man ask you, Why do ye loose him? Thus shall ye say unto him, Because the Lord hath need of him.

Luke 19:31

'Because the Lord hath need of him.' What an irony—that the Lord would have need of anything. But He does, for not only did He need this donkey on which to ride, but...

He needed a boat from which to preach (Luke 5:3).

He needed some loaves and fishes with which to feed the crowd (Matthew 15:34).

He needed a coin through which to make a point (Matthew 22:19).

He needed a tomb from which to rise from the dead (Matthew 27:60).

Our Lord has chosen to place Himself in a position where He has need. Paul said, 'He who was rich became poor for our sakes.'

Why?

I believe one of the reasons was in order that we might partner with Him in what He wants to do on the earth. Whether it's preaching or feeding, the Lord has chosen to say, 'I need you.'

FEBRUARY 12

And after that they durst not ask him any question at all.

Luke 20:40

The scribes and Pharisees did not dare question Jesus anymore. Why? They heard the words He spoke, the logic He displayed—and they were completely silenced in their cynicism. But you and I have an even greater proof before us than the words He spoke, for we, unlike the scribes and Pharisees, can look at the Cross.

You who shrug your shoulders in apathy, look at His shoulder and see it ripped apart by the flagellum, yet bearing a Cross which should have been yours.

You who shake your fist because things aren't happening the way you think they should, see His hand not clenched but open, pierced by a nail.

You who have walked away from the Lord in anger or drifted away in busyness, look at His feet and see them pinned to a beam of wood, bleeding for you.

The word 'crux' meaning 'cross,' the crux of every matter is indeed the Cross. Does God love me even when the job doesn't work out like I thought it would, even when people don't treat me the way I think they should, even if I'm not healed in the way I hoped I would be, even if I'm not understanding what's happening presently? The crux of each of these matters is the Cross.

It is in Cross-examining that which is happening in my life, it is in looking at everything through the lens of Calvary that I have absolute assurance that, although I may not understand it, everything taking place in my life is for my good because if Jesus loved me enough to die for me, surely He will do what's best concerning me.

Dietrich Bonhoeffer, perhaps the greatest of the modern German theologians, said this: 'The words why, when, where, and how are all words of the faithless. The only word spoken by a man or woman of faith is 'Who.' And the 'Who' will lead you to *Him.*'

What gave Bonhoeffer the authority to say this? Living in Germany in the 1940s, he began to publicly call for the overthrow of Hitler. As a result, in 1943, SS officers broke into the church where he was preaching and hauled him off to a concentration camp. Upon his arrival, the commandant said, 'Dietrich Bonhoeffer, the famous preacher and writer, come up here and address the assembly. I will give you two minutes.'

'I don't need two minutes,' Bonhoeffer said, 'just two words: watch me.'

Although the Nazis beat him mercilessly, every time they lifted a hand or used a club, Bonhoeffer would smile, lift his eyes towards heaven, and say, 'Father, forgive them. They know not what they do.' He shared a portion of every meal with either a fellow prisoner or one of the Nazi guards. He was constantly smiling, constantly praying, constantly loving—to the point that revival began to break out in the concentration camp—not because of a word he said, but because of what he did.

Dietrich Bonhoeffer was killed April 9, 1945. He could have asked why, but instead He asked 'Who'—and was satisfied.

If I had the power, I would change the punctuation for the language of the believer. I would eradicate the question mark and replace it with the mark of a cross. Whenever people are asking questions, put the mark of the Cross at the end, and you will find every question answered conclusively.

FEBRUARY 13

And in the day time he was teaching in the temple; and at night he went out, and abode in the mount that is called the mount of Olives. And all the people came early in the morning to hear him in the temple, for to hear him.

Luke 21:37-38

I can so easily be sucked into the cares of this life, bogged down by the things of this world. But when I study the words of Jesus, I am reminded of the big picture all over again. I am reminded that I'm only here for a short time. I am reminded of eternity.

Every single believer who is hurting physically or emotionally, every single saint who is struggling financially will indeed be healed and freed incredibly. It might be tonight; it might be this week. It might be this year. It might not be until heaven. But God's promises to you will be kept perfectly if you don't lose sight of the big picture. Spend consistent time with Jesus.

Be like those in our text. Come *early* to hear Him—early in your day, early in your life, early in the situation before you—and be reminded of heaven all over again.

FEBRUARY 14

And Peter said, Man, I know not what thou sayest.
And immediately, while he yet spake, the cock crew.

Luke 22:60

As a result of the rooster crowing, no longer will Peter ever be so cocky. When he writes his epistles, he will identify himself as Simon Peter, a servant of Jesus Christ. Simon was his name before he became a disciple. It means 'shifting sand' or 'unstable one.' The Lord changed it to Peter, or 'Rock.' But after this event, it was as if he said, 'Yes, I'm Peter in the Lord by His grace. But I'm still also Simon because I know my tendency to fail.'

But I think there's something else here. That is, I believe in using a rooster, the Lord was telling Peter that even though he messed up, even though he denied Him, even though He committed a singularly hideous sin in denying Jesus even as Jesus was about to die for him, there would be a new day dawning—

A new day of humility,
Of brokenness,
Of forgiveness

after which He would use Peter mightily, in a way He would use few others. The same is true of you. You will find that the Lord will do a mighty work in and through you if, even after you've failed miserably, like Peter, you turn to Him.

FEBRUARY 15

Now when the centurion saw what was done, he glorified God, saying, Certainly this was a righteous man.

Luke 23:47

Matthew tells us this centurion would go on to say, 'Truly, this was the Son of God.' What convinced him? It was the way Jesus handled rejection and pain, suffering and death.

Why do we as believers insist on never going through suffering when it is actually the method the Lord uses to bring about the conversion of many a centurion?

In Exodus 14, God positioned His people between Pi-hahiroth and Migdol with their backs to the Red Sea and Pharaoh's army headed right towards them. Why? So He would be glorified among the Egyptians when they saw how He delivered His people.

Oftentimes, we go to great lengths to avoid being boxed in, to avoid hard times, to avoid physical pain. Yet those are the very things which convince the Egyptians, the centurions, and our neighbors of the faithfulness of God when He sees us through.

Yes, we should pray. Yes, we should make our requests and petitions known to our Father. Yes, we should persevere in prayer. But we must also let God be God. We must also allow Him the freedom to do what He wants to do in our lives no matter how painful it might seem. It was for the joy set before Him that Jesus, our Friend, our Lord, our Model *endured* the Cross.

And so must we.

FEBRUARY 16

Now upon the first day of the week, very early in the morning, they came unto the sepulchre, bringing the spices which they had prepared, and certain others with them. And they found the stone rolled away from the sepulchre.

Luke 24:1

When Joseph of Arimathaea placed the body of Jesus in his tomb, there would not have been time for a complete embalming because Passover would begin at sunset during which no work could be done. Consequently, these women were now coming to complete the task. All of the Gospel writers tell us that they came early—always a good time to come to the Lord.

'They that seek Me early shall find Me,' the Lord declares (Proverbs 8:17). Those who seek the Lord early—early in life, early in a situation, early in each and every day—will uniquely find Him. And these precious women would prove to be no exception.

After a grandfather had lost his much-treasured watch during a family gathering, he called his grandchildren together and said,

'I'll pay twenty-five dollars to the one who finds my watch.'

This sent the kids on a mad scramble—running and screaming and turning over every rock. But the youngest grandson just sat and watched his brothers and sisters and cousins all come back empty-handed. The next morning at breakfast, he handed his grandfather the watch.

'How did you find it?' asked the puzzled old man.

'I just got up real early and listened for the ticking,' replied his clever grandson.

There's some timely advice in that little story. Oftentimes, there's so much noise and commotion going on all around us that it's hard to hear the Lord in the middle of the day. The time to hear Him is when these precious women did, these who were last at the Cross and first at the tomb.

The time to hear Him is early in the morning, early in life, early in any and every situation.

FEBRUARY 17

Behold my hands and my feet, that it is I myself: handle me, and see; for a spirit hath not flesh and bones, as ye see me have. And when he had thus spoken, he shewed them his hands and his feet.

Luke 24:39-40

The teaching of present-day American Christianity which says that God wants His children to be healthy and wealthy and that those who walk in faith should never have problems flies in the face of the early Church and the teachings of the apostles. It flies in the face of the martyrs of every continent of every age who knew nothing of such a so-called Gospel.

Shipwrecked on the island of Malta, as Paul gathered sticks to build a fire to warm the drenched soldiers and prisoners, a snake fastened itself to Paul's hand. Recognizing it as a poisonous viper, the villagers thought Paul must have been a murderer to deserve such a fate. So they watched him and waited for him to swell up and die. But Scripture records that, although he was smitten by the same serpent which had killed others on the island, Paul shook it off. And then they thought he was a god (Acts 28).

When will people listen to what you have to say about Christ Jesus? When, although you've been smitten by the same serpents which smite them, you shake it off and go on. When your business goes bankrupt, when your health fails, when problems mount, unbelievers expect you to swell up or fall down, to no longer love God or walk with the Lord. But when, like Paul, you shake off the snake and keep going, keep praising, keep loving, the islanders take notice.

The cynics and skeptics who live on your street and work in your office are not waiting to see how rich you can get. What they are waiting to see is what you do when the serpent strikes, when pain comes, when things get tough. Will you swell up and fall down, or will you keep on? Such are the results of suffering. Even in heaven, Jesus will bear the marks of Calvary to remind us that He loves us so much that He gave everything to see us through, to bring us Home.

FEBRUARY 18

All things were made by him; and without him was not any thing made that was made.

John 1:3

Everything was made by Jesus Christ—even this day. I was outside this morning, enjoying the warmth of the Oregon sun...

Our sun is big—so big that 1.3 million of our earths could fit inside. It is small, however, compared to Antares, a star in our galaxy. Antares is so big that 64 of our suns could fit inside of it. But Antares is a relatively dinky star. Hercules is a big star. One hundred ten million Antares could fit inside Hercules. So, 110 million Antares, each big enough to hold 64 of our suns, which are big enough to hold 1.3 million of our earths could fit into Hercules.

When you stop to consider such things, we on this earth are just specks on a speck in a speck. And yet most of the time we think we're pretty 'speck-tacular,' don't we? Now put down your telescope, pick up your microscope, and consider a drop of water, which is equally amazing...

Think back to junior high science class, and you will recall that each molecule of water is composed of two hydrogen atoms and one oxygen atom. If you were to take all of the atoms in only a single drop of water, and were able to enlarge each to the size of a grain of sand, do you know how much sand you would have? You would have enough sand to make a slab of concrete one foot thick and one half mile high, stretching from San Francisco to New York City.

'All things were created *by* him...' declared Paul, speaking of Jesus (Colossians 1:16, emphasis mine). Scientists call the atomic force which holds together the nucleus of the atom 'atomic glue.' The Bible, however, identifies this mysterious atomic glue as Jesus Christ, for 'by *him* all things consist,' or hold together (Colossians 1: 17, emphasis mine).

There is coming a day when Jesus will let go His hold on the atom, resulting in chaos and utter devastation (II Peter 3). But in this day of grace, He continues to hold the galaxies, the atoms, and our lives together. Why do you exist today? You were made *by* Him. You were made *for* Him. And if you don't give your life *to* Him, like errant atoms, you're going to fall apart. Life is not going to make sense. You're going to wonder what you're doing, where you're going, why you're living.

The secret of life is found here in the prologue of John, for, indeed, all things were made by Him.

February 19

And both Jesus was called, and his disciples, to the marriage. And when they wanted wine, the mother of Jesus saith unto him, They have no wine. Jesus saith unto her, Woman, what have I to do with thee? Mine hour is not yet come.

John 2:2-4

As a young woman of perhaps fourteen or fifteen years of age, Mary had become miraculously pregnant by the Spirit of God. Yes, she was highly favored by God and blessed among women. But she also must have become the subject of speculation and slander, raised eyebrows and wagging tongues. Thus, for thirty years, she had lived with the knowledge that her character had been unjustly maligned.

Is it not possible that at this point, she looked to her Son not only for wine, but for vindication, thinking that if people could only see who He really was, perhaps they would at last see the truth about her as well?

'Woman...Mary...Mother...' Jesus said in response,
'I better than anyone know you have been waiting.
I better than anyone know how you have been hurt.
I better than anyone understand your situation.
But it is not time to rectify everything...
Not quite yet.'

So too, oftentimes, I think we ask the Lord to do something which will get us off the hook or make us look a little better, smooth our road, or lighten our load. Like Mary's, our requests might sound very noble, very generous, very altruistic—but in reality, they're self-centered. And in such instances, Jesus might whisper in our hearts, as He did to Mary, 'What have I to do with thee? This is not the hour. This is not the time. This is not the place. The problem will be solved. Your reputation will be salvaged. The provision will be made. The healing will be enjoyed. But not yet. Mine hour is not yet come.'

Daniel was in a place of prominence and tremendous authority in Nebuchadnezzar's kingdom. Then, when he was about 65-years-old, Nabonidus came into power and Daniel was removed from office. For 20 years, Daniel is not seen in the narrative given to us in the book that bears his name—until the day Belshazzar called for him to interpret the mysterious writing on the wall (Daniel 5:13). When Darius the Mede seized control of the kingdom shortly thereafter, Daniel was placed in a position of prominence once again. Thus, for 20 years, Daniel was not used in ministry, nor did he hold a position of responsibility. But Daniel, being a man of integrity, did what we must do: he remained ready.

Be like Daniel. Don't say, 'I've been saved for two years now,' or 'I've been walking with the Lord for five years, and nothing's happening, so I think I'll just go to the movies, join the city softball league, or take up bird watching.' Folks, it is your job and my job to be ready—to walk with the Lord, spend time in the presence of the Lord, learn about the Lord so that when Belshazzar says, 'What does this mean?' like Daniel, we can say, 'I'll tell you, because for 20 years I've been in touch with God. For 20 years, I've been in the place of prayer. For 20 years, I've been close to the Lord.'

Radical transformation will occur in your walk with the Lord when you realize *He's* the Master and you're not. *He's* the King, and you're the subject. *He's* the Boss, and you're the servant. Your job is not to order Him or even to make suggestions to Him. Your place is to be ready *for* Him and to rest *in* Him.

February 20

There was a man of the Pharisees, named Nicodemus,
a ruler of the Jews: The same came to Jesus by
night...

John 3:1-2

It has been suggested that the reason Nicodemus came to Jesus at night was because he was afraid to be seen with Jesus in the light. I disagree with this assumption. You see, in those pre-air-conditioned days, the most enjoyable part of the day was the evening. For this reason, each home had a flat roof, easily accessible by a narrow, outside stairway which ran along the side of the house. Consequently, rooftop conversations in the cool of the evening were common.

In addition to cooler temperatures, the evening hours provided a calm not found in the heat of the day. Keep in mind that this encounter took place during the Passover season. As a Pharisee and a member of the Sanhedrin, Nicodemus would have been teaching non-stop during this time; and Jesus would have been pressed by crowds due to their familiarity with His miracles. Thus, with the days during Passover particularly busy for both men, perhaps evening was the only time Nicodemus could make private contact with Jesus.

David meditated on the Lord in the night watches (Psalm 63:6). I like that, because sometimes, like Nicodemus, I feel pressed by the busyness of the day. In the 'night watches,' however, my mind is free for concentration and meditation. Just as a radio picks up dozens of extra stations at night, so my heart is sometimes extra-sensitive to Him when the sky is black, the air still, and the house quiet at last. I'm so glad Jesus is One who *welcomes* late-night company.

FEBRUARY 21

For God so loved the world, that he gave his only begotten Son, that whosoever believeth in him should not perish, but have everlasting life.

John 3:16

'In twenty-five words or less, tell us why your mother should be Mother of the Year,' reads the contest rules.

'In twenty-five words or less, explain the importance of the French Revolution upon the economic and social structures of the thirteen colonies,' reads the test question.

Now, although I might not have much trouble with the second question, the first one would be extremely difficult for me because the more we know about any given subject, the harder it is to communicate our thoughts succinctly.

Not so with Jesus. John 3:16 is exactly twenty-five words long, and in these twenty-five words, Jesus communicates the Father's heart, the Father's plan, and the Father's will...

His heart: He loved the world.
His plan: He gave His only begotten Son.
His will: whosoever believes in Him should not perish, but have everlasting life.

I find it interesting, although I know it is somewhat coincidental, that in our English translation of this verse, the middle word is Son. It is no coincidence, however, that those who have experienced God's presence most powerfully are those who have made the Son the center of their lives. For just as Jesus is the center of the greatest verse in all Scripture, He must be central in our hearts and lives if they are to have meaning, purpose, and impact.

This means that any person, pursuit, or passion in my life which cannot be centered on Jesus Christ has no place in my life, for it is God's plan to gather together everything in the heavens and on earth in His Son (Ephesians 1:10).

Surrounding the word 'Son' in this verse, there are nine other key words: God, loved, world, gave, whosoever, believeth, perish, have, and life.

If you want to be really blessed, meditate on John 3:16 every day for ten days, giving emphasis to a different word each day...

    For *God* so loved the world...
      For God so *loved* the world...
      For God so loved the *world*...

Perhaps you memorized this verse when you were three-years-old, but I believe it will come alive for you in new ways, as you contemplate its enormity.

FEBRUARY 22

> *He that hath the bride is the bridegroom: but the friend of the bridegroom, which standeth and heareth him, rejoiceth greatly because of the bridegroom's voice: this my joy therefore is fulfilled.*
>
> John 3:29

When John first 'met' Jesus, both were in their mother's wombs. John leapt for joy when Mary, pregnant with Jesus, entered the room (Luke 1:41). And again in our text, at the zenith of his ministry, John still finds his joy in the sound of Jesus' voice. To explain the reason for his ministry and the basis for his joy, John used an analogy very familiar to his disciples. You see, wedding custom in John's day dictated it was the best man, the 'friend of the bridegroom,' who invited the guests to the wedding, made preparations for the wedding, and finally, upon completion of the wedding, escorted the bride and groom into the bridal chamber.

Thus, it was the voice of the bridegroom, signaling to him that everything was OK within the chamber, which brought joy to the heart of the best man.

Do you know when joy is fulfilled? It is not when we get something *from* the Lord, or do something *for* the Lord, but when we hear the voice *of* the Lord.

If you are expecting your joy to be fulfilled through a nicer husband, faster car, or better job, you are headed for disaster. If you are caught up in thinking, 'If I can move to this place, teach that Bible study, or sing with the other worship team; if I can just be effective here, or used there, *then* I will be joyful'—you are headed for despair and disillusion.

But if you spend time with the Lord, reading His Word, and simply listening for His voice—like John, your joy will be fulfilled. If you are a baby Christian like John in the womb, you will leap for joy at the sound of His voice. And if you are a seasoned saint like John in the desert, your joy will be full when you realize that what you longed for all along is found in Him.

FEBRUARY 23

Jesus therefore, being wearied with his journey...
John 4:6

Hebrews 2 says Jesus was made like unto his brethren—like you. He knows how it feels to be bone-tired. I'm glad about that, because

I feel that way frequently. The battles rage. The problems mount. The struggles continue—and I just feel weary.

Yet it is often at this point, when we are weary or feeling weak, that we will be used to the greatest degree, for, as Paul learned, when we are weakest, we're actually strongest (II Corinthians 12:10).

A couple of nights ago, there was a knock at our door. It was 10:30. After a particularly taxing day, the lights were out, and I was ready to crash. So when I saw a brother at the door who I knew had needs, my heart sank. But I invited him in, and as we began to share, even though my mind was blurry and my body fried, I sensed the Lord's strength flowing through me in a uniquely powerful way.

It's often when you're feeling particularly tired or spiritually dry that suddenly there will be an opportunity the Lord will bring your way. I have found that if, by faith, you begin to share the Lord with others, you'll experience renewed vitality.

FEBRUARY 24

Then saith the woman of Samaria unto him, How is it that thou, being a Jew, askest drink of me...

John 4:9

Why isn't Jesus a Gentleman here? Why doesn't He say, 'Let *Me* draw water for you?' It seems that would be the right thing to do. In actuality, however, Jesus is demonstrating a very important principle. 'Give to Me,' He says to the woman—not because He wants the water, but because He wants her heart. He wants to see her saved. You see, oftentimes, we as believers err on this point. We think, 'What can I do for other people to find a way of entry into witnessing or sharing?' While there certainly is a place for that, often letting people do something for you—humbling yourself and allowing them to make an investment in or give assistance to you—is the most effective way to reach them.

Jesus knew that wherever a person's treasure is, his heart would be there as well (Matthew 6:21). If someone shares with you something of his 'treasure,' something of his heart will be sure to follow— affording you the opportunity of touching his heart with the Gospel. It's hard because we want to be helpers, not help-ees. We want to be the givers because it's truly more blessed to give than to receive. But, as Jesus shows us, sometimes it's imperative to receive in order that another might come into the Kingdom.

The classic Biblical example of this principle is found in Numbers 10. As Moses prepares to lead the people of Israel on their journey towards the Promised Land, he invites his Gentile brother-in-law to join them. 'Hobab, come with us. It's a good land to which we are going, and good things will happen to you if you travel in our company.'

'Sorry,' said Hobab. 'I'm going back to my own people.'

It was then that Moses changed his tactic. 'Hobab,' he said, 'we need you. You understand the wilderness. You can be our eyes. Would you help us?'

Hobab agreed and ended up in the Promised Land with the people of Israel (Judges 4:11).

How important it is that we don't come across simply as those who say, 'We're going to heaven. We're great. Join us.' Rather, sometimes we need to say, 'We need you. The talents you have, the abilities you've been given would be such an asset to us.'

So it is, that, although in Chapter 3, Jesus said to Nicodemus, 'You must be born again,' here in an entirely different situation, He says, 'Woman, give Me to drink.' And both would be saved.

FEBRUARY 25

Say not ye, There are yet four months, and then cometh harvest? behold, I say unto you, Lift up your eyes, and look on the fields; for they are white already to harvest.

John 4:35

See with me in your mind's eye the Samaritan men to whom the women had witnessed coming towards Jesus dressed in turbans and robes of white. What harvest was white and ready to reap? To which field was Jesus referring?—the field of the Samaritans.

The same is true today. The people in our culture who are ignored and forgotten, the ones no one else wants to be around, the ones others pass by—those are the ones who are ripe for the picking. We say, 'How can we win the quarterback of the high school football team or the President of the company?' when the real action lies with the Samaritans—the people others aren't interested in, the people who won't help our business or gain us a reputation in ministry. I am not negating the importance of sharing with those whom the world esteems highly, but here we see our Lord's wisdom in gleaning from a field which was already ripe.

If you find witnessing difficult, reach out to the unlovely, to the unlovable, to the ignored person where you work, at your school, in your neighborhood. Talk to them about Jesus—and you'll see they're prime for harvest.

FEBRUARY 26

The nobleman saith unto him, Sir, come down ere my child die. Jesus saith unto him, Go thy way; thy son liveth.

John 4:49-50

I want you to note something I find very interesting. In Matthew 8, another Gentile nobleman—a Roman centurion—faced sickness in his house. He too was a man of prominence and political power. He too lived in the region of Capernaum. He too came to Jesus. But there the similarities end.

'My servant is dying,' said the Roman centurion.
'I'll come to your house and heal him,' said Jesus.
'Oh, I'm not worthy to have You come into my house,' protested the centurion. 'Just speak the word.'

And Jesus marveled at the centurion's faith.

Contrast this with the account here in John 4, wherein the nobleman directed Jesus to go to his house. Although Jesus did indeed heal his son, He didn't comply with the nobleman's order to go to his house. I wonder how often we are guilty of the nobleman's error—of giving directions to Jesus.

'OK, Lord, here's the bills, here's the need, and here's what You gotta do to make it happen.'

'There he is. I'm single, and so is he. Let's get this going, Lord.'

'Lord, here's the business, and I can see this is a great opportunity, so bless it by next Monday.'

We have a tendency to give instructions and directions. But that is not the finest and highest way to approach our Lord. The centurion in Matthew 8 was a much wiser, deeper fellow. He simply said,

'Lord, here's the situation.' Period. No directions. No instructions. No advice.

Both noblemen experienced the healing power of Jesus. But only one caused Him to marvel.

February 27

I am the living bread which came down from heaven:
if any man eat of this bread, he shall live for ever: and
the bread that I will give is my flesh, which I will give
for the life of the world.

John 6:51

Human beings can survive longer on bread than on any other substance. Although it is baked in different ways and fixed in different forms, bread is truly cross-cultural. It's also extremely palatable, for most of us eat some sort of bread every day.

But the most intriguing aspect about Jesus' identification with bread is the process by which bread is made: a seed of grain is planted in the ground. After some weeks, it springs up and grows into maturity. Then it is cut down, ground up, and placed in the fire. After it has thoroughly baked, it is enjoyed by humanity.

That's exactly what happened to Jesus. A seed was planted in the womb of Mary miraculously. God Incarnate came forth and grew to maturity. He was cut down as He was pinned to the Cross; ground up as He was cursed and spat upon; and placed in the fire of God's wrath as all of our sin was absorbed by Him personally.

And because He had been planted, cut down, ground up, and burned in the very fire of God's wrath, you and I have the opportunity to eat of Him daily—never tiring of Him, always receiving strength and sustenance for the challenges of any given day. Truly, Jesus is the Bread of Life. The analogy is perfect.

FEBRUARY 28

For neither did his brethren believe in him.

John 7:5

Can you imagine growing up with a Brother who never did anything wrong, who never called you a name, never teased you, and never made fun of you? Jesus was the nicest Brother in world history— never sinning, never failing. Yet His brothers didn't believe in Him. We know, however, that later on, Jesus' half-brother Jude came to such a saving knowledge of Jesus that a book in the Bible bears his name. And His half-brother, James, so strong in the faith that he was the leader of the early Church, penned the Book of James. But neither James nor Jude became believers until Jesus was crucified on a Cross and resurrected from the dead.

Many times we think, 'If I'm a nice person, my neighbor is going to get saved. I'll mow his lawn; I'll bake him cookies; I'll smile when he drives by. I'll be a lovely person—and that will convert him.' Gang, there was no lovelier Person than Jesus Christ. Yet His brothers did not believe in Him until the Cross and the Resurrection. I think some of us need a greater aggressiveness in preaching Jesus Christ and Him crucified.

You can wave to your neighbor for 20 years and wave him right into hell. Or you can take the time at some point to say, 'You know what? Jesus Christ died for your sins and rose again from the dead—and you must believe on Him.'

May we be wisely, but aggressively and radically bold in sharing the full story of the Gospel.

February 29

Now about the midst of the feast Jesus went up into the temple, and taught.

John 7:14

The first time Jesus went to Jerusalem, He cleansed the temple (John 2:13-16). This time, He's teaching in the temple. And that's always the way it is: before Jesus can impart His Word effectively *to* me, there must first be a cleansing *within* me.

The moneychangers must be driven out, the cattle chased away. That is why when you study the Word whether here corporately or in your devotions individually, it's always good to say, 'Lord, before I even begin reading, search my heart. Show me that which needs to be confessed.'

'If I regard iniquity in my heart, the Lord will not hear me,' declared the Psalmist (Psalm 66:18).

Why?

Because our Father won't allow us to live in sin which will hurt us and those around us and still continue in an intimate relationship with Him. He loves you and me too much for that. So He says,

'I'm going to break communication with you not because I'm angry with you, not because I'm giving up on you, but because something's amiss in your life—and if it's not changed, it will bring pain into your life and problems into the lives of those around you. So when you don't sense I'm listening, if your prayers aren't being answered, or the Word isn't speaking, call upon Me; let Me come in and cleanse your temple.

And *then* I will teach;
   Then you will hear My voice;
      Then you will see My face.'

I think that too many of us minimize the importance of quietly waiting on the Lord and asking Him to search our hearts. Before teaching, there must be cleansing.

MARCH 1

And as Jesus passed by, he saw a man which was blind from his birth. And his disciples asked him, saying, Master, who did sin, this man, or his parents, that he was born blind?

John 9:1-2

Incensed by His claim to deity, the Jews took up stones to throw at Jesus (John 8:59). But not more than a stone's throw away sat this man whose life was about to change radically and eternally.

The disciples voice the foundational question of all suffering: 'Why?'—and then give Jesus two possible answers. According to their reasoning, the blindness was the result either of the blind man's sin or his parents' sin.

'The issue is not sin,' Jesus would explain in verses 3-5. 'Rather, this man's misery gives Me opportunity for ministry.'

That's the way it always is. Misery always opens the door for ministry. If you are going through difficulty, tragedy, sickness, or a hard time, be careful that you don't become introspective and wonder what you've done wrong to deserve it. Just as He did to His disciples, Jesus would say to you today, 'Sin is not the issue.' The question is not, 'Who caused the misery?' The question is, 'Will you allow Me to use it? Will You allow Me to demonstrate My glory through it in order that a blind world might see My reality and be made whole?'

MARCH 2

Therefore doth my Father love me, because I lay down my life, that I might take it again. No man taketh it from me, but I lay it down of myself.

John 10:17-18

As an Old Testament believer, if you wanted to be touched by God, you would bring a lamb to the temple. There the priests would carefully inspect and scrutinize it for any spot or blemish. It was not the worshipper who was judged, it was the lamb.

Herein lies a fabulous truth. You see, I can be guided by the Father tonight; I can be led by the Father tomorrow. I can expect to receive abundant life. I can look forward to His blessing upon me and upon my family. I can trust He will anoint my head with oil, that He will take care of the predators who are coming out to get me, that He will lead me through the valley of darkness. I can expect a table set before me; I can expect to truly fellowship with God—not because of my spotlessness, but because the Lamb has been inspected and found perfect. Worthy is the *Lamb*.

I can receive blessing tonight not because I've attended church, not because I've read fifteen chapters in my Bible, not because I didn't watch television. I enjoy the blessing of God upon my life solely because of the Lamb.

'I lay down My life,' Jesus said. He didn't say, 'You better lay down your life if you expect to be blessed.' While it is true that He would call us in discipleship to take up our cross daily and follow Him, my entry into the presence of the Father is not based upon who I am, what I do, or what I don't do. It is based upon who *He* is and what He did on the Cross.

The Shepherd became a Lamb that we dumb sheep might know the Shepherd. Worthy *indeed* is the Lamb.

MARCH 3

The Jews then which were with her in the house, and comforted her, when they saw Mary, that she rose up hastily and went out, followed her, saying, She goeth unto the grave to weep there. Then when Mary was come where Jesus was, and saw him, she fell down at his feet...

John 11:31-32

How special Mary is. In Luke 10, we see her at the feet of the Lord in a happy time. Here, we see her at His feet during a hard time. Mary is one who, both in days of delight and days of difficulty, positioned herself at the feet of Jesus Christ.

I have found that some are inclined to spend time with the Lord in easy times. 'Oh, Lord, You're so good to me. I'll sing Your praises; I'll be at church on Sunday.' But when the hard times come, they pull away. In anger and frustration and confusion, they say, 'Why expend the energy? Why pay the gas money? I'll just stay home and watch TV.'

Others run to church in hard times. We saw that all across this nation during Desert Storm. In hard times, many seek the Lord and sit at His feet. But when things are back to normal, they disappear.

Like many of you, however, there are some like Mary who, regardless of the circumstances, find themselves *always* at Jesus' feet.

People often wonder how they can experience intimacy with the Lord to the degree Mary did. The answer is simple: spend time at His feet.

MARCH 4

Jesus wept.

John 11:35

As the mourners wail, as Mary weeps, as Jesus is at the scene, He finds Himself also crying, which intrigues me because He knew what would be happening. Why, then, does He weep?

Perhaps it is because He was reminded that sin destroys, sin kills, sin stinks. Aren't you finding this to be so? Aren't you seeing heartache and sadness all around because of sin? Doesn't it make you heavy of heart sometimes when you realize that precious people are hurting because of sin?

Perhaps Jesus wept because of the unbelief which surrounded Him. He had given a promise that Lazarus would rise, but no one embraced or believed it. On the contrary, they were all mourning. Jesus said, 'It's going to be all right.' But they said, 'No it's not.'

So too, when He says all things are working together for good (Romans 8:28), and we say, 'No they're not,' our unbelief must break His heart as well.

Perhaps Jesus wept because He knew He was going to pull Lazarus out of paradise and bring him back to this planet. Poor Lazarus!

Perhaps Jesus wept because, although He knew everything would turn out well eventually, those around Him were hurting presently. We are told in the Book of Hebrews that Jesus is a High Priest who sympathizes with us, feels for us, and prays on behalf of us. Therefore, even though I should be stronger in faith, when I'm hurting, Jesus hurts too.

So it is that the shortest verse in Scripture becomes the most powerful when seen in light of both the deity and humanity of our Lord.

MARCH 5

And when he thus had spoken, he cried with a loud voice, Lazarus, come forth. And he that was dead came forth, bound hand and foot with graveclothes: and his face was bound about with a napkin. Jesus saith unto them, Loose him, and let him go. Then many of the Jews which came to Mary, and had seen the things which Jesus did, believed on him.

John 11:43-45

'Where are You, Lord?' we cry. 'I sent a message to You in prayer. I've cried out to You in sincerity. But You're not working. You're not coming. Where are You?' This story teaches you and me that delays are determined by the Lord for His glory.

'Lord, come and heal our brother,' cry Mary and Martha.

'I'm going to do something a whole lot more impacting than that,' answers Jesus. 'I'm going to resurrect him. But that means he has to die first.'

I have found that the longer the Lord waits to do His work in my life, oftentimes the greater blessing it is for His glory and my good. You more mature believers have sung, 'Lord, use my life.' But what if that means tragedy? What if it means setback, bankruptcy, cancer, pain, or death? What if God can get the maximum amount of glory when a world who doesn't believe watches you go through terrible times and sees His strength see you through? Samson's greatest victory did not take place until he stood as a blind man in the temple of Dagon and brought the roof down upon himself and the Philistines (Judges 16:30).

'Use my life, Lord,' I pray. 'I'm ready for the Jon Courson Evangelistic Association, or the 'Jon Courson's Greatest Hits' album.'

But the Lord says, 'OK. I'll use you. I'll show My goodness and reality as you go through horrendous difficulty—for when the roof caves in and the house comes down,

> The demons will flee;
>> The Philistines will fall;
>>> And I will be glorified.'

If you really want your life to be used, precious people, let the Lord do what He knows will bring Him the greatest glory. Be one who says, 'To God be the glory—*whatever* that may mean in my life.'

MARCH 6

Then took Mary a pound of ointment of spikenard, very costly, and anointed the feet of Jesus, and wiped his feet with her hair: and the house was filled with the odour of the ointment.

John 12:3

Worship can be costly. For Mary, the cost would not only be her alabaster box and oil, but she would also be analyzed and criticized by Judas. So will you, and so will I.

When David danced before the Lord with all his might, stripped down to his undergarments, his wife mocked him (II Samuel 6:20). David went on to continue worshipping the Lord all the days of his life; but Michal 'had no child unto the day of her death' (II Samuel 6:23).

Truly, those who critique or find fault with worship will experience barrenness, dryness, and uselessness. Ask Michal. Ask Judas. Then ask Mary about worshipping...

You see, the ointment she poured out upon Jesus was not used several days earlier on her brother Lazarus because she was saving it for Jesus' burial. Yet she did not use it at His burial either, for it was Mary Magdalene who went to anoint His body with perfume and spice on Easter morning—not Mary of Bethany. Nor was Mary of Bethany at the foot of the Cross. Mary, the mother of Jesus was there—but not Mary of Bethany.

Why?

Why did Mary of Bethany seemingly have no part in the death and burial of her Lord?—because Mary understood something no one else comprehended. Although Jesus had spoken directly to His disciples, saying, 'I'm going to die, be buried, and rise again after three days,' they didn't get it. Mary is the only one who understood what was going to happen. She alone saw the big picture. She alone understood there was no need to save the ointment for Jesus' burial—because He wasn't going to stay buried. There was no need to go to the Cross with the other Marys—because that wouldn't be the end of the story.

Why did Mary alone have such profound insight?—because she alone was at His feet constantly, expressively, expectantly.

Be a worshipper in your morning devotions, in your evening watches; be a worshipper on Sundays and throughout the week. Be a worshipper and watch and see what will happen, for, like Mary, you'll hear the Lord's heart; you'll know things that would be otherwise unknowable.

MARCH 7

These things understood not his disciples at the first:
but when Jesus was glorified, then remembered they
that these things were written of him, and that they
had done these things unto him.

John 12:16

Jesus riding into Jerusalem on a donkey, the people waving palm branches and shouting 'Hosanna' meant nothing to the disciples until Jesus was glorified. Are the Scriptures confusing to you? Do they make no sense? Keep reading; keep studying—for as Jesus is glorified in your life, you will have a greater and greater understanding of Scripture. The problem is we want understanding, but we don't want to glorify the Lord by obeying Him. Charles Spurgeon was right when he said, 'Man has a desire to preach new doctrine, to set up a new Church, to be an original thinker, to judge, to consider—to do anything but obey.'

We want to understand esoteric insights; we want to grasp the meaning of this verse or that chapter—but it is only when we glorify the Lord in obedience that we will understand what's being said in any given passage...

'Husbands, love your wives,'—there's a start.
'Be kind one to another,'—is that hard to comprehend?
'Judge not,'—is that mysterious?

As we simply do what we already know the Scripture to say and glorify the Lord in obedience, then more and more understanding will be given us. I like this. The disciples didn't understand initially, but when Jesus was glorified, they understood eventually.

MARCH 8

If any man serve me, let him follow me; and where I am, there shall also my servant be: if any man serve me, him will my Father honour.

John 12:26

A prince and his servant traveling through a hostile region were taken captive by the enemy. After being beaten and thrown into a dungeon, the prince developed a terrible fever, and it looked as though his days were numbered. Semiconscious as he was, however, he didn't miss the opportunity to alert his servant when their guard fell asleep one day.

'Get his keys and get out of here,' he said. 'I'm too weak; I can't make it. But you go. This is your chance.'

'My prince,' answered the servant, 'where you are, there I will be. If need be, we'll both die here together.'

Two weeks later, the prince's father launched an invasion and freed his imprisoned son in the process.

'Oh, Father,' said the prince immediately upon his return, 'even as my servant stayed with me in my danger, suffered with me in my sickness, stood by me in my imprisonment, honor now him.'

And the servant was honored throughout the kingdom.

So too with you. The Lord knows you could opt to escape, that His way of the Cross and obedience is not always easy. The Lord knows many of you are truly paying a price to follow Him. You've been passed by for promotions at work because you've stood for integrity; or you've stayed in a relationship because you committed yourself maritally.

'Forget it,' the world says. 'Here's a key. Get out. Go on. Be free.'

But you've said, 'No, my Master, my Prince, my Savior has called me to follow Him. And even when it's not easy, I will stay by Him.' I've got good news for you who have taken this stand by the Father's Son, the Prince of Peace. After the invasion, when He brings you safely home to heaven, you will be honored greatly, for the Father honors those who honor His Son.

MARCH 9

Therefore, when he was gone out, Jesus said, Now is the Son of man glorified, and God is glorified in him. If God be glorified in him, God shall also glorify him in himself, and shall straightway glorify him. Little children, yet a little while I am with you. Ye shall seek me: and as I said unto the Jews, Whither I go, ye cannot come; so now I say to you. A new commandment I give unto you, That ye love one another; as I have loved you, that ye also love one another. By this shall all men know that ye are my disciples, if ye have love one to another.

John 13:31-35

As Judas goes out, and it is dark, Jesus turns to His boys and says, 'This is the hour of glory. It's all coming down. I'm going to be going, and where I'm going, you can't come now. So in the meantime, I'm giving you a new commandment: Love one another.'

A *new* commandment? Doesn't it say way back in Leviticus that we are to love God and that we are to love our neighbor? Isn't that the message, really, of the Scriptures in their entirety? Hadn't Jesus Himself said that upon these two commandments—to love God and to love people—hang all the Law and the Prophets? What does He mean a *new* commandment?

Look carefully at what Jesus is saying because it's radical. Yes, the Old Testament is filled with commandments and exhortations to love. But Jesus here makes everything new when He says, 'Love one another *as I have loved you.*' How did Jesus love them? How does Jesus love us? *That's* what's new. Paul tells us how He loves us when he writes, 'Husbands love your wives even as Christ loved the church and *gave Himself for it*' (Ephesians 5:25, emphasis mine).

The newness, the unfolding, the fullness of this new commandment is that you are to love in a way that costs you your life—not just loving generally, but loving sacrificially to the place of death.

You see, Biblically there is never true reconciliation apart from someone or something dying. In the Old Testament, reconciliation was impossible without the sacrifice of an animal. In the New Testament, we see Old Testament typology become reality with the death of the innocent Lamb of God, Jesus Christ.

Gang, there will never be true reconciliation between you and the person who's mad at you or estranged from you until you die, until you say, 'I'm not going to grind my ax any longer. I'm not going to press my point any further. I'm not going to prove I'm right anymore. I'm just going to die.'

The question is, will you?

'But I'm innocent,' you say.
So was Jesus.

'But I'm right.'
Wasn't He?

A new commandment He gave us: to die—to our pride, our complaints, our position, our proof.

'What if I die?' you ask. 'Does laying down my life and giving up my rights guarantee reconciliation?'

Was everyone reconciled to Jesus? No.

Not everyone is born again. Not everyone says, 'Thank You, Lord, for laying down Your life for me.' When you love like Jesus, some will respond and there will be reconciliation.

Others, however, will continue to spit and curse and mock—even as they did to Jesus as He was in the very act of dying for their sins. But if we are to love as Jesus loved, like Him, we'll pray, 'Father, forgive them. They just don't know what they're doing.'

'By this kind of love shall all men know you are My disciples,' said Jesus, 'when you love like I do—when you love to the point of death.'

MARCH 10

If ye abide in me, and my words abide in you...
John 15:7

The word 'abide' means to 'be at home in.' The Psalmist didn't say 'Thy Word have I hid in my mind' or even 'in my memory.' He said, 'Thy Word have I hid in Mine *heart*...' (Psalm 119:11, emphasis mine).

Paul echoed him when he prayed in Ephesians 3:17, 'that Christ may dwell in your *hearts*...' [Emphasis mine.]

Why does the Lord want Himself and His Word to abide in our hearts and not just in our heads? Because, affected by data, discussions, and information, the mind is incredibly fickle. I can change my mind 100 times in a single day concerning a single issue. So can you. But not so the heart.

Think back to your dating days and you know how this works. If someone dumped you, even though you knew in your head that you were glad to be free of him or her, you would still find yourself feeling for him or caring about her. Why? Because the heart holds on. That's why the Lord wants His Word to dwell there.

How does this happen?

For me the most practical way knowledge moves from the head to the heart is through meditation and contemplation. Spending time in the Word—in morning and evening devotions, in corporate study, in times when I'm waiting in line or waiting at a stoplight allows it to sink in and permeate my inner man, to be at home in my life, to abide in my heart.

MARCH 11

...Ye shall ask what ye will, and it shall be done unto you.

John 15:7

Our culture has lost the meaning of what real love is. Consequently, husbands and wives are saying, 'I don't have feelings for him or her anymore, so I'm leaving.' But feelings aren't the issue. Love is not an emotion or a feeling. It's a decision. It's an action.

'My commandment,' Jesus said, 'is that you make the decision to love.'

Fighting the flu and not thinking very clearly as I was at my desk preparing for tonight's study, I decided to take five minutes to rake some leaves and get some fresh air. No sooner had I walked out the door than a sister walked by, pushing her granddaughter in a stroller. 'Do you have a minute, Jon?' she said.

'Well, yeah, a minute is just about what I've got,' I answered. But as soon as I spoke those words, I was convicted of an attitude that was amiss, so I walked over and began to converse with her. What she shared with me blessed my heart so deeply that I went back into my study totally refreshed.

So too, you will come across people today who might initially seem to be an interruption in the raking of your leaves. But if you say, 'Wait a minute. Here's an opportunity for me to love,' you know what will happen? As you make that decision, there will be a change in your emotions. The Lord will meet you in that place. I guarantee it.

MARCH 12

Greater love hath no man than this, that a man lay down his life for his friends.

John 15:13

An entire nation was revived when John Knox prayed, 'Lord give me Scotland, or I die.'

But what many people don't know is what Knox wrote concerning the answer to that prayer. The Lord responded in his heart saying, 'First die, then I'll give you Scotland.'

'Make this relationship work, or I'm going to die,' we pray.
'Die first,' the Lord says.

Lay down your life for your wife, your neighbor, your friend. That is not only the proof *of* your love, but the pathway *to* love because love is not some feeling you hope returns, not some kind of elusive mystical emotion. It's the decision to die to your dreams, your desires, your needs, for your friend, your husband, your neighbor, your kids.

MARCH 13

...That whatsoever ye shall ask of the Father in my name, he may give it you.

John 15:16

If you walked into Costco, made $100,000 worth of purchases, and then pulled out a check upon which was written at the top 'Jon Courson,' you would be laughed out of the store. But if you walked into that same store with an authorized check from Donald Trump, there would be no problem because the issue isn't how rich you are, but how rich the person is upon whose account you've drawn.

And that's the beautiful thing about prayer. My request isn't based upon how many devotions I've had this week, how many folks I've witnessed to this month, how many hours I've spent in prayer today. No, that's all irrelevant. I draw from the bank of heaven based solely upon the riches of Jesus Christ, who gave me His name to use.

How free your prayer life will be when you understand what it means to use Jesus' name with the Father.

Go to my parents' house on Steeplechase Drive in Moreno Valley, knock on the door and say, 'I'm here. Where's the pool? When's dinner?'

'Pardon me?' they'd say.

Then say you're a close friend of their son Jon, and their response will be, 'Come in! There's the pool; dinner's at 6; and here's a hot fudge sundae while you're waiting'—all on the basis of your linkage to me.

Approach the Father solely on the basis of your relationship with His Son, and watch prayer become a pleasure and a joy.

March 14

...The hour is come; glorify thy Son, that thy Son also may glorify thee.

John 17:1

Prayer is not the way to get God to do our will in heaven. Prayer is the way to get us to do His will on earth.

Once this is understood, you will find yourself praying in an entirely different manner. And that's what Jesus is doing here. 'Glorify Me,' He prays, 'so that You might be glorified—even if that means being pinned to the Cross of Calvary.'

'That sounds sadistic,' you say.

Not at all, because on the other side of the Cross is a crown—joy unspeakable, full of great glory. We only see five months or ten years down the road. But God sees the next ten zillion years.

You see, Jesus allowing the Father to be glorified *through* Him ultimately bought a Bride *for* Him for all eternity.

It's so radical when a believer finally gets the big picture and stops saying, 'God do it my way.' God is not Burger King. We can't give orders about how things should be done and then complain when we don't get the lettuce and onions we asked for. God is not Burger King—He's the King of Kings, and He sees what is going to be absolutely best in the long run.

MARCH 15

I have finished the work...

John 17:4

'I have finished the work.' Not, 'I started it'; not, 'I thought about it'; not 'I was going to get to it.' The roads from Bible studies and Bible conferences are strewn with the broken commitments of men and women who began but never finished what God told them to do. I'm sure glad that after Noah finished the frame on the ark, he didn't say, 'Close enough. We don't need a roof.' No, he *finished* the work. He *completed* the task. If he hadn't, we would all be sunk.

What about you? If you knew you only had a few hours to live, could you say, 'Father, I finished the work You gave me to do'? Or would you say, 'I know You put this on my heart last year, and I meant to get to it, but...'?

Have you finished the work? Saul didn't...

'Let not one Amalekite remain,' Samuel told Saul (I Samuel 15:3). And Saul killed *almost* everyone—but he decided to keep Agag, king of the Amalekites, as a trophy. Twenty-five years later, wounded in battle, rather than being captured by the enemy, Saul turns to a young man on the field and says, 'Kill me.' And the young man—an Amalekite—did just that. Where did he come from? Somewhere along the way, Agag fathered a son.

What has God called you to do? What has He spoken to your heart about? Maybe it's some sin, or something that's got to go, and you think, 'Well, I've got it pretty much taken care of. I know the Lord's told me not to do this, but I've cut way back.'

'Have you finished it?'
'No, but I've got it under control.'

Watch out. Agag is out to get you.

'*IT IS FINISHED*,' cried Jesus from the Cross. I'm so glad He didn't say, 'I almost did it, but I'm going to come down now'—because if He had come down from the Cross, we would go down to hell. He paid the price. He *finished* the work.

MARCH 16

...Which thou gavest me to do.

John 17:4

'The whole city wants You,' Jesus was told in Mark 1:37. Having spent the morning in prayer, however, He knew that the directive of His Father was for Him to minister in the backwoods region of Galilee. Thus, He went in the opposite direction of the clamor of the crowd.

I believe this is why you never see Jesus accused of being busy. His enemies accused Him of being a winebibber, a glutton, demon-possessed, crazy—but never busy. Jesus moved with a paced peace and an ordered steadiness because He knew the heart of the Father.

People's burdens will give you an ulcer. People's expectations will drive you crazy. Whenever the burden is not light, I know I'm not doing the will of the Father. But when I'm being directed by Him morning by morning, I find His yoke easy (Matthew 11:30).

MARCH 17

*As thou hast sent me into the world, even so have I
also sent them into the world.*

John 17:18

Jesus not only kept those entrusted to Him, He sent them out; He made opportunities for them. Earlier, He had said, 'They are not of the world,'—but yet He sends them into the world. Christian, listen carefully. We are not to be of the world—but we must be in the world. The mistake of the monastery movement lies in isolation from the world. You can get away, yes, but don't stay away.

Jesus ripped into that wrong understanding when He told the parable of the Good Samaritan. You can't walk on the other side of the street to avoid the stench and infection of the world. The answer lies not in isolation, but in incarnation—for just as God became Man yet retained His deity, so we are a people who, although we live among humanity, are linked to eternity. We're here in the flesh, but we are really living in heaven. That's where our hope, our destiny, our source of strength lie.

In the aftermath of the December 7th bombing of Pearl Harbor, divers were sent to rescue the survivors. In one compartment of the USS Utah, however, it was impossible to get to the men trapped inside. The divers could hear men tapping 'Is there any hope?' in Morse Code—but rescue was impossible with the technology then available. The tapping finally stopped December 27th.

We're deep-sea divers, gang—down here on earth, but connected to heaven. We don't fit in here; we don't belong here; and we're not going to stay here. But the Lord has allowed us to be here, pumping the oxygen of the Spirit and the Scriptures to us saying, 'There are people to rescue. Do what you can as I guide and lead you.'

MARCH 18

Now there stood by the cross of Jesus his mother, and his mother's sister, Mary the wife of Cleophas, and Mary Magdalene. When Jesus therefore saw his mother, and the disciple standing by, whom he loved...

John 19:25-26

When Jesus was healing the sick and feeding the multitudes, He captivated people's attention. Like a magnet, the masses were drawn to Him. But as His ministry progressed, when His teaching became a little more intense, no longer did thousands follow Him, but seemingly, hundreds. And from there, only 70 chose to be engaged in service and to share the Gospel of the Kingdom (Luke 10:1). From there, only 12 left everything to follow Him. And of the 12, only 3 would be with Him on the Mount of Transfiguration where He spoke of His death and in the Garden of Gethsemane where He prayed with such intensity. And of the three, only one would be at the foot of the Cross.

But there were four women there—although it was not easy for them. It was not easy for Mary to watch her Son convulsing in pain, or for her sister to hear the curses hurled at Him. It was not easy for the wife of Cleophas to see the spit of the crowd running down His face, or for Mary Magdalene to see His blood flowing from His wounds. But these four women, lovers of the Lord and followers of Him, were there at the foot of the Cross no matter how great the price, no matter how deep the pain.

Let us be like John. Let us be like these four women. Let us spend time at the Cross—and then go out and impact our world as they did.

MARCH 19

And stooping down, and looking in, saw the linen clothes lying; yet went he not in. Then cometh Simon Peter following him, and went into the sepulchre, and seeth the linen clothes lie, And the napkin, that was about his head, not lying with the linen clothes, but wrapped together in a place by itself. Then went in also that other disciple, which came first to the sepulchre, and he saw, and believed.

John 20:8

First, John came to the tomb and saw the linen clothes lying. The word translated 'saw' is *blepei*, meaning, 'to look at, to see visibly.'

In verse 6, Peter 'saw' the linen clothes lie, and the word used is *theoreo*, meaning 'to study more carefully,' and from which we get our word 'theory.'

Finally, in verse 8, the word translated 'saw' is *eiden* from which we get the word 'idea'—or 'I get it.'

I find it interesting that most of the time our faith progresses according to this pattern. That is, first you're exposed to some piece of information. You hear what the teacher is saying. Then you give it some more thought down the road. And finally comes that moment when you really get it. More than merely a concept theologically, it becomes part of your life personally.

But if you never hear the information, you'll never be able to embrace it. And that is why you'll never see the process unfold if you don't come to the place where you can investigate the claims of Christ. Keep in the Word, gang.

'But I'm not getting much out of it,' you say.

You wait. Eventually it will begin to stir something in your thinking, and finally it will become part of your being. Read your Bible. Stay in the Scriptures, and see the process unfold for you even as it did for Peter and John.

MARCH 20

And he said unto them, Cast the net on the right side of the ship, and ye shall find. They cast therefore, and now they were not able to draw it for the multitude of fishes.

John 21:6

Think about this, you who have been toiling, working, wondering when it's going to happen. Success for these disciples was only a boat's width away. Three, perhaps four feet from one side of the boat to the other—that's how close they were to success in this fishing endeavor. And you might be just three, four feet away from seeing success happen in your life, in your ministry, in your occupation. How do you move the three or four feet that make all the difference?

'Mr. Getty,' asked an eager young man, 'what's the secret of success?'

'It's very simple,' answered the billionaire. 'Rise early, work late, and strike oil.'

How do you strike oil? How do you find success? You do what Jesus says. Listen to what He's telling you in your heart. Perhaps He's been dealing with you, speaking to you, but you've thought His direction doesn't relate to the challenge you face or the endeavor you've undertaken.

The disciples could have said, 'We've been fishing all night. We're experts. What do three feet have to do with anything?' But when they did what He said, they were immediately on the right side.

So too, you might be real close to success in the best sense of the word. All you have to do is decide to obey what God has told you to do. It's not mystical. It's not difficult. It's just a matter of saying, 'Lord, You've been telling me in my heart, placing on my mind that I am to do a certain thing, and I now, by Your grace, am purposing to do it.'

MARCH 21

This is the disciple which testifieth of these things, and wrote these things: and we know that his testimony is true. And there are also many other things which Jesus did, the which, if they should be written every one, I suppose that even the world itself could not contain the books that should be written. Amen.

John 21:24-25

The world could not even hold all that should be written of Jesus. But Ephesians 2 indicates that in the ages to come, we will at last be able to explore more fully His grace and mercy.

John tells us in Revelation that there are four creatures in heaven who praise the Lord ceaselessly, perpetually, eternally. This goes on day and night because they're continually seeing different facets, different sides, and different aspects of the Person of Jesus (4:8).

And the same thing is going to happen eternally with you. Jesus will so captivate your heart and expand your mind that as you explore and experience the exceeding riches of His grace and goodness, you will praise Him throughout eternity.

But why wait until heaven? Learn more of Jesus this morning; walk with Him today; worship Him this evening—and you'll add your own pages to the volumes yet to be written about Him.

MARCH 22

For he was numbered with us, and had obtained part of this ministry. Now this man purchased a field with the reward of iniquity; and falling headlong, he burst asunder in the midst, and all his bowels gushed out. And it was known unto all the dwellers at Jerusalem; insomuch as that field is called in their proper tongue, Aceldama, that is to say, The field of blood.

Acts 1:17-19

We know from Matthew 27:10 and Zechariah 11:13 that this field was originally a potter's field—the field outside the house of every potter wherein he would throw any of his marred creations which, because they had become hardened, could not be re-shaped. Over the years, due to the accumulation of broken pottery, the potter's field would thus be useless for anything but a burial ground.

What happened to the money for which Jesus was betrayed?

It was used to purchase a potter's field—a useless field full of broken pots and dead bodies. The picture to me is powerful: the blood money of Jesus—His work on the Cross—was spent to redeem,

Useless vessels,
  Lifeless bodies,
    Us.

Therefore, next time you feel like a cracked pot,

When you feel useless,
   When you feel there's no hope for you,
      Remember Aceldama, the field of blood—

for even the place where the traitor died was purchased with the blood of Jesus Christ.

MARCH 23

And they gave forth their lots; and the lot fell upon Matthias; and he was numbered with the eleven apostles.

Acts 1:26

Although Peter knew the Word and was right on in discerning that Judas needed to be replaced, I believe he and the other disciples erred when they chose two men and said, 'Now Lord, which of these two do You want?'

I believe God's choice was neither man. Revelation 21:14 tells us that the names of the apostles are written on the twelve foundations in heaven. My personal conviction is that we won't see Matthias' name on any of those foundations. We'll see Paul's name. I believe Paul was the one who should have filled Judas' office.

I believe the disciples got ahead of the Lord by trying to make something happen before the power of the Spirit came upon them on the Day of Pentecost.

That's a mistake I make frequently. I'll see a principle in the Word and say, 'OK now how can I make this happen?' instead of saying, 'I see the principle, Lord. Now I'm going to wait on You and for the power of Your Spirit to bring it about.'

Maybe you're wrestling with a decision right now, saying, 'Which one is it, Lord? Is it him or him? This or that? Here or there? What do You want, Lord? Here are Your choices...'

Turn to Numbers 11. This is so typical of what we do...

The Israelites were murmuring, saying, 'We're sick and tired of this manna.'

Hearing their complaints, Moses said to the Lord, 'What am I supposed to do? You told me You would give them meat. Do You want me to kill the flocks and the herds we're bringing into the Promised Land? Or do You want us to fish all the fish out of the Red Sea? Which is it, Lord?'

But the Lord said, 'Trust Me, Moses, and you'll see that I have more choices than just those two. I have options you would never think about even in your wildest dreams.'

And, sure enough, suddenly, quail by the thousands flew into the camp two feet off the ground—right in the strike zone. The Israelites grabbed sticks and batted them down. I know that's what happened because verse 32 says, 'He that gathered least gathered ten *homers*.'

Be careful about saying, 'OK, Lord, is it this—or is it that?' because the Lord has options we've never even heard of. Wait on Him; listen for *His* answer—and, like the children of Israel, you'll hit one out of the park every time!

MARCH 24

And he took him by the right hand, and lifted him up: and immediately his feet and ankle bones received strength. And he leaping up stood, and walked, and entered with them into the temple, walking, and leaping, and praising God.

Acts 3:7-8

Like the crippled man, we too were lame from birth. Our father in the flesh, Adam, fell—and so great was his fall, that all of his descendants were born lame. Unable to walk with God, or after the things of God, we sat outside the temple—alienated from God because of our sin—and begged enough silver or gold to get us by for one more day. Maybe we weren't bitter about life, but every one of us realized our handicap to some extent.

And then something happened.

Through a brother or sister, a church or a fellowship—perhaps when we least expected it, Jesus grabbed us by the hand and said, 'Stand up and walk. I'm calling you into the Kingdom. I'm taking you to heaven.'

Thus, it is no wonder that, like the crippled man, we not only walk—but we leap and praise God for His goodness and grace to us lame-brains.

MARCH 25

And when they heard that, they entered into the temple early in the morning, and taught.

Acts 5:21

'They entered into the temple early in the morning.' I like that! It doesn't say, 'They went into the temple the first chance they had,' or 'They waited until noon...' No, following their release from prison the night before, the apostles headed straight for the temple early the next morning.

The largest nation in the world today is procrasti-nation. No doubt about it! Our tendency is to say:

'Thank You, Lord. You freed me from prison. You freed me from eternal damnation, from meaningless existence, from emotional depression. You opened the door for Me, Lord, and I'm going to share Your Gospel with others real soon—maybe at noon, maybe tomorrow night. I know You told me to go and share the Word with everyone. And I'll get right on it, Lord—pretty soon.'

Procrastination is a real problem in spiritual life and spiritual discipline. When the Lord speaks to your heart, be it in Bible study, in devotions, through a book you read, or through a sister or brother—learn to respond immediately.

I read of one very wealthy inventor who said, 'Without exception, after I have invented something and patented it, at least ten men come to me and say, "I thought of that a long time ago." But the difference between their poverty and my wealth is that they thought about it, but I *did* it.'

The same thing is true spiritually. There are those who think,

'I really should share my faith,' or,
'I really should intercede,' or,

'I really should get involved.'

And they think and they think and they think and they think...
while they remain poor spiritually. The ones who are used by the
Lord are those who hear and *do*.

MARCH 26

And Stephen, full of faith and power, did great
wonders and miracles among the people.

Acts 6:8

In Matthew 25, Jesus taught that those who are faithful in little
things will be made rulers over greater things. If we desire to be
used by the Lord, we must be faithful in the things He gives us to do
in the beginning days of our service, of our ministry. The Scripture
tells us not to despise the days of small things (Zechariah 4:10),
yet many people find themselves reluctant to do the seemingly
insignificant tasks. Desirous of something grander, they feel as
though it's beneath them to involve themselves in menial service.
But the way of the Lord is that we first prove ourselves in smaller
things and, as we are faithful in them, He will give us greater things
to do.

The reward for faithfulness in service is greater service. Jesus
came on the scene and stated something radical when He said,
'Happiness is found in losing your life, in giving yourself away.
Happiness is found in serving, not in being served; in giving, not in
getting' (Matthew 10:39).

Today if you're feeling somewhat blue, perhaps it's because you're
not engaging yourself in serving others. When you feel like throwing
in the towel, take up the towel instead. Wash someone's feet and
suddenly you'll be refreshed.

Stephen modeled this beautifully. He began by serving tables, helping feed widows—not necessarily a glorious position, not an exalted kind of ministry. But because he was faithful, he was then elected to the office of deacon (Acts 6:5)—one of seven men chosen by the early Church as being a man full of the Holy Ghost, full of wisdom, and full of good works. And here, three verses later, we see him doing 'great wonders and miracles among the people.'

Stephen went from being a table server to a deacon to a miracle worker because he was faithful at each step.

MARCH 27

When they heard these things, they were cut to the heart, and they gnashed on him with their teeth. But he, being full of the Holy Ghost, looked up stedfastly into heaven, and saw the glory of God...

Acts 7:54-55

Stephen began his sermon by speaking of the God of glory (7:2). He ended his sermon seeing the glory of God. That's the way it always is.

Whenever you start talking to people about some quality of the Lord, by the time you've finished the conversation, you find that very quality in your own heart. It's incredible how that works. Start telling someone how awesome Jesus is, and by the time you conclude, you'll be totally in awe of Jesus. Start sharing about the God of grace and you'll find yourself receiving the grace of God. That is why I encourage you to share your faith—not because it is a job to do—but because it is a joy to experience.

'I'm so dry,' you say.
When was the last time you talked to someone about Jesus?

'Jesus doesn't seem very real to me.'
When was the last time you got into an interesting full-on dialogue with someone about what you believe?

'I'm just not experiencing joy.'
When was the last time you ministered to someone who was depressed?

'I just don't know if I really have faith.'
When was the last time you shared what faith you do have with someone who had less than you?

Be like Stephen. Share the Lord with others, and you'll be the one to see His glory.

MARCH 28

And they stoned Stephen, calling upon God, and saying, Lord Jesus, receive my spirit. And he kneeled down, and cried with a loud voice, Lord, lay not this sin to their charge. And when he had said this, he fell asleep.

Acts 7:59-60

How could Stephen be so peaceful—dying without fighting back, without lashing out, crying, 'O, Lord, don't hold this against these guys'?

He looked into heaven and saw Jesus.

You see, Revelation 5:6 tells us that when we see Him, we will see Him as a Lamb having been slain. Therefore, if I'm looking up to heaven and seeing the Lord, inevitably I will understand that the scars He still bears were caused by me. *My* sin, *my* rebellion, *my* carnality, *my* depravity caused Him to be slaughtered on Calvary. And as I look into heaven and see what my sin did, what my sin wrought, I have no other alternative but to say even to those who are gnashing their teeth and throwing stones at me. 'Lord Jesus, forgive them. Don't hold this against them.'

When I truly see Jesus, I have no other choice but to be amazed at His grace and to be at peace with others. It's only when I lower my sight and begin to look at people horizontally that I want to say, 'Who do you think you are to say that about me?' It's only when I take my eyes off Jesus that I become defensive and antagonistic, uptight and combative, abrasive, callous, and critical.

What about you? Are you tense? Nervous? Uptight? The solution is so simple: don't look down on people. Look up into heaven and see the Lord. See how He has forgiven you. See the grace He has shown to you. See His mercies extended in your direction.

In II Kings, we read the account of a battle between Israel and Moab. Losing the battle and realizing his number was up, the king of Moab in desperation took his eldest son and sacrificed him on the wall of his city.

When the people of Israel saw the sacrifice of the king's own son, they departed from him and returned to their own land (II Kings 3: 27). They lost the will to fight when they saw the sacrifice the king made.

So too, when we see the sacrifice of our King's Son, when we see clearly the price that was paid, we lose the will to fight. And like Stephen, we're at peace even when the enemy throws stones.

MARCH 29

And Saul was consenting...

Acts 8:1

This Saul, of course, would later become known as the Apostle Paul. The word 'consenting' actually means 'voting,' implying that Saul was a voting member of the Sanhedrin, the Jewish Supreme Court.

This interests me because marriage was one of the requirements for a position on the Sanhedrin—and yet Paul wrote to the church at Corinth that it was good for the unmarried and the widows to remain in a single state—even as he was (I Corinthians 7:8). If Paul was married in Acts and single in I Corinthians—what happened to his wife? Some suggest she died—that he was a widower who chose to remain single in order to give himself more fully to ministry.

Much more probable, however, based upon the writings of early Church history, is that Paul's wife left him. When he was converted, she walked out and never came back.

Either way, it's interesting that Paul doesn't tell the story. Truly, he practiced what he preached when he wrote: 'Forgetting those things which are behind, and reaching forth unto those things which are before, I press toward the mark for the prize of the high calling of God in Christ Jesus' (Philippians 3:13-14).

If you've been hurt in the past, perhaps Paul can be an example to you today. I know it's not easy, but Paul shows us the possibility of forgetting the past, pressing on, and seeing how the Lord can do something unique and special in your situation presently.

MARCH 30

And at that time there was a great persecution against the church which was at Jerusalem; and they were all scattered abroad throughout the regions of Judaea and Samaria...

Acts 8:1

'You shall receive power when the Holy Ghost comes upon you and you shall be witnesses in Jerusalem, Judaea, Samaria, and to the uttermost parts of the earth,' promised Jesus (Acts 1:8). In other words, 'My work starts here in Jerusalem, but it must not only stay here.'

We all have a tendency to camp out where it's comfortable. So did the early Church. Jerusalem was the 'happening spot.' It was the center of spiritual activity, and for six years, no one wanted to leave. It took persecution to get the believers moving, to scatter them to Judaea and Samaria. It was persecution in Acts 8:1 which moved the Church to obey the command of Acts 1:8.

Maybe you face a job transfer, a relational change, or something else which makes you unsettled or unsure. Maybe doors are closing and you're wondering why. Although it would be wonderful if we were all so spiritually sensitive that we would feel the prompting of the Lord and respond immediately, most of us don't have that kind of sensitivity. For most of us, it takes a pink slip, a job transfer, a broken romance to get us moving. Perhaps you'd rather stay where you are, but in reality, the Lord sees where He can use you most effectively. Trust Him.

MARCH 31

And the angel of the Lord spake unto Philip, saying, Arise, and go toward the south unto the way that goeth down from Jerusalem unto Gaza, which is desert. And he arose and went...

Acts 8:26-27

Philip, whose ministry had brought about the wonderful work of the Lord in Samaria, was now being called to Gaza. 'But Lord, what about the posters?' he could have protested. 'What about the book-signings? Lord, I'm so influential here in Samaria. The entire city is getting turned on to You. Why are You asking me to go to the desert? There's nothing down there.'

Please note that the Lord didn't say why He was sending Philip to the desert. He just said, 'Arise and go.' And Philip arose and went. If you struggle with finding God's will, know this: God's will is for you to obey what He tells you to do one step at a time. He doesn't give us the full story. He just says, 'I want you to go down to the desert. And once you do that, I'll show you the next step.' That's why the Christian life is so incredibly exciting—we never know what's ahead.

A scientist placed caterpillars on the rim of a large pot containing dirt and several of their favorite plants. The caterpillars began to move along the rim of the pot—each one following the one in front, every caterpillar thinking the one ahead of him knew where he was going. Around and around and around they went until they all died of starvation.

Do you feel like you're drying up and getting dizzy? Could it be because the Lord spoke to you at some point but, because you were so intent on following the caterpillar in front of you, you missed the adventure? The key to the exciting, impacting Christian life is to be like Philip and obey when you hear the Lord's voice or feel His pull—even though you don't know the end of the story at the beginning.

April 1

But Philip was found at Azotus: and passing through
he preached in all the cities, till he came to Caesarea.

Acts 8:40

As a deacon, Philip served tables. In Samaria, he became an evangelist. In Gaza, he was removed from the public arena to minister one-on-one to the Ethiopian eunuch. In Caesarea, he found himself raising a family of four daughters who became prophetesses (Acts 21:9).

Wherever he was, Philip flowed in ministry. I'm sure he was as thrilled serving tables as he was preaching to multitudes; as enthusiastic talking to the Ethiopian as he was raising daughters to be godly women.

In your walk with the Lord and your work for the Lord, like Philip, you will go through different seasons. There will be times when you'll wait tables and minister practically. There will be other times when the Lord might use you to speak to multitudes as you minister publicly. Other times, you will work one-on-one as you minister personally. Still other times, you'll invest in your kids as you minister to your family.

Solomon was right: to everything there is a time and a purpose. Trust the Lord. Go with the flow. Walk with Him one step at a time, and He'll lead you in paths you could never have imagined.

APRIL 2

Then had the churches rest throughout all Judaea and Galilee and Samaria, and were edified; and walking in the fear of the Lord, and in the comfort of the Holy Ghost, were multiplied.

Acts 9:31

The churches were edified and multiplied—when?—when they got rid of Paul. Paul, who had such a heart for the people of Israel, was finally sent out of Israel, into Gentile territory, where he would spend the next seven to ten years living in obscurity in Tarsus.

Maybe you can relate. Maybe you were saved ten years ago, and you had such vision, such desire to be used in ministry or service. You thought, 'I'm tailor-made to do this,' or, 'I've got a call upon my life for this,' and you tried—but it just didn't work out. Maybe for the past ten years, you've been just waiting, wondering, 'Is the Lord *ever* going to use me?'

Be of good cheer! The man who would turn the world upside down—the most important preacher of all time, the most powerful person who has ever lived except for the Lord Jesus Christ—had to first experience shut doors, shut doors, shut doors, and ten years of sitting in Tarsus while the Lord reworked and rewired him. If the Lord is doing that in your life, don't be discouraged. Don't throw in the towel. Don't walk away. Let Him do His work and have His way. Go with the flow. Put away your agenda. Get back to basics and say, 'Lord, what wilt *Thou* have me to do?'

Maybe you can relate. Maybe you were saved ten years ago and you had such vision, such desire to be used in ministry or service. You thought, 'I'm tailor-made to do this,' or, 'I've got a call upon my life for that,' and you tried—but it just didn't work out. Maybe for the past ten years, you've been just waiting, wondering, 'Is the Lord *ever* going to use me?'

Be of good cheer! The man who would turn the world upside down—the most important preacher of all time, the most powerful person who has ever lived except for the Lord Jesus Christ—had to first experience shut doors, shut doors, shut doors, and ten years of sitting in Tarsus while the Lord reworked and rewired him. If the Lord is doing that in your life, don't be discouraged. Don't throw in the towel. Don't walk away. Let Him do His work and have His way. Put away your agenda. Get back to basics and say, 'Lord, what wilt *Thou* have me to do?'

APRIL 3

> *He saw in a vision evidently about the ninth hour of the day an angel of God coming in to him, and saying unto him, Cornelius. And when he looked on him, he was afraid, and said, What is it, Lord? And he said unto him, Thy prayers and thine alms are come up for a memorial before God. And now send men to Joppa, and call for one Simon, whose surname is Peter.*
>
> Acts 10:3-5

Why did the Lord send an angel to tell Cornelius to find Peter? Why didn't the angel himself share the Gospel with Cornelius? I believe the reason is that it is not the job of angels to share the Gospel. It's ours. God could thunder the Gospel from heaven if He so desired. But He's chosen to use you and me as instruments to tell people His Good News. If we ever get it through our heads that the Gospel really is good news, we wouldn't need classes or motivational seminars on witnessing. Telling people that the Lord loves them—that every sin they've ever committed, are committing, or will ever commit is forgiven because of Jesus' death on the Cross—is not a burden. It's a privilege! Talking about religion is a pain; but sharing the Gospel is pure joy.

Daniel 12:3 says those who turn many to righteousness shall shine as the stars forever. If you're a soul-winner, a Good News-sharer, you're going to shine—not only in heaven, but here on earth as well. How long has it been since you looked someone in the eye and said, 'I've got Good News for you!'? A week? A month? If you feel kind of dull and burned-out, share the Gospel and shine once again!

APRIL 4

While Peter yet spake these words, the Holy Ghost fell on all them which heard the word. And they of the circumcision which believed were astonished, as many as came with Peter, because that on the Gentiles also was poured out the gift of the Holy Ghost.
Acts 10:44-45

When did the Spirit move?—when Peter spoke the Word.

There was no mumbo jumbo. There was no seminar entitled, 'How To Speak In Tongues.' It was simply when Peter taught the Word that the Spirit began to move. People often say, 'You guys out there at the Fellowship spend too much time teaching and not enough time moving in the Spirit.' My answer to them is that the Biblical pattern is that of the Spirit moving *through* the teaching of the Word.

Colossians 3 says, 'Let the word of Christ dwell in you richly, speaking to yourselves in psalms and hymns and spiritual songs. Singing and making melody in your heart to the Lord. Wives submit to your husbands. Husbands love your wives. Children obey your parents. Employees obey your employers.'

Ephesians 5 and 6 say, 'Be not drunk with wine but be filled with the Spirit, speaking to each other with psalms and hymns and spiritual songs, singing and making melody in your heart to the

Lord. In everything, give thanks. Wives submit to your husbands. Husbands love your wives. Children obey your parents. Employees obey your employers.'

The results of 'letting the Word of Christ dwell in you richly' (Colossians 3) being exactly the same as being 'filled with the Spirit' (Ephesians 5), it follows that the Word and the Spirit are intimately linked together. If you want to live in the Spirit, keep in the Word. Become totally saturated with the Scriptures, and you'll find yourself overflowing with the Spirit.

APRIL 5

And I heard a voice saying unto me, Arise, Peter; slay and eat. But I said, Not so, Lord: for nothing common or unclean hath at any time entered into my mouth. But the voice answered me again from heaven, What God hath cleansed, that call not thou common.

Acts 11:7-9

Isaiah wrote, 'I will greatly rejoice in the Lord, my soul shall be joyful in my God; for he hath clothed me with the garments of salvation, he hath covered me with the robe of righteousness, as a bridegroom decketh himself with ornaments, and as a bride adorneth herself with her jewels' (Isaiah 61:10). What a fabulous day it is when we say, 'I'm righteous because I'm in Christ Jesus and because of what He has done for me on the Cross of Calvary. I'm His Bride. I am aware of my uncleanness, my four-footed beastiness, and my "fowl" mentality—but God has cleansed me eternally.'

Why is it that we beat ourselves when, in so doing, we only cast aspersions on the work Jesus did on Calvary? Salvation is so wonderful! What the Lord has done for us is incredible! But it's so hard for us to receive grace graciously because there's something in us that says, 'I don't deserve that kind of unconditional, unmerited love. I've got to earn it. I've got to prove myself worthy of it.'

Whenever you talk to the Lord freely and cast your care upon Him joyfully, expect Satan to whisper in your ear, 'You're a creep, a four-footed beast, foul, and unclean. You don't deserve to even enter God's presence, much less stay there!'

But may your answer always be: 'What He has cleansed, don't call uncommon. And He has cleansed *me.*'

APRIL 6

...And they sent forth Barnabas, that he would go as far as Antioch. Who, when he came, and had seen the grace of God, was glad, and exhorted them all, that with purpose of heart they would cleave unto the Lord.

Acts 11:22-23

Barnabas didn't exhort people to cleave unto the Law, but to cleave unto the *Lord*! He didn't lay down rules and trips on them. He said,

'Cleave to the Lord Jesus.
   Enjoy Him;
      Hang on to Him;
         Abide in Him
            With purpose of heart.'

It's the heart that's important, folks—not the mind. 'For with the *heart* man believeth unto righteousness' (Romans 10:10, emphasis mine).

Why is the Lord so interested in the heart? Because the mind can change very quickly and very easily. I can change my mind about something 100 times in a given day. I can go back and forth and back and forth depending on what I hear, the conclusions I make, the information I have. But the heart does not change easily. Think of that time, guys, when the girl of your dreams told you to pack sand—or girls, when your boyfriend walked out of your life. Your mind may have accepted it—but your heart didn't let go that easily.

So too with the Lord. He's not after an intellectual assertion. He desires heartfelt unification. That's why He says, 'Open your *heart* to Me—not your brain, but your heart.' You see, the Lord knows that if my faith is intellectual only, academic arguments about evolution or existentialism will cause me to get confused and to vacillate.

But if my *heart* is His, even though I may not be able to counter intellectual assaults, my relationship with Him will remain secure.

APRIL 7

Then departed Barnabas to Tarsus, for to seek Saul.
Acts 11:25

Anazeteo, the word translated 'to seek' means 'to search up and down, high and low.' It's used only one other time by Luke—in Luke 2 where he wrote that Mary and Joseph searched diligently for Jesus after Passover. The idea of *anazeteo* is that of a parent frantically, desperately, energetically searching for a lost child. And that's exactly what Barnabas, the Son of Consolation, the quintessential discipler, the ultimate encourager, did. He searched high and low for Saul, who had been in Tarsus for seven to ten years, living in obscurity.

I know some of you have been gifted and graced by the Lord to be Barnabases. Blessings on you—what a wonderful calling! You're encouragers, Sons and Daughters of Consolation. You're one-on-one kind of people. You have no need to be the big gun or the head hog at the trough. And because, like Barnabas, you're 'good men and women—full of the Holy Ghost and of faith'—I encourage you to search high and low for that one who, like Paul, is stuck off in obscurity—loving the Lord and committed to the Word, but in need of someone to throw an arm around him and draw him back to the fold, back to fellowship, back to ministry.

APRIL 8

Peter therefore was kept in prison: but prayer was made without ceasing of the church unto God for him.

Acts 12:5

Prayer was made on Peter's behalf, and what a difference it would make! What would have happened had they prayed when James was in prison? I wonder. Why didn't the Church pray for James? Perhaps they thought, 'Why pray? God's will is going to be done anyway.' The Bible says we have not because we ask not (James 4: 2). Why are we so dumb? Why do we have to learn the hard way? Why does there have to be difficulty, sadness, and tragedy before we say, 'You know what? I better pray'?

What difference does it make if you pray? All I know is this: the Church didn't pray for James, and he was sawn in half. They prayed for Peter, and he is about to be spared.

You see, the Lord has sovereignly chosen to work through the avenue of prayer in order to teach us how to talk *to* Him and depend *on* Him so that in the ages to come when we rule on behalf *of* Him, we will already have established communication *with* Him.

APRIL 9

When they were past the first and the second ward, they came unto the iron gate that leadeth unto the city; which opened to them of his own accord: and they went out, and passed on through one street; and forthwith the angel departed from him. And when Peter was come to himself, he said, Now I know of a surety, that the Lord hath sent his angel, and hath delivered me out of the hand of Herod, and from all the expectation of the people of the Jews.

Acts 12:10-11

What if, sitting in prison, Peter had said, 'Wow, what a dream,' and then continued sitting there? He would have been dead before his time. You see, even though Peter wasn't sure what he was seeing was reality, he acted on it as if it were. I wonder how many of us remain imprisoned because, although we hear teachings and exhortations, prophecies and illuminations—although we take notes and nod our heads in agreement, we just sit in our cells thinking they must be dreams. Our culture says, 'Take it easy.' Christianity says, 'Take a chance.' We'll never experience what God intends us to enjoy until we follow what He lays on our hearts by stepping out in faith.

Now sometimes when we step out, we find it was only a vision after all. That's OK. Proverbs says an empty stable stays clean, but an empty stable brings no profits (Proverbs 14:4). Some people say, 'I've never messed up. I've never made the mistake of following a vision. Look how clean my barn is. The floor is spotless.' But the farmer who has some meadow muffins on the floor and a few flies swarming around is the one who is productive.

Follow the Lord's leading even if it seems like only a vision. The worst that could happen is that a pasture patty or two could appear in your barn. But the best that could happen is, like Peter, you could be set free!

APRIL 10

And when she knew Peter's voice, she opened not the gate for gladness, but ran in, and told how Peter stood before the gate. And they said unto her, Thou art mad.

Acts 12:14-15

This story encourages me greatly because it shows that the Lord responds to prayer even when it's not accompanied by a great deal of faith. These believers were praying fervently and intensely, but you cannot say they were praying the prayer of faith since they didn't even have enough faith to believe Peter was free when he was knocking at their gate!

I like this story because I find myself praying a whole lot like them. I pray fervently, even intensely—but a lot of times I'm not sure anything's going to happen. This story tells me that's OK. God can still work through a tiny smattering of faith. Jesus said faith the size of a mustard seed—just a tiny bit of faith—can move mountains (Matthew 17:20). If you have faith enough just to pray, things can happen. Doors can open. Ask Peter!

You who feel imprisoned, boxed in, and like nothing's happening in your job, in your family, in your ministry—take heart and take hope and pray anyway. Sometimes it takes only enough faith to pray for a miracle to happen.

APRIL 11

Now there were in the church that was at Antioch certain prophets and teachers; as Barnabas, and Simeon that was called Niger, and Lucius of Cyrene, and Manaen, which had been brought up with Herod the tetrarch, and Saul.

Acts 13:1

The word 'Saul' means 'Requested One'—even as King Saul was requested by the people (I Samuel 8:6). What does 'Paul' mean? 'Little.' You see, something happened in Paul's life when he was converted to Christ. No longer did he identify himself as Saul, the Requested One, the Man in Demand. No, he said, 'Call me Little.'

In the early part of his ministry, Paul said, 'I am the least of the apostles' (I Corinthians 15:9).

In the middle of his ministry, he said, 'I am less than the least of all saints' (Ephesians 3:8).

At the end of his life, he said, 'I am the chief of sinners' (I Timothy 1:15).

I find it interesting that the longer Paul walked with the Lord, the more he realized how far he was from Him. That's always the way it is. The Pharisee, praying on the street corner said, 'God, I thank thee, I am not as other men,' while the true convert beat his breast and said, 'God be merciful to me a sinner' (Luke 18:11-13).

If you feel less than adequate for the challenge before you, for the day facing you, rejoice. You're in good company and in the perfect position for the Lord to do something wonderful in and through you.

APRIL 12

But he, whom God raised again, saw no corruption. Be it known unto you therefore, men and brethren, that through this man is preached unto you the forgiveness of sins: And by him all that believe are justified from all things, from which ye could not be justified by the law of Moses.

Acts 13:37-39

You are justified from all things. The word 'all' in Greek means '**all**'!

Last Sunday, before I baptized a young man, I told him, 'By your being here, you're testifying to everyone that you're serious about Jesus Christ. And because of that, any compromise that you're involved in, any sin or stuff that's going on in your life which is not right —' At this point, the guy started weeping, no doubt thinking that the sin in his life presently would disqualify him from salvation eternally. I said, 'You're here because you're serious about the Lord, and I want you to know any sin you're now committing is forgiven.'

With a look of amazement on his face, he looked up at me and said, 'Really? You mean I'm forgiven of the sin I'm *presently* involved in?'

And great was my joy when I could answer, 'Yes!'

We don't get it. We know our old sins are forgiven, but we think, 'Now I've got to toe the line and make sure I don't mess up from here on out.'

That's not salvation. That's not justification. True salvation, true justification means that *every* sin you've ever committed, are presently committing, or ever will commit in the future is forgiven and forgotten because where sin abounded, grace did much more abound (Romans 5:20) The full price has been paid. And all that remains is for us to believe it.

APRIL 13

And there came thither certain Jews from Antioch and Iconium, who persuaded the people, and, having stoned Paul, drew him out of the city, supposing he had been dead. Howbeit, as the disciples stood round about him, he rose up...

Acts 14:19-20

These disciples were risking their own lives by standing around Paul's corpse. What were they doing?

Were they praying?
Was Dr. Luke trying to revive him?
Were they crying?
Were they having a memorial service?

The Bible doesn't say. It just says they were *there*.

My mom, who lives in Southern California and who's been a widow for just about a month, told me her days have been very, very challenging. Yesterday, following an earthquake, she told me she felt helpless as the house and pool were rocking and rolling. When it was over, she went outside and started walking around her neighborhood, looking for someone to talk to. Since no one was outside, she went back to her house, only to feel a second quake. Just then, she said, the phone rang and on the other end was a sister from the Fellowship saying, 'Mary, I know you know God's promises, so you don't need a sermon. I just want to talk with you. No sermon, no promises—just talk.' My mom was deeply touched and greatly encouraged.

We all have experienced times when we have felt wiped out, finished, dead. And then some precious people gathered around us and we felt our hearts resurrected, our spirits revived. You can't stand with everyone who's down, but there are those whom the Lord will lead you to stand by, hang out with, and be there for—be it in person, over the phone, or through a letter. Be sensitive to the Lord's leading in this oh, so important avenue of ministry.

APRIL 14

...And came into the city: and the next day he departed with Barnabas to Derbe. And when they had preached the gospel to that city, and had taught many, they returned again to Lystra, and to Iconium, and Antioch.

Acts 14:20-21

Wrapping up their yearlong tour, which began in Acts 13, Paul and Barnabas doubled back on their return trip. In II Timothy 3:11, Paul made mention of Lystra, Iconium, and Antioch, when he wrote of the persecutions and afflictions he suffered there.

In Antioch, he was expelled.
In Iconium, he narrowly escaped.
In Lystra, he was stoned.

The Lord delivered Paul out of all of these dangerous traps—but in each case, it was in an entirely different way.

In Antioch, he was kicked out.
In Iconium, he caught wind of a plot.
In Lystra, he was left for dead.

I point this out because our tendency is to say, 'If I'm going to get out of my dilemma, it must be in this way, or according to these ten steps.' But God will not be boxed in by any program, agenda, or formula. He has promised to deliver us (II Corinthians 1:10)—but He has not predicted how He'll do it.

APRIL 15

Confirming the souls of the disciples, and exhorting them to continue in the faith, and that we must through much tribulation enter into the kingdom of God.

Acts 14:22

How do we enter into the Kingdom?—through much tribulation.

Shadrach, Meshach, and Abed-nego knew this. They were in a fiery trial indeed, yet they didn't come out until they were ordered out (Daniel 3:26) because they preferred walking in the fire with the Lord to sitting in the shade without Him.

What happened to the fourth Man in the furnace?
He remained in the fire (Daniel 3:25).

Where is Jesus—the fourth Man—today?
In the fire.

We have a tendency to try to avoid the fire whenever possible—and it's a great mistake. I'm not saying we should be masochists. I am, however, saying:

It's in the fire,
When times are tough,
When your heart is breaking

That Jesus is most visible,
Most real,
Most precious.

April 16

And they came and besought them, and brought
them out, and desired them to depart out of the city.
And they went out of the prison, and entered into the
house of Lydia: and when they had seen the brethren,
they comforted them, and departed.

Acts 16:39-40

Notice that Paul and Silas comforted the *brethren.* This poses an interesting question: up until the time Paul and Silas landed in prison, all they had seen in Macedonia were women. Who, then, were these *brethren?*

I suggest they were the prisoners who, in the dungeon with Paul, were converted by him when they heard his songs of praise. Paul's mindset concerning himself was, 'Go ahead. Beat me. Throw me in prison. I've been looking for some men to work with—now I can begin a jail ministry!'

But his mindset concerning others seemed to say, 'I am a Roman citizen, and I'll be watching you, so you had better watch your step with my brothers' (Acts 16:38).

When you and I come to the point where we can say, 'I don't care what happens to me—but when it comes to my brothers and sisters, I'll go to the wall for them and do whatever I can to cover and protect them,' *that's* maturity. Most of us protect ourselves and figure whatever happens to others is God's will. Paul did just the opposite.

No wonder the Lord used him so mightily.

APRIL 17

Therefore disputed he in the synagogue with the Jews, and with the devout persons, and in the market daily with them that met with him.

Acts 17:17

What did Paul do about the idolatry which broke his heart? He talked. In the church and on the street, Paul dialogued daily concerning the idolatry which gripped the city. So too, I am discovering that it's my job as both a pastor and as a father to dispute, to dialogue, and to discuss in depth.

Mom and Dad, we have the responsibility and the privilege:

To talk to our kids constantly,
  To share with our kids consistently,
    To invest in our kids wisely—

not so much telling them what to do, but teaching them how to think so that, slowly but surely, they will make the right decisions eventually.

How do we teach our kids how to think? Through the Scriptures.

How long has it been since, like Paul, you've talked with your kids in depth concerning issues as they relate to the Scriptures? In II Kings 4, we read that the responsibility of one of the young men who studied under Elisha was to prepare breakfast. But when the other students dove into the meal, they spit it out saying, 'This stuff is terrible. There's poison in the pot.' Spitting and sputtering, they were about to dump out the whole thing, when Elisha said, 'Hold on. Don't dump it out. Take the meal—the good stuff—and pour it into the bad stuff.' They did, and a miracle transpired, for when the good was poured in, the poison dissipated.

That's the key, Mom and Dad: we are not to pick the poison out of our kids' lives, for that will only lead to legalism and result in resentment and rebellion. Instead, we're to pour in the meal of the Word when our kids are poisoned by the pottage of the world, for greater is He that is in us than he that is in the world (I John 4:4).

Not only are we to pour in the meal, but we are to let the dirt go, for in II Kings 5, we see another relevant example in the life of Elisha. Naaman, a Syrian who had leprosy, was told by Elisha to dip in the Jordan River seven times. When Naaman obeyed, he was healed immediately. He then said to Elisha, 'I must go back to Syria, but I want to take some soil from Israel with me so I can worship Jehovah at home.' You see, in this region of the world, the prevalent point of view was that gods were local and could only be worshipped on the soil of the country of their origin. That is why Naaman wanted to take dirt from Israel back to Syria. Elisha's response? 'Go in peace. Do it.'

'Elisha, what are you doing?' I protest. 'You know that the God of Israel is not a local deity to be worshipped superstitiously. Why didn't you correct Naaman?' But upon further reflection, I believe there's a wise reason Elisha let Naaman return to Syria with dirt from Israel: Elisha knew Naaman's understanding of God was very limited. Naaman had been touched by God, had received healing from God, but he was not yet very deep in his knowledge of God. Did Elisha give him a lecture on theology? No. Elisha simply let him go his way, knowing that as a brand new baby believer, Naaman in time would discover he didn't need the dirt at all.

So too, mom and dad, if we fight every side-issue our kids struggle with, when they face the crucial issues—the ones dealing with sin and black and white matters—we will not have their attention. We see a lot of Christian young people whose circuits are blown because a well-meaning parent pushed too hard on non-essential matters and fought the wrong battles. Consequently, as a father I have to pray, 'Heavenly Father, help me to know what issues are essential for my kids. Help me see which questions need to be addressed, and help me, Lord, to let the bags of dirt go.'

Folks, our Father delights in dilemmas without easy answers because they make us go to Him. A lot of us would rather talk to a pastor, read a book, or seek counsel from a friend—but in so doing, we are robbed of the opportunity of cultivating a deep, intimate, eternal relationship with a Father who says, 'See Me for specific instructions. Search the Scriptures daily, and I'll guide you and show you what battles need to be fought, for I alone know the hearts of your children.'

APRIL 18

God that made the world and all things therein, seeing that he is Lord of heaven and earth, dwelleth not in temples made with hands.

Acts 17:24

God is our Creator. 'The Unknown God is the God who made everything,' Paul declared. 'He's too big for any singular temple or any carved altar no matter how beautiful or impressive it might appear.'

In Exodus 20, the Lord said, 'An altar of earth thou shalt make unto me...And if thou wilt make me an altar of stone, thou shalt not build it of hewn stone: for if thou lift up thy tool upon it, thou hast polluted it' (Exodus 20:24-25). In other words, the Lord said, 'If you build Me an altar, make it very simple—preferably of dirt. If you use rock, don't carve or polish it. Keep it simple so that the attention of the people will remain focused upon Me instead of on the altar.'

This gives me great hope because, although I want my life to be used by the Lord, I am increasingly aware of my plainness, my earthiness. I'm not very polished. I don't know if I'm 'cut out' to do great things for God. Yet, according to Exodus 20, these very doubts make me eminently qualified! Paul said, 'We have this treasure [Jesus Christ] in *earthen* vessels' (II Corinthians 4:7, emphasis mine). We're not fancy vases. We're just plain canning jars, boasting not of our exterior—but of whom we have within. If you don't feel capable to share, witness, teach, or minister, you are an ideal candidate because God will get the glory, not you.

APRIL 19

> *Because he hath appointed a day, in the which he will judge the world in righteousness by that man whom he hath ordained; whereof he hath given assurance unto all men, in that he hath raised him from the dead.*
>
> Acts 17:31

In John's Gospel, Jesus said the Father had committed to Him all judgment (John 5:22). Therefore, Jesus is 'that man' to whom Paul referred. I'm so grateful Jesus is my Judge because, having been 'tempted in all points like as we are' (Hebrews 4:15), He understands what I'm going through and the battles I wage.

Before he began his ministry, Ezekiel was caught up by the hand of the Lord and brought to the river Chebar, where the people of Judah were held captive (Ezekiel 3:15). Before Ezekiel delivered his heavy message of judgment, God first had him sit with the captives. So too, Jesus looked on the multitude with compassion (Matthew 9:36). He didn't come down *on* the sheep—He felt *for* them. Why? Because He sat where they sat. He walked where they walked.

Our leader, Jesus Christ, has gone through everything we're going through or will ever face. He understands it. Others might say, 'What's wrong with you?' Not our Lord. He says, 'I understand. I was tempted in the same way. I know exactly what you're struggling with.'

Before I can be effective in ministry, I must first sit where others have sat. It's easy to come down on people, easy to find fault with people, easy to be critical of people. But when you sit where they've sat, you have a ministry based on compassion and mercy, forgiveness and love.

I believe the Lord allows us to go through hurts, pains, and struggles—physically, emotionally, and spiritually—because they alone are what give us hearts of compassion.

APRIL 20

So Paul departed from among them. Howbeit certain
men clave unto him, and believed: among the which
was Dionysius the Areopagite, and a woman named
Damaris, and others with them.

Acts 17:33-34

Paul left Athens. And I personally believe that the message he gave there is recorded not as a model to copy, but as an example of failure. Why? In most of the other cities Paul visited, a church was born as a result of his ministry. Not so in Athens. Even though Paul gave an incredibly polished sermon, only a couple of folks believed. Why? I believe it is because in Acts 17, Paul mentioned neither the crucifixion of Christ, nor even the name of Jesus. Why? Could it be that, knowing he was in the company of brilliant men, Paul thought the coarseness of the crucifixion might not have been culturally correct?

In Church leadership journals and seminars today, the overriding message is: 'You must be culturally relevant. Relate to the culture; quote their poets; and be careful that you don't be too offensive or too simple.' That is why we see ministries, churches, Bible studies, and witnesses trying to be careful that they are relatable philosophically and relevant culturally. But, as a result, very few believe.

From Athens, Paul went to Corinth where he came 'not with excellency of speech or of wisdom, declaring unto you the testimony of God, determined not to know anything among you, save Jesus Christ, and him crucified' (I Corinthians 2:1-2).

A great church was born in Corinth, a powerful, impacting work of God took place there because Paul said, 'After Athens, I came to you in weakness, fear, and trembling, preaching nothing but Jesus and Him crucified.'

Regardless of whether you're preaching in South America, south central Los Angeles, or south Medford—wherever you go, whomever you're with, whether it be college grads or high-school drop-outs, liberals or conservatives, teenagers or golden-agers—the key to relating to anyone and everyone is to preach the Cross of Jesus Christ. That's where the power is; that is how we will truly be 'Cross-cultural.'

I have found that every single question and problem in life and ministry is always answered at the foot of the Cross and in the Person of Christ Jesus. Jesus said, 'If *I* be lifted up, I will draw all men to Myself' (John 12:32). Preach Jesus Christ and the power of the Cross, saints. Learn the lesson of Paul...

> Keep your ministry focused.
> Keep your message simple.
> Point people to the Cross.
> And they'll find Jesus.

APRIL 21

For I am with thee, and no man shall set on thee to hurt thee...

Acts 18:10

'Paul,' said the Lord, 'I'm giving you this promise: I am with thee, and no man shall set on thee to hurt thee.' So too, the Lord has given over 3,000 promises to you and me in His Word. He has already given them—the only thing that remains to be done is for us to believe them. Consequently, we have a choice to make: to bail out in the night, or, like Paul, to continue in the city.

You see, contrary to Paul's typical pattern of making short stops in the cities to which he ministered, Paul stayed in Corinth a year and a half. Why? I suggest he was established because of the Lord's promise. So too, we don't need to be on an emotional roller coaster—rejoicing one moment and fearful the next. Like Paul, we can say, 'The Lord gave a promise to me. Therefore I will continue on steadfastly.'

Turn to Isaiah 7 and contrast Paul with another man who also received a promise from the Lord...

Rezin, king of Syria, and Pekah, king of the ten northern tribes of Israel, formed an alliance and planned an attack against Judah, the two southern tribes. The Lord told Isaiah to speak to Ahaz, king of Judah, who was fearful and upset about the upcoming battle. 'Your response to the promise of God will have no effect on the outcome of the battle,' Isaiah told Ahaz, 'for God has already determined that Israel and Syria will be unsuccessful. *However*, your response to God's promise will have great effect upon you, for if you don't believe God, you won't be established. You'll be unstable. You'll be emotional. You'll cave in.'

So too with us. The Lord says to you and me...

> *In my Father's house are many mansions: if it were not so, I would have told you. I go to prepare a place for you. And if I go and prepare a place for you, I will come again, and receive you unto myself, that where I am, there ye may be also.*
>
> —John 14:2-3

And we know that all things work together for good
to them that love God, to them who are the called
according to His purpose.

—Romans 8:28

Like Paul, we can be established and strengthened in such promises, or, like Ahaz, we can fret and fear needlessly. Whether we choose to claim them or ignore them, God will keep His Word. He will prepare a place for us as believers, return for us, and work all things together for good regardless of whether we believe Him or not. But if we don't take Him at His Word, we will live a life of instability, inconsistency, and anxiety—totally needlessly.

'But what if I'm misunderstanding the promises?' you ask. 'What if I'm misreading the Bible? What if I'm misinterpreting the context? So often I come across a promise and I believe it's for me—but what if it's not?'

Consider Isaiah's words to Ahaz: 'Therefore the Lord himself shall give you a sign; Behold, a virgin shall conceive, and bear a son, and shall call his name Immanuel' (Isaiah 7:14). The word 'you' in this verse being plural, the sign was not only for Ahaz but for everyone. 'Ahaz,' the Lord declared, 'a sign will be given to you—and not to you only, but to all people. A virgin shall conceive, and a Son shall be born whose name will be Immanuel—God with us.'

God still says to the Ahaz in you and me, 'I am Immanuel. I am the ultimate source of stability.' You see, I might question if I understand the Scriptures properly. I might wonder if what I'm reading is applicable to me personally. I might doubt whether I interpret the theology correctly. But the Lord says to me, 'Know this: even if you're not sure if the promises apply to you, I, Immanuel, am with you.'

On a trip to Los Angeles recently, Mary Elizabeth rode in the front seat between Tammy and me. Fascinated by a map of California, she kept busy trying to figure out where we were and where we were going. At five years of age, Mary can barely read. So, even if she was confused about where we were in relationship to her map or if we were going the right way according to her interpretation of the map—guess what? It didn't matter at all because she wasn't driving. I, her father, was in the driver's seat. She could have been reading the map backwards and upside down and it would have had no effect whatsoever on my ability to get her to L.A.

So too, even if we're not reading the map of God's Word correctly— even if sometimes we feel like we're holding it upside down and backwards—the fact remains that Immanuel is with us, and *He's* in the driver's seat.

The only thing that could have gone wrong on our trip to L.A. would have been if Mary suddenly lurched out of her seat and grabbed the wheel, saying, 'Let me steer. Let me steer.' You see, gang, anytime we grab the wheel of our lives and say, 'Let me steer; I gotta figure this out; I have to make this happen,' our lives begin to career and swerve—and we end up wondering why we crash unnecessarily.

Read the Word, saints. Saturate yourselves in Scripture and look for His promises as you rest in His presence.

APRIL 22

And he sailed from Ephesus. And when he had landed at Caesarea, and gone up, and saluted the church, he went down to Antioch.

Acts 18:21-22

Although he was determined to go to Jerusalem, and although he had taken a vow in order to fit in *at* Jerusalem, Paul didn't stay in Jerusalem. You see, Paul was not always real popular in Jerusalem.

The Jerusalem boys—Peter, James, and John—had a different flavor than the Antioch boys—Paul and Barnabas, Timothy and Silas...

James would stress that faith without works is dead (James 2:20). John would say, 'Children, keep yourself from idols' (I John 5:21). Peter would write, 'Be sober, be vigilant; because your adversary the devil, as a roaring lion, walketh about, seeking whom he may devour' (I Peter 5:8).

But Paul just went on chapter after chapter celebrating the finished work of the Cross of Calvary.

As you read the New Testament, you can feel the healthy tension between the brothers in Antioch and the brothers in Jerusalem.

I share this with you not simply as a historical note, but to realize that even today different people will have different flavors within the Body of Christ. There will be Pauls and Barnabases who will comfort you by reminding you that you're perfect in Christ, that the veil is rent, and that the work is done.

And just when you begin to settle in maybe a bit too much, a James or a Peter will remind you that faith without works is dead, that you must be sober and vigilant.

Like the tension on a trampoline, this balance is healthy and important, for without it, we would hit bottom in one extreme or the other.

APRIL 23

And he began to speak boldly in the synagogue: whom when Aquila and Priscilla had heard, they took him unto them, and expounded unto him the way of God more perfectly.

Acts 18:26

Realizing Apollos didn't have the full story, Aquila and Priscilla took him aside. They didn't interrupt the service, but they privately shared with him the message of the Gospel.

I love Aquila and Priscilla for being there with hearts to serve in humility. And I love Apollos for being teachable. After all, he could have said, 'Who are you, you tentmakers? I am a man mighty in the Scriptures, eloquent of speech, fervent of spirit—read Acts 18 if you don't believe me.' But that wasn't his heart. Apollos shared what he had, and the Lord sent Aquila and Priscilla to give him more.

How can you know more about the way and heart of the Lord? Share what you already know.

I read about an Army paratrooper who recently completed his 2,000th jump. Asked by one of his students why he got into parachuting, he answered, 'I was an infantryman 15,000 feet in the air when the third engine on our plane went out. I jumped because I had no other choice.'

When do you become a teacher, a Bible student, an evangelist? When you take the jump, knowing you are the person on your street, in your office, or at your school who knows more about the Kingdom than does the person next to you.

God will give you opportunity to minister tomorrow if you choose to take it because I guarantee you will find yourself next to someone who is dumber than you concerning the things of the Lord. And when He does, you can either say, 'I'm not a pastor. I don't have a lot of knowledge theologically. I don't know that much about the Bible, so I won't say anything,'—or you can be a Priscilla or an Aquila and say, 'I may not be a pastor or a theologian, but I know more than this guy next to me, so I'm going to jump in and share with him because his plane is going down.'

April 24

...He said unto them, Ye know, from the first day that I came into Asia after what manner I have been with you...

Acts 20:18

Paul said, 'From the day I arrived in your city, you knew what kind of man I was.'

In talking to a couple moving to a different part of the country, I said, 'You're going 1,500 miles away from here. No one will know you. You don't have to live down, worry about, or explain any mistakes and misunderstandings of the past. So from day one, identify yourself as a radical Jesus Person.' If you carry your Bible to your new job or school the first day, people are not going to say to you, 'Hey, want to do some crack? Want to watch a porno flick? Want to party?' They'll know from the very beginning that you're a follower of the Lord.

Parents, help your kids understand this. When they graduate from elementary school and go to junior high, say, 'Guess what? You have a new start. Go radical for the Lord.' And when they get through junior high, say, 'You're going off to high school. Here's another chance for a first impression. Be extreme for Jesus.' At each stage of life, encourage your kids or your grandkids to go for it from the first day. I don't know where we get this idea that we should 'fit in' and 'relate,' because if people don't know where we stand, there will be temptations coming our direction that wouldn't have been there had we taken a stand the first day.

APRIL 25

...At all seasons...

Acts 20:18

In ministry and in service, you will inevitably go through various seasons...

There is the excitement of spring when you get new understandings from the Word and fresh insights into the Lord. Things blossom and bud; new growth abounds.

Spring leads to the fruitfulness of summer, when you start to see ministry opportunities open. The Lord uses your life and you say, 'Wow! Fruit!'

Then comes fall when the Lord says, 'There are some dead leaves that need to be knocked off.' The winds blow, trials come, and you wonder what's going on.

Fall is followed by winter—long periods where you feel nothing and hear very little.

Early in my walk, not understanding the necessity of seasons, I used to freak out when winter came. 'Oh, my,' I thought, 'I must be backsliding. I must be doing something terrible because I don't feel the Lord's presence.' In reality, however, it was in the wintertime that the Lord was giving me the opportunity to walk by faith and not by feeling.

What are we to do during the winter times in our lives? Worship. Praise. Sing. Why? Because in the wintertime, we have unique opportunities to worship the Lord without immediately receiving more than we give.

As I sat in the Sanctuary in early morning worship, I saw a brother in the winter season of his life come towards the Communion table and go to his knees in prayer while lifting his hands in praise. A few hours earlier this man's wife had been taken home to heaven, yet he didn't call for counseling; he didn't ask for pity; he came to worship.

How I pray we will walk in this kind of maturity.

APRIL 26

Serving the Lord with all humility of mind...
                                          Acts 20:19

Paul's gifts were great. His abilities were mind-boggling. Intellectually, theologically, oratorically, the guy was incredible. Yet he said, 'I served you with humility of mind' because he knew every ability he had was a gift from God.

Humility of mind means truly esteeming others better than yourself (Philippians 2:3). Humility of mind means not finding fault with a brother or sister, but finding fruit—approving those things which are excellent within them. Humility of mind means realizing it's the grace of God, not our own merit, which allows us to know Him and walk with Him.

I recall driving Highway 42 from San Bernardino to Twin Peaks where I was to address a group of spiritual leaders. As I wound my way up the road, I found myself praying, 'Lord, I want to be like You when I talk to my brothers at the conference.'

I thought it was a pretty good prayer—until the Lord spoke to my heart so clearly that I literally had to pull of the road.

'You want to be like Me?' He asked.
'Yes,' I answered.

'Why do you want to be like Me, Jon?'

'Well, Lord, because You're so awesome.'

'Did you ask to be like Me when you were with your kids two mornings ago?'

'No.'

'But you're asking to be like Me now—when you're about to talk to a group of pastors?'

I was busted. I had prayed that prayer hundreds, if not thousands of times before. It was a noble request, but you see, my motivation was amiss. I didn't necessarily want to be like Him so I could serve my kids humbly. No, I wanted to be like Him so I could minister powerfully.

Watch out for those times when you think you are being spiritual, lest an entirely different form of pride surface. Instead, be like Paul. Serve the Lord with humility of mind.

APRIL 27

...So that I might finish my course with joy, and the ministry, which I have received of the Lord Jesus, to testify the gospel of the grace of God.

Acts 20:24

The word 'joy' means 'exceedingly happy.' The way to happiness is to testify of the grace of God. Many people grew up in an atmosphere or in a church which said, 'It's your responsibility to pray, to study, to serve.' And they became burdened by a weight of responsibilities they could never fulfill.

Then, at some point in their walk, they understood that, on the basis of the finished work of Jesus Christ, they didn't *have* to study; they didn't *have* to pray; they didn't *have* to worship.

'You mean, Lord, my sin is forgiven?' they said. 'I'm robed in Your righteousness? I don't have to work to try and attain Your favor or merit Your blessing?'

'Yes,' answered God. 'It's all grace.'

'You mean You love me as much when I'm not doing so well as when I'm studying Leviticus and Deuteronomy?'

'Yes.'

'Wouldn't You love me more if I was studying Leviticus and Deuteronomy?'

'No, I can't love you anymore than I love you right now.'

And what does that do? 'Wow,' we say, 'I wonder what Leviticus says. Where is Deuteronomy, anyway?' We find ourselves *wanting* to study. We find ourselves *enjoying* worship. We find ourselves freely talking to the Lord. Our Christian walk changes from responsibility to response—and that's when it becomes a whole lot of fun.

If you want an explosion of joy in your heart today, be like Paul—'testify the gospel of the grace of God.' Go to the person you work with and say, 'Every sin you committed last weekend is forgiven. Every sin you're thinking about today is paid for. You're free because, when Jesus died on the Cross, He died for every sin every man has ever done. There's only one unpardonable sin, and that is refusing to receive His forgiveness.'

An interesting thing happens to a person who's sharing his faith: he becomes a channel through which the joy and power of the Lord flows. For just as electricity will not enter an object unless there's an outflow from that object, the power of the Lord will not enter a church or an individual in whom there is no conduit for evangelism. When people say, 'The electricity is gone from our church corporately or from my life personally,' invariably it's because there's no outflow.

Paul was one who was charged-up, red-hot, and turned-on because he was one who continually testified of the Gospel. He never stopped sharing his faith in Christ Jesus.

APRIL 28

Take heed therefore unto yourselves, and to all the flock...

Acts 20:28

Notice the order: take heed to yourself first. Make sure you're cultivating a personal devotional life; that you're a man or a woman of prayer. Make sure you're one who is engaged in consistent communion with the Lord personally.

Abraham was a lover of God. On his way to the Promised Land, wherever he went, he built an altar. As he traveled, because the Lord prospered him more and more, his flocks began to increase. So he dug wells to ensure that his flocks were sufficiently watered.

When Abraham's son, Isaac, came on the scene, seeing his father's expansive flocks, he decided the key to his father's success was digging wells. So Isaac dug many wells—but he built only one altar. Consequently, his wells were named Sitnah and Esek, or 'Strife' and 'Contention.'

When Isaac's son, Jacob—the third generation from Abraham— appeared, he built no altars and dug no wells. Instead, he said, 'The key to seeing the flock grow is ingenuity, creativity, and genetic engineering' (Genesis 30).

That's what often happens: a man or woman loves God and, from that love, there's an overflow whereby the flock grows. Then the second generation says, 'I too want to be in ministry and see a flock grow'—so they copy the outward activity of the generation before them—but it only produces tension, strife, and agony. Why? Because they're not altar-builders.

Finally, the third generation comes along and says, 'Programs— that's the key. We'll have excellent entertainment. We'll have relevant, current messages which, although they aren't necessarily

Biblical, speak to the needs of the people.' And it's exciting for awhile, but it's not sustaining. They have to try harder and harder in their Jacob mentality to keep everything going with creativity and ingenuity.

True ministry begins with an altar-building man or woman loving God and enjoying the Lord. All too often, however, the lover of God is followed by a well-digger—one who wants to see the flock watered, but who has lost the understanding of the altar and a personal, private passion for the Lord. The third generation, the program people, the Jacobs, then come on the scene and say, 'We're going to really wow the world with our creativity.'

I see this happening not only in churches, but in my own life as well. Quite frankly, I can go through all three generations in one day. I can start the morning as an altar-builder, a lover of God. Then, sometime around noon, I can become a well-digger saying, 'Lord, I don't have time to talk to You. I've got to water these sheep.' As a result, in the evening, I find myself thinking, 'Oh, no. My ministry's slipping. I better do something creative and ingenious.'

What happened to Jacob? Finally, this clever heel-snatcher came to the end of his rope when he heard his estranged brother, Esau, was coming with 400 men to meet him. After Jacob crossed a little creek called Jabok, he wrestled the angel of the Lord and said, 'I'm not going to let You go until You bless me' (Genesis 32:26). Talk about close contact and a restoration of intimacy! Jacob was no longer striping stakes; he was wrestling with God all night long.

In the morning, the Lord said, 'Jacob you have prevailed. No longer will you be called Jacob, or, 'Clever One.' You'll now be called Israel, which means 'Governed by God,' because at last you understand it's staying close to *Me*; it's wrestling with *Me*; it's depending on *Me* that matters.'

I've seen people finally get to the place of being exhausted from 'Jacob-ing' it. They get back to the altar, back to saying, 'Lord, we just want to know You.' People like that get used by the Lord time after time as they touch people from the overflow of an 'altered' life.

APRIL 29

...And to all the flock...

Acts 20:28

Take heed to yourself first and then to the flock, because if you're in right relationship with the Lord, blessings will flow through you to the flock of your family, the Sunday school kids you teach, the people to whom you witness.

Towards the end of his life, David was surrounded by a group of men who are recorded as being men who killed giants (II Samuel 21:15-22). Saul, on the other hand, who had been afraid of Goliath, was surrounded by men who never engaged in battle against a giant. Therein lies an extremely important principle as it relates to ministry: if I want those around me to be giant-killers, I must kill giants myself.

If you're not worshipping or witnessing, chances are, your family, congregation, and friends won't worship or witness because, as seen in the lives of David and Saul, what you are is what those around you will become.

I cannot stress too heavily the importance of a secret, personal devotional life. 'Take heed to yourself and to the flock,' wrote Paul—not because the priority is to be on self, but because a preparation of self will allow you to see those around you kill giants.

APRIL 30

...To feed the church of God...

Acts 20:28

After shepherding sheep on the backside of the desert, the Lord called Moses to shepherd three million people through the wilderness. On their way to the Promised Land, his authority was questioned time after time. In Numbers 16, we read that Dathan, Abiram, and Korah brought 250 leaders of the nation of Israel to Moses, saying, 'Who gave you authority to lead us?"

In response to their question, the Lord instructed Aaron to have one leader from each tribe place a rod in the tabernacle along with his. They did so, and the next morning, the rods looked just as they had left them—all except for Aaron's, which had blossomed.

From whence comes authority in ministry or in your family?—from the blossom of fruitfulness.

What is fruit? Galatians 5:22 defines it as love—love which is joy, love which is peace, love which is longsuffering, love which is gentle, good, faithful, meek, and temperate. If we truly love people, we will have authority to give direction to them because they will see the fruitfulness of the Lord's love blossoming in us.

The story of Moses continues. The years passed and the people began complaining once again saying, 'We're out of water, Moses. You've brought us out here to die.' In response to their complaint, the Lord instructed Moses to speak to the rock from which water would flow (Numbers 20:8). Instead of speaking to the rock, however, Moses struck it with the rod, while saying to the people, 'You rebels. Must we fetch water for you?'

What happened to the rod as he smote the rock?

No doubt, the blossoms fell off;
Most likely, the fragrance was diminished;
Surely, the fruitfulness was lost.

Whenever I beat one of God's people verbally or in my heart, I'm smiting Christ, the Rock of my salvation, and destroying the fruit of His Spirit in the process. Therefore, it is not my job to beat the flock—to analyze, scrutinize, or criticize. It is my job to feed the flock—to encourage, nourish, and love. Certainly feeding includes warning and exhorting—but it does not include beating, bruising, or wounding.

'Feed the flock,' said Paul, not, 'Beat the flock,' because there has already been One who was bloodied, bruised, and beaten on our behalf.

They beat His face.
 They beat a crown of thorns into His scalp.
  They beat Him with rods.
   They beat Him with fists.
    They beat Him with words.

Therefore, because He was beaten in our place, I must not beat myself or beat others.

May 1

And the Lord said unto me, Arise, and go into Damascus; and there it shall be told thee of all things which are appointed for thee to do.

Acts 22:10

'Go into the city, Paul, and when you get there, further instructions will be given.' That's always the way of the Lord: one step at a time. He gives His people one instruction and waits until they obey it before more information is given.

In the midst of a great revival taking place through Philip's ministry in Samaria, the Lord told him to go to Gaza. Philip obeyed, and the Ethiopian eunuch was saved (Acts 8).

While Peter was praying on his rooftop, the Lord instructed him to follow three men who would knock on his door. Peter obeyed, and the house of Cornelius was converted (Acts 10).

The Lord called Abraham from Ur and told him to follow Him one step at a time. Abraham obeyed, and a nation was born (Hebrews 11:8).

Every time the Lord calls a man or a woman, every time He wants to bless someone, He does it by encouraging them to take a step of faith. Many times a lot of us miss out on years, or even a lifetime, of being in God's will because we don't act on the singular instruction He gives us. Precious people, we must obey the one thing the Lord has made known to us either through His Word, through times of prayer, or through the desires He has placed within our hearts.

If we knew how it was going to work—it wouldn't be faith.
If we knew where the supplies would come from—it wouldn't be faith.
If we had it all mapped out—it wouldn't be faith.

Faith says, 'OK, Lord. Like Abraham I don't know exactly how it's all going to work out—but here we go!'

In I Samuel 14, the Israelites were at a standoff in a battle against the Philistines. Perhaps looking up at the stars one night, Jonathan was reminded that the Creator who made such beauty and displayed such glory was with him constantly. Perhaps pondering God's promise that one could chase 1,000 and two could put to flight 10,000 if they were in God's will (Deuteronomy 32:30), he poked his armor-bearer and said, 'Let's sneak over to the Philistine camp and see what the Lord might want to do.'

So while the other guys snoozed, Jonathan and his armor-bearer made their way to the camp of the Philistines. As they approached the Philistine garrison, Jonathan said to his armor-bearer, 'Now wait a minute. We want to be men of faith, but we don't want to be fools. I'll yell to the Philistines, and if they say, 'Stay there, you guys. We see you, and we're coming to get you,'—we'll split and make our way back to camp as fast as we can. But if they say, 'Come up here you guys. We'll take you on'—we'll take that as a word from the Lord, and we'll go get them.'

That's the way I believe the Christian life should be lived: by taking steps of faith without being foolish. We should put on our armor, get ready for battle, go out to the edge and say, 'Here we are, Lord. What do You want to do?'

Jonathan called out. The Philistine answered, 'Hey, come up here, and we'll teach you guys a lesson,'—and Jonathan said to his armor-bearer, 'God is with us. Let's go get 'em.'

God was indeed with them, and a great, miraculous victory took place that day when two guys took on an entire army—and won.

Stepping out in faith and yet always being willing to pull back if God isn't in it—that's the key. Step out in faith—but if you sense the Lord's not in it, re-group, and see what else He might want to do. Be a Jonathan. Take a step of faith. You'll never regret it.

MAY 2

And they came to the chief priests and elders, and said, We have bound ourselves under a great curse, that we will eat nothing until we have slain Paul. Now therefore ye with the council signify to the chief captain that he bring him down unto you tomorrow, as though ye would enquire something more perfectly concerning him: and we, or ever he come near, are ready to kill him. And when Paul's sister's son heard of their lying in wait, he went and entered into the castle, and told Paul.

Acts 23:14-16

It was neither coincidence nor accident that Paul's nephew was in earshot of the plan to kill Paul. It was part of God's program for Paul.

At some point in their walk, most believers ask, 'How can I know what God wants me to do?' And like Elijah in I Kings 19, they sit in a cave wondering. Like Elijah, they feel the earth shaking—but the Lord is not in the earthquake. They see the fire glowing—but the Lord is not in the fire. They watch the wind blowing—but the Lord is not in the wind. Many people are still looking for an earth-shaking confirmation, a fiery illumination, or a wind to blow them in Divine direction.

But it's much simpler than that: as Elijah discovered, God's is a still, small voice (I Kings 19:12). The Lord whispers in your heart, writes desires upon your heart, and then gives confirmation to your heart through situations and people around you. Accuse me of being simplistic, but I find it so wonderful to say, 'Father, this is the desire of my heart. I'm going to pursue this course, knowing You will close and open doors—as You lead me in a supernaturally natural way.'

For whatever question you face presently, just make sure your heart is open to the Lord—and He'll have a nephew in the right place at the right time who will overhear a conversation, go to the Roman captain, and set events in motion which the world will call luck, but in which you'll see the hand of God.

MAY 3

And after certain days, when Felix came with his wife Drusilla, which was a Jewess, he sent for Paul, and heard him concerning the faith in Christ. And as he reasoned...

Acts 24:24-25

Paul, an intellectual giant of theology, a lover of God, and a lover of people, begins to *reason* with Felix and Drusilla. Our faith is exceedingly reasonable. That is why I welcome opportunities to go into high school classes or college seminars to discuss the faith with so-called intellectuals.

The longer I walk with the Lord, the more I understand that our faith is reasonable in every way—logically, philosophically, scientifically.

The cover story in *TIME* magazine two weeks ago was about a 6,000-year-old frozen corpse discovered in the crevice of a glacier in the Alps last summer. I chuckled my way through this very interesting article as I read that the scientific world was shocked to find out that the 'Ice Man' wasn't bowed over with sloping forehead and thick jaw, as had been hypothesized and accepted as fact for decades—but that he looked just like us. He had lined shoes, sewn clothes, and sophisticated tools centuries before he was 'supposed' to have been able to do any of those things.

Prior to this discovery, ancient man was regarded as little more than a glorified ape at best. But the discovery of Ice Man calls all previous suppositions into question. If only these scientists had read their Bibles—they wouldn't have been surprised.

Concerning the things of the Lord, Paul could reason with complete assurance, knowing that our faith can withstand any question and every argument.

MAY 4

...Of righteousness...

Acts 24:25

Felix and Drusilla were not righteous. Their life was filthy, their history diabolical. They were not liked by the people they ruled and were not trusted by even their own household of slaves, servants, and companions. But Paul must have told them that if any man be in Christ, he is a new creature. Old things pass away; all things become new (II Corinthians 5:17). 'Felix, Drusilla, you can have a new beginning. You can become righteous in Christ Jesus,' Paul must have said.

When I was saved, not only did Jesus come into me, but just as wonderful, just as fabulous is the fact that I was hidden in Him (Colossians 3:3). Therefore, when the Father looks at me, He doesn't see sin. He sees Jesus.

When a believer finally understands this concept, how his walk will change. No longer will he think, 'God won't listen to me or be kind to me because I'm such an idiot.' No, he'll say, 'When God looks at me, He doesn't see my sin. He sees His Son.'

May 5

*But after two years Porcius Festus came into Felix'
room: and Felix, willing to shew the Jews a pleasure,
left Paul bound.*

Acts 24:27

Felix and his wife, Drusilla, both had an opportunity to hear the
Gospel, but they put off making a decision. This is not surprising.
Eighty-two percent of all Christians are saved at the age of 19 or
younger. The lower the age, the higher the percentage of those who
make a commitment to Jesus Christ. Why? Because a person who
puts off a decision, saying,

'I'll think about it;
I'll wait until later;
I want more information,'

will find himself falling into a pattern that becomes more and more
difficult to break.

He trembles when he says 'No' to the Holy Spirit the first time.
The next time he hears the Gospel and says 'No', he trembles less.
The third time, it's pretty easy to say 'No'.
The fourth time it's a piece of cake.

This happens not only when the Spirit is convicting unbelievers, but
also when He convicts Christians. The first time we are tempted to
do wrong, we tremble. The second time the temptation comes our
way, it still kind of bothers us, but not as much as it did the first
time. The third time bothers us a little less. And the fourth time,
giving in to temptation doesn't bother us at all.

Folks, the conscience must be guarded very carefully because it
can become seared very easily (I Timothy 4:2). In fact, not only will
our conscience become seared or desensitized, it will become evil
(Hebrews 10:22), justifying wrong by whispering to us, 'Don't worry
about what you're doing or the show you're watching. That's simply
the way society is. There's nothing wrong with it. It's just life.'

Felix and Drusilla went from having a tender conscience—shaken when they felt the convicting work of the Spirit (Acts 24:25), to having a seared conscience—when they didn't tremble quite so easily, to having an evil conscience—where they were only interested in making a deal monetarily. The result?—their lives were destroyed, and they were damned eternally.

You might be saying, 'What if I'm doing things which used to bother me but don't anymore? What if I have a seared or an evil conscience? Is there any hope for me?'

Yes. The Lord is so faithful. He comes to us over and over again, giving us opportunity to get right with Him. But in Genesis 6:3, God said, 'My Spirit shall not always strive with man. I'll come to you. I'll speak to you. But I'm not always going to wrestle with you.'

Therefore, if you are so graced to hear His voice in your heart speaking to you about an issue—don't follow the folly of Felix. Respond immediately, and you'll be blessed eternally.

You really will.

MAY 6

Unto which promise our twelve tribes, instantly serving God day and night, hope to come. For which hope's sake, king Agrippa, I am accused of the Jews. Why should it be thought a thing incredible with you, that God should raise the dead?

Acts 26:7-8

'Oh, Agrippa, you who know the stories of the Bible, you who are aware of our history, why should it seem like an amazing thing to you that God could raise the dead?' asked Paul, referring to the resurrection of Jesus Christ.

The same question could be asked today. People have trouble with miracles because they fail to comprehend the power and the reality of God. You see, the difficulty of a task can only be determined when measured against the agent who attempts to accomplish it.

If Benjamin, my five-year-old, went into the YMCA and tried to press 300 pounds, we would all get uptight and tell him not to even try. But if a weightlifter took up the challenge, we'd say, 'No problem!'

J.B. Phillips was right in his contention that sometimes our God is too small. If we get hung up on the problems and the challenges before us, it's because we fail to realize the size, strength, and heart of our Father.

The God who made 100 billion stars in the Milky Way Galaxy and 100 million galaxies at least the size of the Milky Way, spans the entire universe between His thumb and little finger (Isaiah 40:12). Our Father is big! Yet He is the same God who made the atom—a miniature planetary system so small it takes 1 million bunched together to equal the thickness of a single strand of human hair.

Most of us do not doubt the power of God physically. Instead, we doubt His willingness to intervene in our situations personally.

Why should He care about us? The answer lies in the Cross. 'If God did not spare His only Son that we might be saved, shall He not freely give us all things pertaining to life?' asked Paul (Romans 8:32). He will supply everything that's good for me. How do I know?—because He already gave me the very best when He gave me His Son.

MAY 7

*And the soldiers' counsel was to kill the prisoners,
lest any of them should swim out, and escape. But
the centurion, willing to save Paul, kept them from
their purpose; and commanded that they which could
swim should cast themselves first into the sea, and
get to land: And the rest, some on boards, and some
on broken pieces of the ship. And so it came to pass,
that they escaped all safe to land.*

Acts 27:42-44

Just as the Lord promised, everyone on board survived the storm.
Following are four reasons why storms come into our lives...

1. Storms of correction. Ask brother Jonah about these. When a
storm arose and he was tossed overboard and swallowed by a great
fish, it was because he was rebelling against the Lord (Jonah 1:10).
So too, sometimes when I'm in a place of disobedience or rebellion,
the Lord will allow a storm to get me on track again.

2. Storms of perfection. After Jesus fed the five thousand, He sent
His disciples across the Sea of Galilee (Matthew 14). Midway through
their journey, a storm arose around them. Why? For their perfection.
You see, Jesus knew it wouldn't be too many months before these
same disciples would see another multitude of five thousand—not
fed, but saved (Acts 4:4)—followed by another storm—not on the
sea, but of persecution within the Church (Acts 8: 1). Thus, Jesus
was training His boys to endure the storms of persecution which
inevitably follow the seasons of blessing.

Faith is not a pill we take, folks. It's a muscle we work. Therefore, the
Lord will send me into a storm from time to time not for correction,
but for perfection, because the way I react to storms internally will
tell me where I'm at spiritually. Storms provide a unique opportunity
for me to see where I'm at and to grow in my understanding that the
Lord will come through at the right time, saying, 'Be of good cheer.
We're going to make it.'

3. Storms of protection. Because 'Noah found grace in the eyes of the Lord' (Genesis 6:8), God sent a storm to drown out all of the carnality, sin, and iniquity which surrounded him. The storm raged for forty days and nights, but Noah and his family were not only protected in the storm—they were protected by the storm.

'Oh, no!' we cry. 'My TV blew up,' or 'My stereo doesn't work. What a storm I'm in.' But, as in Noah's case, it might be a storm of protection—protecting us from the carnality and iniquity which surround us continually.

4. Storms of direction. Knowing there was a group of people on the island of Malta in need of ministry, the Lord said, 'Before you go to Rome, Paul, I'm going to allow you to be blown off course because of something I want you to do for Me—something you never would have thought of on your own, something that wasn't part of your agenda. I have some people to whom I want to minister, so I'll allow a storm to arise, which, although it looks like it's blowing you off course, will put you in the very place I want to use you.'

'How come I got canned?'
 'Why did she dump me?'
  'How come it's not working out?' we ask.

Don't be blown away. Realize that the Lord is changing your direction because there's something He wants to do that will ultimately be a blessing.

Storms of correction and perfection, storms of protection and direction—how can you know which one you might be in? Talk to the Father. Say, 'Why am I in this storm, Lord? Is it correction—or are You perfecting me for what You see is coming my way? Is there a new direction for my life—or are You protecting me from something which would be very damaging?'

How long has it been since you got away to spend time with the Lord? Clear your schedule and seek Him—and you'll be blown away by His goodness rather than by the storm.

MAY 8

And when Paul had gathered a bundle of sticks, and laid them on the fire, there came a viper out of the heat, and fastened on his hand.

Acts 28:3

Sometimes Satan tries to destroy or discourage us with sizable storms. Other times, he uses sneaky little snakes. While Paul was helping people, the snake struck. And you can be sure that's when the serpent will strike you. When you are helping others, serving others, loving others—from out of the heat of hell, Satan will strike.

Paul, however, would use this opportunity to share the Gospel with these people in a uniquely powerful way. You see, the fallacy of the over-emphasis of the faith movement—the mentality which says we should never be smitten by snakes—is that it robs us of opportunities to share the Gospel. While the Maltese people knew about these snakes and had watched their families and loved ones succumb to their poison—now they were about to see how Paul would handle the power, the danger, the pain of their venom.

So too, the Lord will allow you to go through difficulties. The doctor may say, 'It's inoperable.' And no matter how you name it and claim it, folks, it may be the Lord's plan for you to navigate that pain and venom in such a way that those around you who are also losing their loved ones to cancer will change their minds about who God is as a result. Jesus said to Thomas,

>   not—'Watch this miracle,'
>   not—'Listen to this sermon,'
>   but 'Touch My wounds.'

The world is rarely impacted and drawn to Jesus Christ through the sight of Christians prospering. No, it's through seeing believers suffering but not giving up that the skeptics change their minds.

Perhaps the most important ministry you'll ever have is when people see how you react to the pain they go through all of the time. Difficulty is the agent which often allows people an opportunity to see the reality of Jesus Christ most clearly.

MAY 9

And some believed the things which were spoken, and some believed not.

Acts 28:24

Some believed and some didn't. That's still the way it is—even among Christians.

You see, we as believers know our sins are forgiven. We know Jesus is the Messiah and that we'll soon be with Him in heaven. Yet in the meantime, we might be in hellish situations of depression, defeat, and despair because of unbelief.

The Word of God says, 'In everything give thanks' (Ephesians 5:20). Why? Because all things are working together for good (Romans 8: 28).

'Oh, but you haven't seen the stack of bills on my desk,' we say.

Well, the Word says, 'My God shall supply all your need according to His riches' (Philippians 4:19).

'Yeah, but you don't understand the hurt I feel because she dumped me,' we say.

The Bible says even if she meant it for evil, God will use it for good (Genesis 50:20).

'But I feel so bad about my son. He's not walking with the Lord,' we say.

The Bible says we can be confident that He who began a good work in him will perform it until the day of Christ Jesus—He'll finish what He started (Philippians 1:6).

Some Christians believe what God says and some don't. Those who don't, find themselves engulfed in despair, defeat, and discouragement. You see, it's not enough just to know the Scriptures, gang. It's not enough just to hear the Word. It's not enough just to come to Bible study. You and I must *believe.* And 'believe' is not a noun—it's a verb.

We can be the happiest, most carefree people in the world if we believe—and act on that belief. You might know the Scriptures backward and forward—but Jesus said, 'Happy are you if you *do* them' (John 13:17).

It's what you *do*—not what you know that matters, and it all begins by saying, 'Today I'm going to believe that God is working and that He is fulfilling what He has promised. You are faithful, Lord; and I will live in that today. I will proclaim Your faithfulness; and I will choose to rejoice in You.'

MAY 10

Paul, a servant of Jesus Christ...

Romans 1:1

The word 'servant' is *doúlos*, meaning 'bond slave.' Exodus 21:2 sheds light on what this means: in Israel, a slave was required to serve only six years before he was set free. If, however, at the end of six years, he said, 'I like it here. I want to become a bond slave,' the master would drive a nail through his right earlobe and place an earring in it, signifying he was a doúlos, a slave by choice.

It's a wise decision to give yourself fully to the Lord as His bond slave because He takes excellent care of those committed to Him. Their lives are filled with purpose and focus, their hearts with peace and joy.

Perhaps you're saying, 'I'm my own man—captain of my destiny, master of my fate. I don't serve anyone.' But reality says otherwise. *Everyone* will serve someone. Bob Dylan was right: 'It may be the devil or it may be the Lord but you're gonna have to serve somebody.' And Paul made a wise decision indeed when he chose to serve the Lord.

MAY 11

...Called to be an apostle...

Romans 1:1

To this day, the Spirit continues to appoint apostles—missionaries who are 'sent out' with the message of the Gospel. 'What a great calling that is,' you say. But you know what? A call to be a drywaller, a science teacher, or a repairman is just as holy and just as important if you're doing what God has opened up for you and you're doing it for Him. Whether you're a baker, banker, mechanic, or cook, yours is an important calling because of the need for brothers and sisters to serve in all kinds of arenas and locations.

Please don't think you're missing it if you're not a missionary. If the Lord wants you selling insurance or pouring cement, be at peace about it, saying, 'Lord, if this is what You have for me, I'll do it for Your glory. I'll be salt and light, and I'll do it as unto You.'

Herein is a problem, folks: there's a tendency for us to think everyone should have our calling. If I'm called to be a missionary—everyone should be a missionary; if I'm called to be a teacher—everyone should be a teacher. Not true. That's not the way it works in the Body of Christ. The Lord calls each of us uniquely, individually, personally.

How can you know what your calling is? Very simple: what's flowing from your life presently? What comes easy to you? What's working out supernaturally for you?

Isaac dug a well in order to water his flock. But the inhabitants of the land challenged his right to be there. So he called that well 'Esek' or 'Contention,' moved down the road, dug another well, and struck water once more. A second time, the inhabitants came out and said, 'This is our territory. Get out of here.' So Jacob named the well 'Sitnah,' or 'Hatred,' and went down the road a little further. He dug a third well, and this time no one bothered him—so he called the name of this well 'Rehoboth' or 'There's room for me' (Genesis 26).

I have found life basically follows such a pattern: you dig and strike some water. There's some refreshment and good things happen—but it becomes strife or hatred. So you go down the road and dig a second time, and again there are problems. Eventually, however, if you don't give up, you'll find your Rehoboth.

Isaac had the job of watering sheep. He didn't agonize over it. He didn't complain about it. He just tended to what was at hand—and he ended up at Rehoboth. That's the key. Do what's before you. Say, 'Lord, here I am. You've allowed me to do this, and I'm going to do it as unto You. And if there's strife or hatred, I'll just move down the road and dig again until I find Rehoboth.'

God has a Rehoboth for every one of us. Don't give up on seeking yours.

MAY 12

*Grace to you and peace from God our Father, and the
Lord Jesus Christ.*

Romans 1:7

Peace from God has two components. First of all, peace *from* God
implies peace with God, which is positional and unconditional
because Jesus Christ took all of our shortcomings and sins,
problems, weaknesses, and rebellions—and absorbed them
(Romans 5:1).

Most of us really believe the Lord is disappointed in us because
we haven't spent time in the Word, because we don't pray like we
should, because we're not doing very much for Him. But here, Paul
the apostle says, 'There is grace and peace for all because Jesus did
it *all*!'

Secondly, we have the peace *of* God, which is experiential and
comes through prayer (Philippians 4:7). Let me tell you what
happened to you today: the kids didn't behave. The job didn't go
well. Your parents didn't come through, or your friends let you
down. The burdens began to come, the tension began to build, and
you thought, 'I should pray.'

But no sooner did you think this than the enemy was there, saying,
'Pray? Now that you have a problem, you want to pray? What
about devotions, Mr. Prayer Person? You didn't have devotions this
morning, did you? And you think you can pray *now*?'

You see, gang, we know we have problems, and we are all too aware
of our failures. But we think the Father won't hear us if we haven't
talked to Him for a day or two or three or ten if we haven't been
doing what we should do or going where we should go.

Nothing is further from the truth. Look at our Lord, our Friend,
Jesus Christ. After He had prayed in the Garden of Gethsemane so

intensely that He was bleeding physically, He looked up and saw a group of soldiers coming toward Him, led by His disciple, Judas. As Jesus looked at Judas and said, 'Friend, what seekest thou?' His heart was revealed in that moment—for if Jesus looked at Judas at the moment of His betrayal and said, 'Friend what can I do for you?' don't you know He feels the same way about you today?

'Oh,' you say, 'but I've ignored Him,' or, 'I've not been bold in sharing Him,' or, 'I haven't been walking closely to Him.'

Was Judas? Judas was at the lowest ebb possible, yet Jesus still said, 'Friend, what seekest thou?' (Matthew 26:50). This One with whom we walk is so incredibly gracious. He'll respond to you and work with you *anytime* you call upon Him.

MAY 13

Making request, if by any means now at length I might have a prosperous journey by the will of God to come unto you.

Romans 1:10

By 'making request if by any means I might come to you,' Paul was giving God a blank check. He was giving God permission to use any means He chose to get him to Rome. How different that is from the way I often pray. I say, 'I'm the quarterback, Lord; You're my offensive line. Run interference for me, and we'll make this happen.'

Are your prayers direct—or are they directive? Watch out for directive prayers in which you tell the Father what to do. Instead, be one who prays directly, saying, 'Lord, You know the needs I have. You've asked me to share them with You. I know You know them, Father, but to enjoy fellowshipping with You, I give them to You. This is my desire, my burden, and my concern. Now, Lord, Your will be done by any means You see fit.'

'But aren't we supposed to name it and claim it?' you ask.

Ask Hezekiah about that...

'O Lord, let me live,' he prayed. 'I know Isaiah said I was supposed to die, but Lord, let me live. I name it and claim it.' In Hebrew, the account reads that he turned his face to the wall and chirped like a bird incessantly, demanding his own way until finally the Lord said, 'OK. Live' (II Kings 20:1-6). When messengers from Babylon came to congratulate him on his recovery, Hezekiah responded by taking them on a tour of the treasures of Israel. And it was this report which led Nebuchadnezzar to subsequently invade Israel. Meanwhile, Hezekiah fathered a son named Manasseh, who would become the worst king in Israel's history.

The Lord did indeed answer Hezekiah's prayer by prolonging his life fifteen years. But those fifteen years were disastrous both to Hezekiah personally and to the kingdom nationally. How much better it would have been had Hezekiah simply shared his heart with the Father and said, 'Not my will, but Thy will be done.'

That's the way to pray, gang, because that's how Jesus prayed in the hour of His greatest need (Luke 22:42). Our faith is not to be in our own plans but in the goodness and wisdom of our Father.

MAY 14

For not the hearers of the law are just before God, but the doers of the law shall be justified.

Romans 2:13

I believe one of the great hazards for those who love to study the Scriptures and who take seriously the privilege of plowing through God's Word is this: we can begin to think that hearing the Word automatically implies obeying the Word. It's a very subtle, but a very real danger.

How do you know if you're obeying the Word?

Well, if you're grumpy, you're not obeying because Jesus said, '*Happy are you if you do these things*' (John 13:17). The word 'happy' in Greek means 'happy.' It means 'elated.' It speaks of emotion. You will be happy if you're obeying the Word, but if you're just hearing about it or being analytical of it, you will not be happy. So Paul would say to the self-righteous, to the Hebrew, to the Biblical scholar, 'It's not what you hear or know, it's what you *do* that will affect you.'

In your morning devotions, during Wednesday night study, in a Sunday morning service, or whenever you're in the Word, ask the Lord to give you one thing to do. Not just to journal or to ponder, but one thing through His Word to do by His Spirit. And happy will you be if you do it.

MAY 15

...Yea, let God be true, but every man a liar...
Romans 3:4

There are times when people say, 'I prayed and nothing happened.' 'I had devotions and it's not working.' 'I go to church and don't receive anything.' 'I'm doing all the things Scripture tells me to, but it's just not happening.'

And I have to respond in love, 'You're a liar because God promises that if we draw close to Him, He'll draw close to us' (James 4:8). Therefore, somebody's lying—and it's not God.

Feeling a bit dry in my spirit and a bit distanced from the Lord in my heart, I grabbed my Bible one Monday evening and strolled through

Jacksonville, reading the books of Amos and Joel as I walked. And you know what happened? Even though Amos and Joel are far from lighthearted reading, I found myself smiling. Why? Because the Lord used His Word to minister to my heart in a beautifully satisfying way. Truly, the Lord will meet anyone who will take time to open the Word and seek Him.

We're so fortunate, gang. We don't have to answer everyone's questions or solve their problems. But with great confidence, we can just tell them that if they seek Him, the Lord *will* draw near to them.

MAY 16

Now to him that worketh is the reward not reckoned
of grace, but of debt.

Romans 4:4

If Abraham had been pronounced righteous because he left Ur or because he was willing to sacrifice his son, then he would have been given salvation as a reward. God would have been paying off a debt. But Paul's argument is that it was nothing Abraham did or didn't do—other than believe what God said was true—which justified him.

So too, if you are attempting to work your way into God's favor—either prior or subsequent to your salvation—then He owes justification to you. Whenever we subconsciously think, 'Now, Lord, I prayed a whole bunch today, so I know it's going to be a great day,' the implication is, 'Lord, You owe me.' And that nullifies grace. God will not be a debtor to any man. He won't owe us anything.

That is why there will be no boasting in heaven—not only with regard to our salvation, but with regard to any of God's blessings. A lot of times we forget that and think it's because of our great faith or our prevailing prayer, our diligent works or our dedicated devotion that God has blessed our life.

It's a hard thing to say, but it's true: some of the greatest blessings both *in* my life and flowing *through* my life have come when I have not been in prayer, when I have not had strong faith, when I've not been what I should or want to be. God's blessings during those times remind me that *everything* which comes my way is because of grace—unmerited, undeserved, unearned favor—and they create in me a heart that wants to love the Lord and worship Him rather than a tendency to say, 'If I've accomplished this with three hours of prayer, just think what I could do with six hours!'

Am I saying we should **never** pray? If you're praying to earn a reward, give it up. But if you're praying because you enjoy the Lord, you are amazed at His goodness, you want to participate with Him in what He's doing on the earth, you love to spend time with Him, or you are thankful for Him and want to be close to Him—pray on!

If you get up at 3:00 tomorrow morning to pray in order to fulfill an obligation, God won't be impressed a whit. But if you get up at 3:00 in the morning just to enjoy Him, He'll be blessed. Great is the day when a man, a woman, a church learns that it's all grace, for they will find themselves praying, worshipping, studying, witnessing—not because they're trying to earn God's blessing, but because they're responding to the One who's been so good to them and loves them so deeply.

MAY 17

Blessed is the man to whom the Lord will not impute sin.
Romans 4:8

Once we receive the work God did redemptively in order that we might be pronounced righteous, He no longer sees us as sinners. For me to utter this would be presumption. But because David said it, it's inspiration. It's interesting to me that in David's early Psalms, he talked about how righteous he was, how there was no vanity in his life, no iniquity on his hands. But then what happened? David had a little lapse, a small problem—as does every man, as does every woman. As a result, he discovered he was not as righteous as he thought he was previously—and his later Psalms reflect this discovery.

A young married couple in Portland moved into an upstairs apartment and bought a waterbed. Forgetting to bring a hose, they bought one at True Value and hooked it from their sink to their waterbed before going out for about an hour. The surprised couple returned to find their floor had collapsed and fallen onto the apartment below—not because of the weight of the waterbed, but because they had accidentally purchased a sprinkler hose with holes in it.

That's so much like me! I think I've got my act so together—until I find a few holes I wasn't counting on. Maybe you think you've got it all wired, but you watch. Sooner or later, you'll discover your floor has collapsed; you're not together; you're a sinner.

That is why David says, 'Happy is the man who's not trying to prove his worth or merit God's blessing. Happy is the one whose sins are forgiven.' It doesn't matter how long you've walked with the Lord or how much you know about the Lord. The fact is, the man who is happy, the woman who succeeds in her walk with God is the one who is not working, but simply believing in the goodness and lovingkindness of the Father revealed through the Son on Calvary's Cross.

MAY 18

And he received the sign of circumcision, a seal of the righteousness of the faith which he had yet being uncircumcised: that he might be the father of all them that believe, though they be not circumcised; that righteousness might be imputed unto them also.

Romans 4:11

Paul here is saying Abraham is the father not only of the circumcised Jew, but of the uncircumcised Gentile because he was pronounced righteous before his circumcision. Thus, circumcision did not *confer* righteous. It *confirmed* righteousness.

So too, you can be baptized 1,000 times next summer, but it won't save you if you don't believe in your heart that the work is done, the price is already paid for your sin. The basis of *everything* we enjoy is based upon what God has done for us and how He looks on us through the lens of His Son.

So I get baptized because I want to go on record externally, declaring what I know is already true internally.

I come to Communion because I want to do outwardly what I'm excited about inwardly.

I have devotions not to earn His favor, but because He has already shown me such favor.

It's not responsibility, folks. It's *response.* Why is it so hard for us to understand this? Could it be because our culture says, 'There's no free lunch,' and 'God helps those who help themselves'? Could it be because our flesh says, 'Set the alarm earlier. Stay up later. Memorize more. Study harder. And maybe, just maybe, you'll be blessed'?

If I could communicate one thing to you, precious people, it would be this: quit trying to give God a reason to bless you. It'll never work because God will be a debtor to no man. Just marvel at His goodness. Enjoy an intimate relationship with Him, and watch what He can pour out on you because you won't be taking the credit.

MAY 19

...And calleth those things which be not as though they were.

Romans 4:17

God called Abraham a father even before the birth of Isaac because, from His perspective, Abraham was already a father. Read Ecclesiastes 3:15 for a glimpse into the great mystery of God calling things which are not yet as though they already were. The implications are fabulous.

Romans 8:29-30 tells us that God foreknew those who would want to know Him, so, on the basis of His foreknowledge, He predestined them to become believers. Because they're predestined, they're called by Him. And when they respond to His call, they're justified— declared righteous—and they're glorified.

The implication is staggering. God views us as already glorified. What does this do? It frees me incredibly, knowing the Father sees me not in my cruddy humanity, but in my glorified state. I see myself flailing, faltering, and failing—but the Father sees me as already glorified.

Think of it this way...

Picture yourself in New York City, watching the St. Patrick's Day parade. A band marches by, followed by some floats and big balloons. Your buddy, standing a mile down the road has not yet seen the band, the floats, or balloons which pass before you. You're enjoying them presently and you know he's going to enjoy them eventually when the parade works its way to him.

That's the way the time/space continuum works. But suppose on this St. Patrick's Day, you were invited to sit in the Goodyear blimp. Suddenly you would see the whole parade simultaneously. The people down below would be watching the parade go by. But not you. You would see the whole thing in its entirety. That which is yet to be for your buddy, you'd already see. And that which already was past for him would still be in your sight. From your vantage point, it would all be happening in the present.

That's how it is for the Father. We're marching through the parade of life, trying hard, doing well sometimes, and stumbling other times. But He sees our whole life—past, present, and future. He sees the whole thing in totality. Thus, He views us as already glorified, as already in the Kingdom of heaven.

Consequently, we have beautiful freedom today. We can just enjoy the Lord because He has said we are already glorified. We're not a disappointment or an embarrassment to Him—but already perfect in Him.

MAY 20

Who was delivered for our offences, and was raised again for our justification.

Romans 4:25

Jesus died for our sins redemptively, and He was raised for our justification advocationally. Furthermore, I John 2 and Hebrews 8 tell us that He lives to make intercession for us continually. He is our Advocate, our Defense Attorney. Satan condemns us not only in our hearts day and night, but before the very Throne of God

(Revelation 12:10), saying, 'Look at those people down there. They're hypocritical, weak, faltering.'

But the moment he hisses these accusations, Jesus is literally there, saying, 'Depart, Satan. They're washed in My blood and robed in My righteousness.'

And the Father says, 'Case dismissed for lack of evidence,' as He casts our sins into the depths of the sea (Micah 7:19). Why the depths of the sea?—because as a people, the Jews were terrified of the ocean. Therefore, the Lord put their sins in the last place a Jew would have gone looking for them.

To our culture, He would say, 'I have cast your sin into the bottom of a toxic waste dump. Your sins are not only forgotten by Me, but I'm putting them in a place where there's no danger of anybody looking at, digging up, or talking about them. On the basis of the finished work of Calvary, every sin you've ever committed, are committing, or will commit is forgiven, forgotten, and out of sight.'

That's forgiveness.
That's justification.
That's *Good* News!

MAY 21

Therefore being justified by faith, we have peace with
God through our Lord Jesus Christ.

Romans 5:1

By embracing the simple fact that Jesus died for our sins and rose again, we have peace with God. Why then do so many Christians still fight Him?

It was in 1972 that the last Imperial Japanese soldier was discovered on a South Sea island. Because he was living in complete isolation, he hadn't heard the news that the war was over. So there he was—still building fortifications, ready to hold off the American invasion of his little atoll.

'What a waste,' you say. 'He could have been enjoying the Japanese economic boom, but instead he was stuck on an island, fighting malaria—all because he didn't hear that a peace treaty had been signed.'

Yet it's amazing how many of us do the same thing. 'I hope the Lord doesn't come down on me for this or get mad at me for that,' we think. 'He must be really upset with me. I better hide here in the jungle.'

We don't get it! The war is over! We have peace with God. The sin which separated us from God is forgiven and forgotten completely because of what Jesus Christ did for us.

Gang, whether you've prayed for three hours today or you haven't prayed in three months, the war is still over. If you are a believer in what God the Father did for you in sending Jesus Christ to die in place of you, then you are righteous—justified by faith. We have a tendency to fall back into thinking we have to earn something or prove something to the Father. Not so. We can relax in our relationship with Him, talk to Him freely, and fellowship with Him continually because we have peace with Him eternally.

May 22

Moreover the law entered, that the offense might abound. But where sin abounded, grace did much more abound: That as sin hath reigned unto death, even so might grace reign through righteousness unto eternal life by Jesus Christ our Lord.

Romans 5:20-21

Everything wrong with the world today, everything wrong with you, your family, and the people you work with is all due to Adam's failure. Knowing this allows me to see people in an entirely different light. I realize that whether a man is a sly entrepreneur who cheats his way into money he shouldn't have by cutting deals he shouldn't make, or whether he's as obvious and gross in his sin as Charles Manson—I am no less a sinner than he. And it's all because of Adam.

No wonder Jesus could look at the multitudes and have compassion on them—not crusade against them, march to get rid of them, or mobilize to neutralize them. He looked at the multitudes, and in every instance, He had compassion.

You see, when it finally sinks in that by one Man righteousness, justification, and grace came—I stop striving and struggling to prove I'm a notch or two above you, and I stop feeling bad if I'm a notch or two below you. I'm not the issue at all. He is. When I understand this, I stop being a worker and become a worshipper.

Do I find myself trying to earn blessings by intensive prayer or Bible study? Do I try and prove I'm saved by street witnessing or by ministering in Mexico? If I fall into that trap, my Christian experience will always be one of analyzing, scrutinizing, and condemning myself and others.

Salvation is not based upon my knowledge, my deep study, or my 24-hour prayer chain. It's based upon one thing only: the grace and goodness of God in sending One Man, the Last Adam: Jesus Christ.

MAY 23

For when we were in the flesh, the motions of sins,
which were by the law, did work in our members to
bring forth fruit unto death. But now we are delivered
from the law, that being dead wherein we were held;
that we should serve in newness of spirit, and not in
the oldness of the letter.

Romans 7:5-6

'Newness of spirit' speaks of the New Covenant, of an entirely new way of living (Jeremiah 31, Ezekiel 36). 'No longer will I give you tables of stone,' the Lord declares in the New Covenant, 'but I will write My will upon the table of your heart. Every day will be an adventure. Some days I might awaken you at 4:30 to seek My face and to pray, while other times, I might tell you to sleep in.'

That's the way Christianity was meant to be.

But what have we done?

We have constructed legalistic systems and expectations both personally and corporately.

Folks, we were meant to live in a newness of the Spirit, moment by moment obeying and yielding and wondering, 'Lord, what next?'

Throw off the yoke of legalism.
Walk in the Spirit.
Respond to His direction—

and I guarantee you will find yourself on the adventure of a lifetime!

MAY 24

*I thank God through Jesus Christ our Lord. So then
with the mind I myself serve the law of God; but with
the flesh the law of sin.*

Romans 7:25

While we may readily agree with Paul that the answer lies not in
a program or a procedure—it is harder for us to understand that
neither is the answer found in a principle. What do I mean?

At this point in my study of Romans, I can say, 'Wow! I get it. The
penalty for my sin was paid *on* the Cross. The power of my sin
was broken *by* the Cross. Preoccupation with my sin is eliminated
because of the Cross. I'm free! It's a principle I'm going to jot down
in my journal and rejoice in.'

But wait. Even as I have immersed myself in the Book of Romans,
in the past few days I've been on edge; my temper has flared; and
I was taken aback by the ugliness of my own flesh until the Lord
dealt with my heart again, saying, 'You *are* free. But you're missing
out on what only I can produce as you spend time with Me. Even if
you have the principles down and the theology right, without Me,
there will be no self-control and peace, love and joy, gentleness and
goodness, faith and meekness. Those only come from spending time
with *Me.*'

Thus, I have found myself in the past few days more eager than ever
to be in the presence of the Lord—for, while I have always been wary
of programs, I have been prone to intrigue with positional truth. In
recent days, however, the Lord has been reminding me once again,
'The answer lies in spending time with Me—not legalistically, but
just because without Me you can do nothing.'

This afternoon, I was kneeling beside my bed, enjoying the Lord.
As I got up to let in some air, my finger got caught between the two
windows. Now, although this was just the kind of irritation which

had been getting to me in the past few days, this time I didn't get upset at all. Why? It wasn't because I was reading a book on how not to get mad when your finger gets stuck in the window. No, it's because I was simply enjoying the Lord's presence.

Who shall deliver me from my own sin and failure? Not 'How shall I be delivered theologically'—but 'Who shall deliver me personally?'

Like Paul, I declare to you experientially and emphatically that Jesus Christ is the key!

MAY 25

There is therefore now no condemnation to them which are in Christ Jesus...

Romans 8:1

We're in Christ Jesus, folks. That's the key. The Lord said to Noah, 'Rooms shalt thou make in the ark and thou shalt pitch it within and without with pitch' (Genesis 6:14), the word 'pitch' being the same word used in the Old Testament for 'atonement.' The ark is a perfect picture of our salvation, for when the rain began to fall, the Lord shut them *in* (Genesis 7:16).

He didn't say, 'I'm going to put eight pegs on the outside of the ark, Noah. You and your family are to hang on for dear life, and as long as you hang on, you'll make it through.'

No, He said, 'I'm going to put you *in.*' So too with us. It's not a matter of holding on, hoping that if we can keep from sinning, we'll be OK. No, our Ark is Jesus Christ; and we are *in* Him. Therefore, there is no condemnation. No matter how rough the seas might be or how heavy the rain comes down, we're sealed, safe, and secure.

Our youth pastor came by today with a couple boxes of Häagen-Dazs bars—the dark chocolate-covered ones—my favorites. Now, if you've ever read the ingredients on the side panel of a Häagen-Dazs box, you know they're sinful. And yet that sinfully-delicious Häagen-Dazs is now hidden and buried *in* me. You no longer see it.

So too—you are *in* Christ—with all of your sinful tendencies, calories, and fat grams. Thus, when the Father looks on you, He doesn't see you with all of your failings and shortcomings. No, He sees you robed with the righteousness of Christ Jesus (Isaiah 61:10).

God doesn't see you in your sin; He sees you in His Son. Therefore, there's no condemnation whatsoever. I don't care where you've been or how badly you've failed—whoever you are, wherever you are, there is *no* condemnation.

MAY 26

For the law of the Spirit of life in Christ Jesus hath made me free from the law of sin and death.

Romans 8:2

The law of sin and death is comprised of three forces working in conjunction with each other: Satan, the flesh, and the world. Now, in my own energy, I can take on any two. But I'm doomed by the combination of three.

If Satan and the world system were alive and well—but I didn't have a body, sin would have no pull on me.

If I have a body and if I am in the world—but there was no Satan, there would be no problem because Satan is the prince of this world (John 12:31), who activates the world system which plays on my flesh.

If I have a body and Satan is present—but there was no world system, Satan could not have access to me because he would have no way to influence me.

Go to an airport and you'll see planes sitting on the runway not going anywhere because the law of gravity is keeping them on the ground. But as soon as their engines are turned on, the law of aerodynamics takes over. Gravity is still in effect and still pulls on the planes, but there's a higher law, a more powerful force at work which allows them to overcome the law of gravity.

That's what Paul is saying. Are we free from this law of sin and death by possibility thinking? No. By positive mental imaging? No. We're free by the Spirit of Jesus Christ. He lives *in* us, enabling us to fly high and overcome the law of sin and death.

MAY 27

For they that are after the flesh do mind the things of the flesh; but they that are after the Spirit the things of the Spirit. For to be carnally-minded is death; but to be spiritually-minded is life and peace.

Romans 8:5-6

The question then becomes, 'Paul, if this is so, if there's no condemnation, if we're free from rules and regulations, then why shouldn't I just continue in my carnal tendencies and fleshly activities?'

'Wait a minute,' Paul would say. 'To be carnally-minded is death.' Do you want to know how to experience the stench of death in your life? Live carnally. What does it mean to live carnally? Jesus associated it with Gentiles who were concerned with nothing more than what they would eat, what they would wear, and where they would go

(Matthew 6:31-32). A carnal person asks, 'Where can we eat now? What new hobby can we enjoy? What vacation can we take?'

You see, we think living in the flesh is synonymous with shooting heroin or robbing a bank—but that's not the meaning primarily. To live in the flesh simply means to give priority to the things of the material realm.

To be spiritually-minded, on the other hand—to set our sights, thoughts, and hearts on heaven—results in abundant life and true peace.

MAY 28

Because the carnal mind is enmity against God: for it
is not subject to the law of God, neither indeed can be.
So then they that are in the flesh cannot please God.
Romans 8:7-8

With the soul—the mind—lodged between the spirit and the flesh, the question becomes: what is going to control my mind? Is it going to be the spirit, as my spirit is linked to God's Spirit? As the day unfolds, will I be a spiritual man? Or am I going to be carnal, wondering, 'Where am I going to go? How am I going to be entertained? What am I going to eat?' Truly, if my body controls my thoughts, I am carnally-minded and cannot please God.

'What's life about?' wondered Solomon. 'It must be about money.' So he gathered so much gold that even silver had no value in his kingdom. Ever notice how it is the wealthy people in our society who oftentimes end up taking drugs?

Why is this? Because the ones who hit the top find out money isn't the answer, whereas the rest of us think that if we could just make more money, work harder, or invest more wisely, we would be happy. Solomon knew better. He had more money than he knew what to do with, and he still wasn't happy—so he thought happiness must lie in women.

He amassed 1,000 wives and concubines, but found they weren't the answer either. 'Happiness must be found in intellectual pursuit,' he decided. So he became a botanist, a biologist, an ichthyologist. He became so knowledgeable that his books were penned by the hundreds. And he became philosophical in such a way that people traveled from all over the world to hear him share his proverbs. But after all of this, he concluded that much study wearies the flesh (Ecclesiastes 12:12).

The answer must be in partying, he thought. So he brought in peacocks and apes from Africa, and the wine flowed freely during parties so lavish, they would make Hollywood jealous. But it was still empty in his eyes. Deciding the answer to his restlessness must lie in power, he built his empire to be the most powerful empire of his day. Yet he remained empty.

Poor Solomon. Put yourself in his golden sandals. What frustration! All the power he could ever want, more money than he could even count, 1,000 of the most beautiful women at his beck and call, nonstop parties, education, philosophy—he had it all.

But here was his dilemma: it didn't satisfy. Whereas the average person thinks, 'I'm almost happy. If I can just get a bigger house or a newer car, I know I'll be happy,'—Solomon was stuck. He was at the top. There was no bigger car to buy, no other woman to go after, no higher investment to make. He was at the top, and he said, 'It's empty.'

And here little Paul comes along with his bowed legs, hooked nose, and bald head, saying, 'It's real simple. To be carnally-minded is death—but to be spiritually-minded is life and peace.'

Brother Solomon finally did figure it out. After approximately 12 years of women, money, power, and philosophy, he said, 'Let us hear the conclusion of the whole matter: Fear God, and keep his commandments: for this is the whole duty of man' (Ecclesiastes 12: 13). And from that time on, Solomon was known as 'The Preacher.'

I ask you this question: what has been ruling your soul? Has it been the flesh, or has it been the Spirit? If you're going to pursue the material and live for your flesh, you'll never be satisfied. But if you live for the Spirit, you'll know life and peace eternally and presently.

MAY 29

Therefore, brethren, we are debtors, not to the flesh, to live after the flesh. For if ye live after the flesh, ye shall die: but if ye through the Spirit do mortify the deeds of the body, ye shall live.

Romans 8:12-13

'I must mortify the deeds of the body,' some people say. 'I've got to crucify my flesh'—but it's impossible to crucify yourself. If you lay down on a cross and pound a nail through your wrist, even if you somehow endure the pain, you're only half crucified because you can't pound in the other nail. How do you mortify the deeds of the flesh? There's only one way: through the Spirit.

The Philistines had captured the Ark of the Covenant and had placed it in the temple of their fish god, Dagon. The next morning, the Philistine priests got up to find Dagon had fallen down before the Ark (I Samuel 5:3). They stood Dagon up and went their way. The next morning, they came in again, and there was Dagon, face down on the floor with his head and hands cut off. Now at this point, you would think the priests would have said, 'Something's fishy here. This isn't working.' But instead, they chose to side with Dagon. They stood him up, patched him together, and said, 'The Ark's gotta go.'

Precious people, the way to gain victory over whatever it is you're struggling with is not to try to topple Dagon, but to bring in the Ark, for the Ark represents the presence of God. Whatever your Dagon might be, here's the key: bring in the Spirit of the Lord.

What does that mean? Just love the Lord. Get up tomorrow morning, and before your feet hit the ground, drop to your knees and give your life to Him. When He whispers in your heart during your coffee break, 'Pull away and talk with Me,' do it. When you're deciding which dial to press on your radio during lunch, just do what the Spirit tells you to do. Allow the Spirit of God to fill your heart, and you know what will happen? You'll lose interest in the stuff which dominated and controlled you—not because you worked on Dagon, but because you brought in the Ark.

That's why Romans 8 is so thrilling! Too many believers are trying to fight evil habits and tendencies on their own—and it's exhausting. If you walk into a dark room, you don't scream, karate chop, give teachings about, or rebuke the darkness.

You turn on the light.

MAY 30

Likewise the Spirit also helpeth our infirmities: for we know not what we should pray for as we ought: but the Spirit itself maketh intercession for us with groanings which cannot be uttered. And he that searcheth the hearts knoweth what is the mind of the Spirit, because he maketh intercession for the saints according to the will of God.

Romans 8:26-27

I spent some time this week with a man in his early 30's who is on his deathbed. The body of this young man, once a good athlete and a vibrant father, is now racked by cancer. His family asks, understandably, 'Why? Why doesn't the Lord just take him home? Why the suffering? We prayed for his healing and that didn't happen. What's the Father doing?'

In those situations, you wonder. I understand the family saying, 'Take him home.' But what if, in these final days of our brother's difficulty and suffering, the Father is putting on the final touches of the inner person shaping and molding what he will be for the next billion years in heaven? Is that what's happening? I don't know, for like Paul, I know not how to pray. The only thing I do know is that I don't know.

Let us ever remember that while prayer is to be directed to God, it is not to be directing God. Most people, at least for part of their pilgrimage, try to direct the Lord, thinking that's what prayer is about. 'Let me explain the situation, Lord. Here's what you need to do...' we say with great piety and audacity.

Jeremiah, a godly man to be sure, prayed, 'Save Your people, Lord. Restore the nation. Revive us.'

'Quiet thyself,' answered God. 'I will not hear your prayer, for I have determined that My people must be carried into Babylon, into captivity' (Jeremiah 20:4).

Thus, regardless how hard Jeremiah prayed, God had a different plan, for it was through their captivity that Judah was finally healed of her affinity for idolatry.

'We know not how to pray,' said Paul. We feel this as well, don't we?

Someone comes to us and says, 'Pray I'll get the job.' 'Pray this project will prosper.' Wait a minute. So many things I thought would be wonderful proved to be detrimental, a distraction, a curse; and so many things I thought would be terrible and awful proved to be a huge blessing.

The same is true nationally. It might be that the Lord wants to close us down. That's a possibility. Maybe the best thing that could happen to our country would be a collapse economically, politically, or militarily—because that's what it might take to heal us spiritually. I don't know. I'm not God. Therefore, I'm not going to give Him direction on what He should or should not do. Instead, I just groan, 'Lord, You see what's going on in the nation. You see what's going on with that person. You see what's going on in our congregation. I don't know how to pray. I don't know what Your will is. But I just give it all to You to work out according to Your perfect and beautiful plan.'

Now if we don't know how to pray, then why pray at all? Understand this: prayer is not getting my will done in heaven. Prayer is getting God's will done on earth. It's not me giving directions to the Father, but rather me saying, 'Father direct me. I open the door for You to work. I hold up this need to You. I place this situation in Your hand.' I do this all through prayer because the Word tells us that God has chosen to work through prayer and that if we do not pray, we will limit what He would do, what He could do, what He desires to do (James 4:2).

Therefore, if I don't pray, I will never know if God got His way with Peter John, in this congregation, or in our nation. But if I do pray and say, 'Lord, here's the situation. I'm not directing You, but I'm just looking to You to have Your will done'—then I can be at peace. Whatever happens, I know I played my part; I opened the door, and since the Father knows best, I can rest. The Spirit groans through me, the Son intercedes for me, and the Father will do what's right concerning me—but if I don't pray, I'll always wonder if things would have been different if I had.

MAY 31

And we know that all things work together for good to them that love God, to them who are the called according to his purpose.

Romans 8:28

We usually rewrite Romans 8:28 to read: '*Most* things,' or '*Some* things work together for good.' Paul says even though there's groaning and suffering as we're being adapted for heaven, know this: it's *all* working for good.'

'We *know* all things work together for good,' said Paul. You see, it's not something we have to learn—it's something the Spirit witnesses in our hearts. No matter what's coming down, no matter what's going on—we know innately that all things are working together for good.'

Jacob declared just the opposite. Famine was in the land. His wife, Rachel, was dead. He thought his beloved son, Joseph, was dead as well. His oldest son, Simeon, was being held hostage in Egypt. And the man in charge was saying, 'I will give you no more supplies until you bring your youngest son, Benjamin, to Egypt.' It was more than Jacob could bear.

'All things are working against me,' he said (Genesis 42:36). But then what happened? In the next chapter, he did indeed send Benjamin to Egypt. Why? I suggest it was because even though he was murmuring, complaining, and doubting, Jacob knew Benjamin *would* come back, that things *would* work out, that everything *would* be OK. Otherwise, he never would have allowed Benjamin to go.

So too, in the times we have said, 'Everything's working against me,' even then we knew that wasn't true.

That's why Paul said, 'We know'—not 'I want you to know,' not 'I'm going to teach you,'—but 'We already know that all things are working for good.' By the Spirit, we know this intuitively, and by our experience, we see how God has worked everything together for good previously. Therefore, we can trust Him to keep working for our good—and for His glory.

JUNE 1

What shall we then say to these things?

Romans 8:31

In light of the fact that there's no condemnation to those who are in Christ Jesus, in light of the fact that everything is working out for our good because of Christ, in light of the fact that we are already glorified from God's perspective, Paul finds himself speechless.

When Nathan told David that, although he wouldn't be able to build a temple for the Lord, the Lord wanted to establish His royal line through David, David was amazed. 'What can I say?' he said (II Samuel 7:18-20)—which was quite a question for David to ask, considering the Psalmist had a way with words and was perhaps more skilled in expression than anyone else in history. Yet here he was, speechless in response to God's kindness to him.

Do you ever feel that way? The Lord touches you and ministers to you, gives you a verse in your devotional time, or impresses you with a truth as you're driving in your car, or looking at your grandchildren or wife—and you just become overwhelmed at the goodness and mercy of God.

I believe praise often reaches its highest point when we're speechless, blown away by His mercy and grace.

JUNE 2

If God be for us, who can be against us?

Romans 8:31

This verse literally reads, '*Since* God is for us, who can be against us?' We have the tendency to think God is disappointed with us.

Not true. God is *for* you. And He's for me. God views His people very highly and loves His people very deeply. Why? Because He already sees the end product. We're already glorified in His eyes.

If God be for us, who would dare to be against us? Only one: Satan. But Satan is no problem because Satan is not God's counterpart. He's only a fallen angel whose equivalent is, perhaps, Michael. God is so far above Satan and so much greater than this world system that any power which comes against you, any problem which creeps up within you is no match for the One who says, 'I'm *for* you.'

God is *for* you—not because He has to be, but because He really *likes* you. 'That sounds nice,' you say. 'It might even be true theologically. But you don't know where I've been personally. You don't know how weak I am.'

About a week ago, I was reading through the Gospel of John once more, and I had to stop and chuckle. You see, the problem for a lot of us is that, because we are so familiar with the stories in the Gospel, the Gospel loses its impact.

Think with me...

Two stories appear in John 2, both dealing with Jesus and a table. Around the first table, men have been drinking quite heartily—so much so that there was no wine left at the party. Around the second table, men were in the courtyard of the temple, exchanging money into Jewish currency that they might buy doves, lambs, and cattle to offer to Jehovah.

Jesus turned over the table in one of those vignettes. Which one? If you hadn't heard the story, you would say, 'It's obvious. He would be ticked off with the partyers. He would overturn their table. He would drive them out.' But that's not what happened because everything Jesus did was opposite of what people expected Him to do. And the only reason His actions don't shock us is because we're so familiar with them. You see, if you didn't know the story, you would think,

'He dealt harshly with the partyers and gave His blessing to the moneychangers.' But in reality, He made more wine for the partyers and overturned the tables of the outwardly-pious moneychangers.

Jesus is radical, folks. He caused the religious people of His day to be continually shocked and scandalized. They didn't know what to do with Him because He loved to be with real people—

People who had struggled with life,
   People who knew they weren't all that great —
      People just like us.

JUNE 3

He that spared not his own Son, but delivered him up for us all, how shall he not with him also freely give us all things?

Romans 8:32

The word 'spared' is used only one other place in the Septuagint, the Greek translation of the Old Testament. When Abraham took his 33-year-old son, Isaac, to Mt. Moriah (today called Golgotha or Calvary), God said, 'Abraham, lay not your hand upon the lad. Neither do anything unto him for now I know that thou fearest God seeing thou hast not withheld thy son, thine only son from Me' (Genesis 22:12). The word 'withheld' is the same word translated 'spared' here in Romans.

I suggest to you the reason God could pour out so many blessings on Abraham in so many ways was because Abraham was ready to sacrifice the one thing in his life that mattered most. In so doing, Abraham said, 'I'll plunge a knife into my son's chest because I love You, Father, more than I trust my ability to figure out what's going on.'

So too, if the thing that means the most to you—be it your wife, kids, house, car, job, future—doesn't matter at all to you in comparison to your relationship with your Father, God can pour out all kinds of blessings on you because they won't be a distraction to you.

God is saying here, 'If I gave you My Son, I'm going to do what's good for you from this point on. You can be sure of that.' That is why Paul says, when God gave His Son, He proved His magnanimity, His generosity, and His charity. Why, then, question what's going on presently? Anything He shares with us or withholds from us cannot begin to compare with what He's *already* given us in Christ.

JUNE 4

Who shall lay any thing to the charge of God's elect?
It is God that justifieth.

Romans 8:33

I'll tell you who will 'lay anything to the charge of God's elect'— Satan, the accuser of the brethren (Revelation 12:10), points his finger at us constantly.

As Joshua the high priest stood in the presence of the Lord, his garments became filthy (Zechariah 3), because in God's presence, man's spirituality always appears as filthy rags (Isaiah 64). Quick to exploit the situation, Satan pointed his finger at Joshua's sin. 'Is not this a stick I have plucked out of the fire?' said the LORD, as Joshua's garments became dazzling white.

So too with us. We were little sticks headed for the fire of damnation. But the Lord plucked us out, robed us in His righteousness, and gave us the garment of praise for the spirit of heaviness (Isaiah 61).

'Look at his sin,' thunders Satan.

'What sin?' asks God. 'All I see is My Son.'

There is no condemnation to them who are in Christ Jesus. Then what were we doing on our knees this morning confessing sin? Confession is the result of conviction, not condemnation. Conviction is the work of the Spirit. When He convicts me of sin, I say, 'Oh, Father, I realize this is wrong. I agree with You. And I thank You I'm forgiven.'

Conviction draws me to the Father. Condemnation, on the other hand, drives me from the Father. Condemnation makes me say, 'I'm such a wretch. I can't pray, and I sure can't go to church.'

When Adam sinned in the Garden of Eden, God asked him a simple question. He didn't say, 'Where were you? How could you? Why did you?' No, He simply said, 'Where *are* you?'

And that's still the heart of the Father as He asks, 'Where *are* you?' It's not, 'Where have you been?' or 'What did you do?'—but 'Where are you right now? Take off those scratchy fig leaves, and let Me cloak you with My righteousness.'

JUNE 5

Who shall separate us from the love of Christ? shall tribulation, or distress, or persecution, or famine, or nakedness, or peril, or sword? As it is written, For thy sake we are killed all the day long; we are accounted as sheep for the slaughter. Nay, in all these things we are more than conquerors through him that loved us.

Romans 8:35-37

Paul is telling you and saying to me, 'God is for you. He'll never lay any charge against you. He doesn't come down on you. He'll give you every good thing freely because He already gave you the best in Jesus.'

The question then becomes, why, if this be so, do we go through tribulation, famine, distress, nakedness, peril, sword? The answer is because we are like sheep (Psalm 44). Sheep are easily picked off, easily put down, easily done in. It seems the Christian community has forgotten that it is comprised of lambs. We gear up, arm ourselves, and come out swinging. But the imagery is all wrong. After all, which NFL football team goes by the Lambs? Which Marine Corps unit would choose the lamb for its mascot?

'If they hated Me, they'll hate you,' Jesus said (John 15:18). But here's the good news: in all these things we are more than conquerors. What does it mean to be more than a conqueror? It means that, instead of flexing our muscles politically, or marching in protest socially, we draw people's attention to an entirely different dimension spiritually. We're to influence positively—no question about it. But it's not our passion, our purpose, or our priority to conquer the system.

Aren't we to be salt and light?' you ask.

'Yes, but salt is meant to be sprinkled. I had some clam chowder last night and asked for some salt. Now, what if the waiter had said, 'You want salt? Here you go,' and proceeded to unscrew the lid and empty the shaker into my bowl? The chowder would have been ruined.

So too with light. Do you appreciate it when an oncoming car shines its brights in your face? We wonder why the world doesn't listen to us. Could it be because we empty the saltshaker in their soup and shine high beams in their face in our attempt to be salt and light?

We're to be lambs. We're to be salt that's sprinkled to add flavor, create thirst, and bring healing. We're to be light that illuminates, not dominates. And know this: from the world's perspective, we'll never win. If you don't understand this, you'll be frustrated, disillusioned, embittered. We're not conquerors. We're *more* than conquerors.

Shadrach, Meshach, and Abed-nego were tossed into the fiery furnace. But while they were in it, even Nebuchadnezzar saw Jesus Christ in the fire with them (Daniel 3:25).

Do the Nebuchadnezzars of this world look at us and say, 'They went into the furnace without a fight, but somehow they're walking around. They're doing fine. We're the ones who are hurting'?

That's what it means to be more than a conqueror.

JUNE 6

How he maketh intercession to God against Israel, saying, Lord, they have killed thy prophets, and digged down thine altars; and I am left alone, and they seek my life.

Romans 11:2-3

People say, 'Give us a man of passion and power. Give us a man who can pray down fire from heaven. Give us Elijah.' But look how Elijah prayed. He made intercession to God *against* Israel. Yet even this man whom James holds up as an example of one who prevailed in prayer, an example of one who knew how to pray, didn't influence God in this case at all.

Although others may curse you, pray against you, or come down on you, none of those things move God. If God be for us, who can be against us? Elijah was unable to pray successfully against the people of Israel for God had made promises to Israel which still needed to be kept. He had a remnant in Israel Elijah didn't know about.

Next time you, like Elijah, pray God will get someone, remember that there are things about them you don't know. There are qualities in them you are just too blind to see. God sees people in an entirely different light than we do. Yes, He's aware of their failings and frailties—but He also sees what He's doing and the work which has already taken place in their lives.

We miss it. We judge people by what we think they should be. God looks at them and sees what they would have been had He not entered their hearts.

JUNE 7

And be not conformed to this world: but be ye transformed...

Romans 12:2

Every one of us is in one of two categories: conformer or transformer. Right now you're either trying to figure out what she's wearing, what he's driving, or how you can fit in and be cool—or, to paraphrase the J.B. Phillips translation, you're saying, 'I don't care what the world is doing. I'm not going to let it squeeze me into its mould.'

Are you a thermometer—adjusting to the temperature of the culture, or are you a thermostat—changing the climate of the culture? If you are a conformer, a thermometer, here's the problem: you're in for perpetual frustration because by the time you take the temperature and figure out what's hot, by the time you change your look, or buy the car, or redo your house—the world will have moved on, leaving you out of style.

Truly, this is a great mystery to a lot of Christians. They try to make their ministries relatable by analyzing what the world is doing in order to emulate it. But by the time they figure it out and implement it, the world has moved on. That's why Christians are known for being out of style.

What's the key? Don't be a thermometer, be a thermostat. Don't be a conformer, be a transformer. Say, 'I'm in a completely different place than you are, world.

I'm living for eternity.
I'm preparing for the Kingdom.
I'm headed for heaven.'

JUNE 8

...By the renewing of your mind, that ye may prove what is that good, and acceptable, and perfect, will of God.

Romans 12:2

Just as Jesus was transformed or 'metamorphosed,' so too, you can be changed if you keep your *mind* on Him. How do we keep our minds on Him?—by keeping in the Word. 'Lo, I have come in the volume of the book,' Scripture declares concerning Jesus (Psalm 40: 7, Hebrews 10:7).

You see, I can give my body to Him—that's a real key. But it's incomplete in and of itself unless I keep my mind on Him—and that happens through a diligent contemplation of the 'volume of the book,' the Word. However, you can read your Bible every morning for devotions; you can know the Word backwards and forwards and not go through a metamorphosis.

Indeed, Paul would say that, in and of itself, the letter kills (II Corinthians 3:6). If you read the Scriptures just to get insights into theology or practical tips about parenting or relationships, metamorphosis will not take place because transformation occurs only when we study the Word not for the sake of the Word, but in order to touch the Lord.

'In the beginning,' John wrote, 'was the Word. And the Word became flesh and dwelt among us' (John 1:1, 14). It's the Incarnation—the Word becoming flesh, becoming personable, touchable, and relatable—that will transform you. If you approach the Word strictly from an intellectual, academic, theological perspective, you might gain a point or two, but you'll not be changed.

At the stereotypical American breakfast table, the husband reads the *San Francisco Chronicle*. Across from him sits his wife, waiting to talk with him. But the man is interested in the impartation of information, not the intimacy of communication—and I suggest the same thing happens all too often in the devotional life of believers. They read the information in the Word, but completely neglect communication with the Word made flesh.

I am concerned about the great number of people who have a devotional life which is basically informational. Only in the last couple of generations has this happened, because throughout the vast majority of Christian history, Bible study was neither academic nor theological. It was oral; it was relational as people heard the Word being read. Communication transpired as the Living Word was fleshed out in real life.

Those who say, 'Lord, I'm reading this for one purpose: to hear Your voice,' are those who leave their time of devotion metamorphosed—changed from crawling caterpillars to soaring butterflies.

JUNE 9

Let every one of us please his neighbour for his good to edification. For even Christ pleased not himself; but, as it is written, The reproaches of them that reproached thee fell on me.

Romans 15:2-3

While we are to bear the infirmities of the weak, quoting from Psalm 69:9, Paul makes it clear that Jesus did not allow people to remain entrenched in their own legalism. As He healed on the Sabbath Day, the Pharisees began to reproach Him. Did He stop? No. He corrected their misunderstanding and then continued healing (Luke 14).

On the other hand, there were times when Jesus laid aside His liberty.

'Does your Master pay taxes in the temple?' the Pharisees asked Peter. 'Sure He does,' Peter responded.

But when Peter asked this same question of Jesus, Jesus said, 'Do kings charge their own kids taxes? Of course not. But in order that we don't offend, go fishing—and the first fish you catch will have a coin in his mouth which will cover the taxes' (Matthew 17:24-27).

'I'm confused,' you say. 'Do I bear my neighbor's infirmity—or do I correct him for edification?'

Just do what the Lord tells you to do at any given moment. Sometimes He will tell you to bear with those who are weak. Other times, He'll tell you to love them enough to give them a word of correction—even if it means you will suffer reproach. This is Christianity in its essence: it's not rules, principles, or regulations. It's walking with the Lord moment by moment, saying constantly, 'Lord, how do I deal with this situation? Is it a time for backing away and bearing weakness—or is it a time for loving exhortation and confrontation? What do I do?'

It's as though the Lord gives us broad principles in the Word and then says, 'See Me for further instructions. Talk to Me about specific application.' 'If any man lack wisdom, let him ask of God who giveth to all men generously' (James 4:8). *He'll* show you what to do, and it will be right, underscoring *both* love and liberty.

JUNE 10

That I should be the minister of Jesus Christ to the Gentiles, ministering the gospel of God, that the offering up of the Gentiles might be acceptable, being sanctified by the Holy Ghost.

Romans 15:16

D.L. Moody, a shoe salesman captured by Christ who became one of the most effective soul-winners of all time, purposed in his heart as a young man that he would never let a day go by wherein he didn't talk to at least one person about Jesus. One night it was approaching midnight, and because of the events of the day, he had not shared the Gospel with an unbeliever that particular day. So he went out on the streets of Chicago, found a man and said, 'Sir, are you ready for heaven?'

'Mind your own business,' said the startled man.
'This *is* my business,' Moody answered.

And it is our business as well. Walking the hills of Jacksonville yesterday, I found myself in the old Jacksonville cemetery. The tombstones of the early settlers provided an ironic backdrop for the women who were picnicking and the children who were playing hide and go seek. Observing the scene, I felt called back to the simple calling God has given you and me: to minister the Gospel of God— for while the world plays games among the tombstones, eternity is only a heartbeat away.

JUNE 11

Through mighty signs and wonders, by the power of the Spirit of God...

Romans 15:19

Concerning signs and wonders, Jesus said signs shall follow them that believe (Mark 16:17). He said this in the context of evangelism. In other words, 'Get going, and as you're going, I'll be flowing through you. I'll be doing signs and wonders before you.'

Gang, the Holy Spirit is like steam in a locomotive. He's there to move the engine down the track—not to toot the whistle. Too many people look at the power of the Holy Spirit as a whistle-tooter, as an end in itself—but the Lord says, 'You shall receive power when the Holy Ghost comes upon you *to be My witnesses*' (Acts 1:8, emphasis mine).

Thus, when people ask why we don't see more signs and wonders today, I say, 'Go to Honduras. Go to Mexico. Go to Russia. Start evangelizing and watch and see what the Lord will do in you, the miracles which will flow through you.'

But even if you never see an external sign, wonder, or miracle, you're in good company. Jesus said that of all of the men who had lived up to His day, John the Baptist was the greatest of them all. No man was greater—not Elijah, who called down fire from heaven, not Elisha, who raised the dead, not Moses, who parted the Red Sea.

Jesus said, 'Among them that are born of women there hath not risen a greater than John the Baptist' (Matthew 11:11)—and yet John did no miracle (John 10:41). So if you've never performed a miracle or even seen a miracle, take heart. You're in good company.

John did no miracle *but* 'all things John spoke of this Man were true' (John 10:41).

What Man? Jesus Christ. And talking about Jesus is something I can do—and so can you. Yes, I would love to have the powerful, miraculous ministry of Paul. But in the meantime, I'll try to walk in the footsteps of John the Baptist, speaking about the One who has captured my heart.

JUNE 12

Now I beseech you, brethren for the Lord Jesus Christ's sake, and for the love of the Spirit, that ye strive together with me in your prayers to God for me; That I may be delivered from them that do not believe in Judaea; and that my service which I have for Jerusalem may be accepted of the saints; That I may come unto you with joy by the will of God, and may with you be refreshed.

Romans 15:30-32

Paul requested prayer that he might be protected from the unbelievers in Jerusalem who were out to do him in, that he might be accepted by the believers there, and that he might come with joy to Rome.

Was Paul protected?

So severe was the stoning he received at the hands of unbelieving Jews that his life was spared only when he was taken into protective custody by a Roman centurion (Acts 21).

Was he accepted by the believers?

The believers themselves were the underlying reason for the stoning he received (Acts 21:18-25). Furthermore, they never thanked him for the offering he risked his life to deliver to them, nor does

Scripture record any of them speaking with him or caring for him during the two years he was in protective custody.

Did he come to Rome with joy?

He traveled to Rome in the galley of a boat, a prisoner of the Roman Empire.

And so we wonder. It looks like the prayers of the Romans weren't answered—or were they?

Was he protected?

Yes. He didn't die. Bloodied? You bet—but he didn't die.

Was he accepted by the believers?

Oh, not initially—but eventually, for Peter himself instructed the believers to listen to what Paul had to say (II Peter 3:15).

Did he make it to Rome?

While he didn't travel in the way he intended, at least his trip was all-expenses paid!

Gang, like Paul, sometimes we say, 'Pray for me. I'm going through this struggle, and here are three things I need to see happen...' And although we pray with fervency, sometimes initially it seems like just the opposite of what we hoped for happens. But wait. I have discovered that usually when I think prayers are not being answered, it's simply because I have not seen the unique and beautiful way God is working.

This article was in the paper this morning...

Dateline: Vermont. A woman in Alaska recently tried to call her sister in Idaho and mistakenly dialed a house in Vermont. She got through to 89-year-old Mildred Connor, who, at that moment, was suffering a severe heart attack. At that point, the Alaskan woman heard a gasping voice with weak breath saying, 'Help me, help me. Please, God, help me.'

Alice Witt meant to call Area Code 208, but called 802 instead and reached Rutland, Vermont. She and her husband were able to work with telephone operators and emergency personnel, who rushed to the scene and saved Mildred Connor's life.

Sometimes when I pray, I think all I get are busy signals or wrong numbers. But God is working in ways that, if I'll just hang in there, time will prove over and over again His hand throughout. The purpose and the power of prayer is to get the Lord's blessing on your life, not to get your way for your life. The prayers Paul requested on his behalf were truly answered in the best possible way.

Lives were touched;
  Folks were saved;
    And we're encouraged here today—
    Because people prayed.

JUNE 13

Greet Mary, who bestowed much labour on us.
Romans 16:6

The word 'labour' is interesting. The same word is used in Luke 5:5 in reference to the fishermen who toiled all night. It embodies the idea of sweating. Thus, Mary bestowed much 'sweat' upon them, if you would. That is, she gave of herself in a labouring type of ministry.

This intrigues me because there are six Marys mentioned in the New Testament. When you think of Mary, you either think of Mary the mother of Jesus, or Mary of Bethany who sat at the feet of Jesus while her sister Martha toiled in the kitchen (Luke 10:42). This Mary, however, is a worker. I wonder if this Mary ever thought, 'My name is Mary and all these Marys before me were sensitive, 'sitting at the feet' kind of ladies, but I'm a labourer. That's just the way I am.'

I find it's truly a red-letter day in the walk of a believer when he sheds the self-imposed pressures or expectations of what he thinks he should be. Oftentimes, we admire someone else, we want to be like someone else, and we put pressure on ourselves to be what we're not. Great is the day when you realize, 'Even though my name is Mary, the fact is I'm a get-down, get-dirty kind of woman. So I'm just going to be who I am.'

Mary's name is recorded throughout history as one who was noteworthy because she did what she was made to do, regardless of what the other Marys before her were like. Be who you are, and God will use you uniquely.

JUNE 14

Salute Rufus chosen in the Lord, and his mother and mine.

Romans 16:13

Rufus, it seems, is the same Rufus spoken of in Mark 15:21. Rufus' father was Simon of Cyrene—the one who came up from Africa to Jerusalem to celebrate and observe the Passover proceedings. When he lined up along the Via Dolorosa, as the crowd gathered on that Good Friday, he watched the proceedings, no doubt straining his neck and squinting his eyes, trying to get a perspective of what was happening. Suddenly, a Man collapsed before him under the weight of a cross. Instead of forcing Him to carry the burden any further, a soldier on the scene placed the flat head of his spear upon the shoulder of Simon the Cyrene, saying, 'You take the Cross.'

Simon must have thought, 'Oh, no. What a catastrophe. I came to celebrate the Passover, and now I'm going to be defiled by associating with this criminal.' But he discovered that the catastrophe was, in fact, a great opportunity because something happened to Simon when he took up the Cross. Could it be that he understood the prophecy of Isaiah 9:6: 'His government shall be upon His shoulder'? The government of what? The government of the Cross. Simon carried the Cross of Christ, in a sense governed in a way he would have never anticipated nor even wanted. Yet carry the Cross he did, eventually becoming converted to the One whose Cross he carried. For not only was Simon saved, but as can be inferred from this verse, his wife and his sons were saved as well.

What's the point for you and me? Jesus said, 'If any man will come after Me, let him deny himself, and take up his cross' (Matthew 16:24). He didn't say this because He wants us to be miserable or burdened, because He wants to see us squirm or suffer. That's not Jesus.

No, He came to teach us the very important truth that the way to really have happiness and fulfillment in life is to die to self, for the more you live for yourself, the more you focus on yourself, the more you are concerned about yourself, the more miserable and depressed, discouraged, and defeated you'll be. 'I came that you might have life and life abundantly' (John 10:10). He said, 'And this is the way: take up your cross. As for your life, give it up: lay it down; let it go.'

JUNE 15

But God hath chosen the foolish things of the world to confound the wise; and God hath chosen the weak things of the world to confound the things which are mighty; And base things of the world, and things which are despised, hath God chosen, yea, and things which are not, to bring to nought the things that are: That no flesh should glory in his presence.

I Corinthians 1:27-29

The Lord uses weak things so that only He gets credit. Why? Is He on some huge ego trip? Is He saying, 'I don't want anyone else to get any glory because I need to be affirmed'? Obviously not! God uses weak things not because of a lack in His nature, but due to a lack in ours. You see, God knows when He uses someone who is impressive in the eyes of the world, people set themselves up for a huge fall because they look to him rather than to God. Therefore, He says, 'I don't want any flesh to glory because all flesh will fail ultimately.'

It was not until Uzziah died that Isaiah saw the Lord high and lifted up (Isaiah 6:1). Who was Uzziah? One of the most powerful, successful, gifted kings in the history of Judah and Israel, Uzziah increased the boundaries of the nation, ushered in economic prosperity, and invented war machinery. Yet although his name was on the lips of all people (II Chronicles 26:8), it wasn't until he died that Isaiah saw the Lord.

The Lord still allows people to die—not physically—but in the estimation of others in order that our focus can more clearly be upon *Him*. Therefore, wise is the man, mature the church who realizes that Uzziah's death is not a reason to quit, but rather to say, 'Once again, Lord, I see that You are the only One upon whom I can truly and totally rely.'

JUNE 16

I have fed you with milk, and not with meat: for hitherto ye were not able to bear it, neither yet now are ye able.

I Corinthians 3:2

Here's a very simple way to evaluate whether you are carnal or not: how is your appetite? Do you crave the meat of the Word, or are you still only able to digest milk?

According to Hebrews 5:10-14, the milk of the Word deals with what Jesus did for us, while the meat deals with what Jesus is now doing on behalf of us—what's going on in heaven presently, the big plan which will unfold eschatologically. The baby Christian only knows, 'Jesus loves me, this I know.' But as great a truth as that is, he has not gone on to see who Jesus is presently and what's coming down prophetically.

Do you know more about what Jesus is doing today in heaven and on earth through His Church than you did last year? If you do, you're progressing and growing. Good for you! But if you don't, then perhaps you might fall into the category of the carnal believer who still has to be fed with milk, who can't get the meat on his own.

Is there any hope for you? Of course there is! The Lord would have you simply confess your carnality. And the good news is that, following confession *to* the Lord, there is liberation *by* the Lord. He sets you free. How? Not by positive thinking, not by determining to try harder or do better, but by His Spirit within you.

Although a pair of shoes used in the movie *The Wizard of Oz* cost only $9 to make, they were auctioned recently for $12,000. Why? Because Judy Garland wore them. So too, to an unspeakably greater degree, it's who's *in* us that brings value and freedom *to* us as He works in us both to will and to do of His good pleasure (Philippians 2:13).

JUNE 17

If any man's work shall be burned, he shall suffer
loss: but he himself shall be saved; yet so as by fire.
                                      I Corinthians 3:15

Everyone who understands that Jesus is the foundation of life will be saved. But some shall be saved as by fire. They'll make it into heaven; they'll be warmed when they see Jesus' face; but they'll look around and say, 'Oh, no, everything on earth I did vaporized before His eyes, and now I have no crown to cast at His feet.'

Because God shall wipe away every tear (Revelation 7:17), there will be tears in heaven. For what will they be shed? Not for the bigger house we wish we had built, not for the newer car we wish we had purchased, not for the nicer clothes we wish we had worn—but for the opportunities we missed to lay up treasure in heaven.

'Dress me up in my best suit,' said the man who knew he was about to die.
His wife complied.
'Now fill my pockets with gold,' he said, 'and sew them closed.'

When he died shortly thereafter, he went to heaven and was pleased to feel the bulges in his pockets.

'I made it! I did it!' he exclaimed. 'Who said you can't take it with you?! Look at this!' he said to Peter, opening his pockets.
And Peter said, 'Why did you bring asphalt up here?'

That which we are so interested in, fighting for, and worried about here on earth is mere asphalt in heaven.

One further note: although the primary reference of verses 13-15 is to the Bema Seat where we will be rewarded for that which we've done on earth, I believe a secondary reference is to the fires which the Lord allows to sweep through our lives presently.

'You're fired,' your boss says to you—and now you get a chance to see how much of your character is gold, silver, and precious stones, and how much is wood, hay, and stubble. So too, in ministry, in relationships, and on the job, fires will break out around you which you might think you have to put out immediately. But I have found that when you sense a wildfire starting, it's a good idea to be careful before you grab your bucket and shovel and try to put it out in your own energy and by your own wisdom. For if you have good people skills, you can meet with people, try to reason with them, and maybe control the fire for a year or two. But more often than not, it will explode eventually with a flame more devastating than the original.

Thus, when fires come, I am slowly but surely learning to let them burn. I don't defend the church or myself. I don't try to soothe feelings or calm tension. I let the fire burn. And when the fire is over, I poke around and see if any gold, silver, or precious stones are left with which to rebuild.

So too, to you who are involved with people in your family or in ministry, I suggest letting any given fire burn. And when you see what's left, you'll either know you were building with gold, silver, and precious stones—or with the wood, hay, and stubble of your own self-importance.

JUNE 18

Know ye not that ye are the temple of God, and that
the Spirit of God dwelleth in you?

I Corinthians 3:16

The Greek word translated 'temple' is not the usual word, *hieron*, which refers to the whole temple, but rather *naos*, which speaks of the holy of holies—the part of the temple wherein dwelt the

Shekinah, the Chabod, the tangible, visible perception of the presence of God enjoyed by the high priest only one day a year on Yom Kippur.

The word 'ye' being plural, Paul is saying, 'Don't you know that together you are the holy of holies where the glory, the weight, the reality of God is enjoyed and perceived?'

Paul develops this analogy further when he tells the Ephesians they '*grow* unto an holy temple in the Lord' (Ephesians 2:21). The Church grows because we are *living* stones—and this presents some interesting challenges. Dead stones fit together nicely, but living, squirming stones tend to rub each other the wrong way. Yet in this we can rejoice, for the Lord knows there are rough edges which need to be knocked off us blockheads.

That is why it is the mature believer who says, 'OK, Lord, I'm not going to change my location or situation. Instead, I'm going to stay right here and allow You to do Your work through people who might irritate me in order that I might be more like You.'

JUNE 19

> *If any man defile the temple of God, him shall God destroy, for the temple of God is holy, which temple ye are.*
>
> I Corinthians 3:17

What does it mean to be holy? When Moses realized he was in the presence of the Lord, he was told to take off his shoes for the ground he was on was holy ground (Exodus 3:5). As Joshua overlooked the city of Jericho, he had an encounter with the Lord and was told to take off his shoes (Joshua 5:15). Therefore, the Church being holy, it would seem fitting that we take off our shoes as well.

How? After walking through mud on their way home from school, our kids take off their shoes before walking into the house so they don't bring the mud in with them. So too, when we come together as a Body, we are to leave the mud of the world at the door. We're to forsake grudges and pride, attitudes which are amiss, hearts that are quick to judge.

But there's another reason to remove our shoes—for not only do I take my shoes off before I go into my house if they are dirty, but even if they are clean, I take them off because I'm comfortable there.

So too, when we fellowship with the Body, we don't have to keep our guard up or our best foot forward. We can relax in God's comforting love for us and for each other.

JUNE 20

Let a man so account of us, as of the ministers of Christ, and stewards of the mysteries of God.
I Corinthians 4:1

As faithful stewards in ministry, we're to be able to identify the riches of Scripture...

Then said he unto them, Therefore every scribe which is instructed unto the kingdom of heaven is like unto a man that is an householder, which bringeth forth out of his treasure things new and old.
Matthew 13:52

Jesus is talking about drawing from the illustrations and pictures, types and stories of the Old Testament and relating them to what the disciples could see being lived out before them in His life as well as to what we see further in the principles of the New Testament. That is why I think it is so important to go through the entire Bible—

to become familiar with the Law, the Prophets, and the poets; to meditate on the Gospel accounts, Paul's teaching, the Apocalypse. Read your Bible, dear brother. Don't give up, precious sister.

'But I'm reading through Leviticus right now, and I don't understand a thing,' you might be thinking.

That's OK. Keep reading because you're feeding your inner man, and in due season, you will understand even the book of Leviticus to a much greater degree than you do now.

With drought ravaging the land, Jehoram, the king of Israel, called for Elisha the prophet.

'Here's what you are to do,' said Elisha. 'Dig ditches here in the dry sand.'

The people did, and the next day, the ditches were filled with water (II Kings 3). So too, water being a type of the Word (Psalm 119:9, John 15:3, Ephesians 5:26), we're to keep digging ditches—even if it's dry. And eventually, the refreshing springs of Scripture will flow into our hearts.

Why did the Lord write the Bible the way He did? Why didn't He simply compose Section I: Marriage. Section II: The Doctrine of the Holy Spirit. Section III: Bible Prophecy, etc. That's the way I would have written it. But the Lord, in His infinite wisdom, says, 'No, analogies and stories, pictures and genealogies will be mysteries to the carnal mind—but will be exciting, applicable, wonderful to any man of any age in any culture who plugs away studying them day after week after month after year after decade.'

JUNE 21

And this I speak for your own profit; not that I may cast a snare upon you, but for that which is comely, and that ye may attend upon the Lord without distraction.

I Corinthians 7:35

There is a woman in Scripture who models this very effectively. Her name is Anna...

And she was a widow of about fourscore and four years, which departed not from the temple, but served God with fastings and prayers night and day. And she coming in that instant gave thanks likewise unto the Lord, and spake of him to all them that looked for redemption in Jerusalem.

Luke 2:37-38

Anna didn't panic about her single state. She didn't lament her situation. Rather, she realized she had an opportunity to serve the Lord without distraction. And what happened? She was given special revelation, for she recognized that which only one other man—a man named Simeon—knew: the Babe in the arms of Mary and Joseph was not an ordinary Child.

How I encourage you who have been widowed or divorced, you who feel alone or abandoned, to follow the example of Anna.

Look *for* the Lord.
Pray *to* the Lord.
Walk *with* the Lord.

Anna didn't hang out in the temple with God's people because she was miserable there. Rather, I suggest she stayed there year after year because she found in the Lord exactly what her soul was craving. And so will you.

JUNE 22

*The wife is bound by the law as long as her husband
liveth; but if her husband be dead, she is at liberty to
be married to whom she will; only in the Lord. But she
is happier if she so abide, after my judgment: and I
think also that I have the Spirit of God.*

I Corinthians 7:39-40

Throughout the centuries, people have read I Corinthians 7 and
concluded that, because he speaks so highly of the single state,
Paul has a problem with marriage. But that is because they fail to
take into account Paul's full counsel—for in his letter to the church
at Ephesus, Paul elevates marriage to a place of utmost glory when
he uses it as an illustration for no less a relationship than that of
Christ and the Church.

The way a husband lays down his life for his wife and the way a
wife submits to her husband is a powerful illustration which can
be seen on every street in every neighborhood. Bunches of people
aren't into church, so the Lord brings the Church to them through
the illustration of marriage wherein people see how much He loves
the Church and how the Church submits to Him. It's an awesome
responsibility for all who are married. That is not to say people need
to see perfection—just something remarkably different than what
they see in society.

And yet, as seen here in I Corinthians 7, Paul says singleness has
its own unique beauty, its own important role to play in the Body.
The single state is not to be looked down upon, dreaded, or merely
endured. Those who are called to a single life or who find themselves
in a single state fulfill a very real function—to serve the Lord with
spontaneity and without distraction.

Marriage is a picture, but, in a sense, singleness can be the reality—
for it is the single person uniquely who can say, 'I am married to
You, Lord. You are my Husband, my Love, my best Friend. And I

will be devoted to you single-heartedly for as long as You have me in this state.'

Whether single or married, widowed or divorced—be content wherever God has you. And whatever your position, make Jesus your Passion.

June 23

But if any man love God, the same is known of him.
I Corinthians 8:3

What was the one tree of which Adam and Eve were forbidden to eat? The tree of the knowledge of good and evil. Yet once they disobeyed God and ate of this tree, they immediately thought they knew good from evil, right from wrong, without having to depend on the Father as they had done before. Suddenly, knowing they were naked, they hid from God.

The result? Intimacy with the Father was broken.

So too, if I'm not oh, so careful, even Biblical knowledge and theological understanding will make me less of a pray-er, less of a lover, less inclined to depend wholly on the Father because I will mistakenly think I can handle any given situation on the basis of my own knowledge or understanding.

> *Thus saith the Lord, Let not the wise man glory in*
> *his wisdom, neither let the mighty man glory in his*
> *might, let not the rich man glory in his riches: But let*
> *him that glorieth glory in this, that he understandeth*
> *and knoweth me, that I am the Lord which exercise*
> *lovingkindness, judgment, and righteousness, in the*
> *earth: for in these things I delight, saith the Lord.*
> *Jeremiah 9:23-24*

The word, 'know' speaks of intimacy, as a man knows his wife. There are many people who know about the Lord—but they don't know Him intimately. 'Lord, Lord,' they will say, 'didn't we prophesy in Your name and do signs and wonders for Your Kingdom?'

Yet He will say, 'Depart from Me. I never knew you. Yes, you worked for Me. Yes, you knew about Me. But we had no relationship intimately' (Matthew 7:21-23).

Be students of the Word, saints. Grow in the knowledge of the Lord. Become solid in theology—but as you do, make sure that love has the priority. Make sure your love for God is preeminent. The Word will confirm His leading and correct your misunderstanding. But it must not be a substitute for walking with Him day by day, talking with Him about every situation. The Word must never take the place of your walking with Him in intimacy and dependency lest it become as the fruit of the tree of knowledge.

JUNE 24

And every man that striveth for the mastery is temperate in all things. Now they do it to obtain a corruptible crown; but we an incorruptible.

I Corinthians 9:25

The Isthmus Games—the second most important athletic games in all of the region—took place in Corinth. And while the Olympics were the Super Bowl, the Isthmus Games were the Pro Bowl and captured the attention of the Corinthians. They watched the athletes arrive a year before the games took place to train single-mindedly in order to win the prize—a little laurel wreath to put on one's head.

'Look at what these athletes do simply to win a crown of leaves,' Paul says. 'But the crown for which you race is incorruptible; it will last forever.'

'So what?' you say. 'If you looked in my closet, you wouldn't fine a single crown because I'm not into them.'

Really? Of the five crowns identified in Scripture, the crown to which Paul refers here is linked to the declaration in Proverbs 11:30 that 'he who wins souls is wise'—and to that of Daniel, that 'they that turn many to righteousness shall shine as the stars for ever and ever' (12:3). To you who are more concerned about seeing people saved than about your own pleasure, ease, or liberty, a crown will be given—not merely to wear on your head, but, according to I Corinthians 15:41-42, which will determine your function and capacity to enjoy eternity.

You see, while everyone in heaven will be completely happy, totally joyful (Psalm 16:11), the crowns we win on earth will have a direct link to our function and our capacity to enjoy eternity.

Benjamin is thrilled. Mrs. Williams, his kindergarten teacher, appointed him Chair Monitor. As Chair Monitor, he gets to make sure all the chairs are slid under the desks when the bell rings. And he couldn't be happier.

If, on the other hand, I was appointed Chair Monitor, I wouldn't jump up and down and say, 'I can't wait to tell Tammy!' For me, the position of Chair Monitor no longer has an impact because at this point, my capacity, understanding, and involvement with life is bigger than that.

So too, in heaven, *everyone* will be happy. But Jesus told us when the Kingdom of heaven is established, some will rule over ten cities, others five cities, others one—and some will be Chair Monitors.

Understanding this, Paul knew that a crown is not a fashion statement, but rather that which reflects what we will be doing for the next zillion years.

What if, like Paul, we really believed this? I guarantee every one of us would be looking for opportunities to be stepped on if it meant that the person for whom we laid down our rights would see something of Jesus or come into a saving knowledge of Him. What you do with your life is oh, so important, gang. Don't bury your talents. Don't waste your time. Don't fritter away your resources and money foolishly. Run to win the prize.

JUNE 25

But I keep under my body, and bring it into subjection: lest that by any means, when I have preached to others, I myself should be a castaway.

I Corinthians 9:27

Newer translations correctly render the word 'castaway' as 'disqualified.' Thus, Paul is saying, 'I let go of my liberty in order that I might win people to Jesus. Why? Because I'm in a race for a prize which will affect who I am and what I do in the ages to come. Therefore, even though I am free to do all things, I can be disqualified if I don't keep my flesh under control, if I cause another to stumble...'

Favored to win the 1,500-meter Olympic event, Mary Decker was in excellent shape and running her best times. But after the gun went off, another talented runner, Zola Budd of South Africa, leaned into Mary Decker on the first curve, causing Decker to trip and fall—and herself to be disqualified.

This is the reason Paul was determined to keep his body under control.

Before you were saved, your body was not under. Your body was on top. That is, your flesh was that which governed both your soul—your mind and emotions—and your spirit—the real you which lives forever. To see how true this is, all you have to do is listen to the conversations which take place at work or on the campus, wherein you'll hear the average person talk only about his body—about his financial concerns and recreational pursuits, his occupational goals and physical needs. But when the natural man gets saved, suddenly everything is different. The flesh no longer dominates him. The spirit is now on top, and suddenly there's peace in his heart and life makes sense.

But because the flesh hates the basement, as time goes on, it demands to be on top again. And when it is, the new believer's life is a mess, for to be carnally-minded is death (Romans 8:6). So eventually, he gets to the place where he says, 'Lord, forgive me. I've given in to the flesh again.' He confesses his sin, turns his life back over to God, and his body is 'under' once more.

Does this war have to go on daily, hourly, constantly? Paul says here's the key: 'I *keep* my body under. I will not allow my body to determine what I watch, read, listen to, or think about. I will keep my body in the basement.'

How can this be accomplished?

Let me suggest to you one very practical way: how long has it been since you've said 'No' to your stomach? How long has it been since you've said, 'I'm going to use the hour I would have spent feeding my growling, demanding stomach in order to pull away and pray for my family, for the community, and for myself because I'm struggling with this temptation or that addiction'? That's called fasting. And I find it interesting that Jesus didn't say, '*If* you fast...' but, '*When* you fast...' (Matthew 6:16). When you say 'No' to your stomach regularly, you'll be amazed how much easier it will be to say 'No' to the other temptations which plague you.

Fasting from food is only one of the many disciplines the Bible teaches—not to be weird, but to be free. Another is saying 'No' when your body says, 'Hit the snooze bar.' It's saying, 'See, body, you're under. You're not ruling me. I'm out of bed. I'm on my knees. I'm in the Word.' It's following the example of Jesus who rose up a great while before morning to seek His Father.

'I keep my body under,' Paul says. 'I'm tired of my body ruling over me and the death it brings inevitably. Therefore, my spirit, ruled by God's Spirit, will be that which controls my soul—my will, my personality, my emotions.'

You'll never regret knocking fleshly pursuits out of your life, gang. I promise you, you'll never regret the things you let go which would have tripped others and disqualified you; those things which would have wiped out your spiritual stamina and affected your endurance.

Are you as disciplined in your spiritual life today as you were a year or five years ago? Or has your appreciation for the finished work of the Cross and your understanding that your salvation is secure apart from anything you do or don't do skewed your thinking?

Yes, you're free, but have you used that liberty in a way that's tripping others and disqualifying yourself?

Use your liberty wisely, precious people. Keep your body under, for to be carnally-minded is death, but to be spiritually-minded brings abundant life and perfect peace.

JUNE 26

Neither murmur ye, as some of them also murmured,
and were destroyed of the destroyer.
I Corinthians 10:10

After being covered by the cloud and provided for by the goodness and graciousness of the Father, as the Israelites were poised to enter the Land of Promise, Moses sent twelve spies to check out the land. And although they returned with reports of its beauty, although they returned with fruit as proof of its productivity, they also returned with reports of Anakim—giants they believed were sure to squish them like bugs should they dare to enter (Numbers 13:26-33).

But there were two spies who had a different perspective. 'Don't rebel against the Lord,' said Joshua and Caleb. 'Don't fear the people of the land for they are our bread' (Numbers 14:9). I love that! Caleb said, 'These giants are bread for us. We'll eat them up. And as a result, we'll actually be stronger for battle.'

Forty years later, it was to an 85-year-old Caleb that Joshua said, 'We made it, Caleb. Out of the original 3 million, it's just you and me. Take any territory you want. It's time to retire.' But what does Caleb say?

> Now therefore give me this mountain, whereof the LORD spake in that day; for thou heardest in that day how the Anakims were there, and that the cities were great and fenced: if so be the LORD will be with me, then I shall be able to drive them out, as the LORD said.
>
> Joshua 14:12

'Don't give me a beach cabin, give me the mountain where giants live,' said Caleb. 'Why? Because I'm hungry for some bread.'

When you pray the Lord's prayer, 'Give us this day our daily bread,' think Anakim. You see, we complain and murmur, 'Why is this trial happening? Why that? Why not the other?' when in reality, the very situations or people about which we murmur are those through which God wants to strengthen us. That which seems so big and so intimidating are Anakim—and it is the wise man or woman who, like Caleb, says, 'You've let them cross my path, Lord, therefore they must be there to make me stronger.'

Can you imagine how different our homes would be if we really believed that the trials which come our way, the giants which loom before us are actually beneficial to us if we would eat them up in faith? 'More bills?' we'd say, 'Great! Keep them coming. Another rejection notice? All right!'

Most will die murmuring in the wilderness. 'If God loves me, why doesn't He...?' or 'How come this giant is marching towards me?' But there will be those—and I pray I might be one and you might be the other—who will say, 'Giants? I smell bread. Pass the butter!'

JUNE 27

To another the working of miracles...
I Corinthians 12:10

When Jesus talked about the miraculous—drinking poisons which would not hurt, handling deadly serpents which would not harm, speaking with new tongues, laying hands on the sick and seeing them recover—it's important to see that these wonderful, miraculous operations and expressions were in connection with the Great Commission (Mark 16:15).

Thus, I believe one of the best ways to see the miraculous happen to a greater degree is to be involved in radical evangelism. The miracles of Mark 16 are not intended for us to huddle together in the sanctuary so we can see a miracle. No, it's as we're going into the jungles, into the inner city, throughout the community sharing the Lord that He will confirm our message with miracles. Consequently, as you study the Book of Acts, you see the operation of miracles most closely linked with the office of evangelism because the operation of miracles is primarily for the unbeliever.

Why? Because the believer's faith is not increased by seeing miracles. In fact, it's stunted. The Lord dedicated an entire segment of history to prove this point. Read Exodus and Numbers, and you will see God continually performing signs and wonders for His people. The Red Sea parted before them. Manna came down from heaven to them. They were directed by a huge cloud each day and a pillar of fire every night. They were bitten by poisonous snakes and miraculously preserved. The earth opened up and swallowed the rebellious among them. They were a people who witnessed miracle after miracle daily. And yet what was the end of the story? They couldn't enter the Promised Land because of—unbelief (Hebrews 3:17-19).

People think if they could just see a miracle or 2 or 10 or 20, their faith would soar. Not so. Faith comes by hearing, and hearing by the Word of God (Romans 10:17). For the believer, the way to grow in faith is not to see the miraculous but to take in the Scriptures. It is for the *unbeliever* that God will confirm His Word with signs and wonders. That is why it's as we're involved in missions, in evangelism, in service to the unbeliever and the skeptic that the Lord will most often confirm His Word through the arena of the miraculous.

JUNE 28

Though I speak with the tongues of men and of angels,
and have not charity, I am become as sounding brass,
or a tinkling cymbal.

I Corinthians 13:1

Without love, whatever I say is just noise. The word 'charity' appears here rather than the word 'love' because the Greek word *agape* was translated *charitas* in the Latin Vulgate, the first translation of the original Greek manuscripts. John Wycliffe, the man responsible for translating the Latin Vulgate in to English, used a similar-sounding English word for *charitas* when he used 'charity'—a word which spoke of giving simply for the sake of giving. Unfortunately, however, in our day, charity has come to be associated with pity. So modern translators have rightly chosen the word 'love' rather than the maligned 'charity.' Yet even the word 'love' is not without its problems.

I love my wife. I love my kids. I love Big Macs. I love walks in the park on summer evenings. We use the word 'love' so freely that we diminish its meaning. The Greeks circumvented this problem by employing four words for love in their vocabulary...

Storgé means affection. It's the kind of love one feels towards his cat or dog. *Eros* refers to sexual, physical love. *Phileo*, from which we get the name 'Philadelphia,' speaks of brotherly love. Phileo says, 'If you're nice to me, I'll be nice to you.'

It wasn't until the New Testament apostles introduced the concept of unconditional love that the Greeks added *agape* to their vocabulary. Agape is a love which gives simply for the sake of giving, never expecting anything in return. Agape gives anonymously—and it doesn't leave the price tag on. People who don't know the Lord can experience all of the other kinds of love. But for them, agape is impossible, for it is found only in God. Agape is the love of which Paul speaks when he says, 'If I don't have love, I'm just making noise even if I speak in tongues fluently.'

In the year 1647, during England's Civil War, a deserter in Cromwell's army was captured and brought before him.

'When the curfew bell sounds tonight, he shall be executed,' ordered the General.

But that night, the curfew bell was not heard. Upon investigation, it was discovered that, receiving news of her fiancé's sentence, his betrothed made her way quickly to the camp and hid in the bell tower. As curfew neared, she positioned herself within the bell in such a way that when the rope was pulled, the clapper hit her body rather than the inside of the bell. Seeing the bruised and battered lady standing before him, Cromwell was so deeply touched by her love that the soldier's life was spared.

Jesus Christ climbed not a bell tower, but the hill of Calvary in order that you and I would be spared the execution we so rightfully deserve. Whether the word is charity, love, or agape, the love Jesus showed us, the love we are to extend to each other is spelled one way:

S-a-c-r-i-f-i-c-e.

JUNE 29

...Beareth all things, believeth all things, hopeth all things, endureth all things.

I Corinthians 13:7

If you are one who bears all things, believes all things, hopes all things, endures all things, people will accuse you of being blind to certain situations. Not so. Agape love is not blind. Quite the opposite. Because love sees *more*, it's willing to see less.

What does love see? It sees the price that was paid on the Cross of Calvary for the person or situation which threatens to make us mad or bitter. The older I get, the more clearly I see the work of the Cross. I see the reality of the Holy Spirit's power to convict people. I see the promise of the Father being worked out—that in due season, if they choose not to listen to the Word and respond to the Spirit, their sin will track them down (Numbers 32:23). Therefore, rather than feeling I have to solve every problem and deal with every situation, I can simply bear with, believe in, and hope the best for people because of the commitment Jesus made to them when He died for them.

How can we live in this kind of love? The only way is to let Jesus Christ live it through us, for He is the Embodiment of these characteristics. We can't psyche ourselves into this, gang. This kind of love is nothing less than the fruit of the Spirit. But as I walk with the Lord, talk to the Lord, and learn about the Lord, His Spirit produces this character in me ever so slowly, but ever so surely.

'If you abide in Me,' Jesus said, 'you shall bring forth much fruit' (John 15:5). What fruit? Love. He told us we're branches and that He is the Vine. What do branches do? Just hang in there, close to the vine. Therefore, as I stay connected to the Vine by getting to know Him and enjoying Him, the fruit will come.

Fruit comes when you continue doing just what you're doing now—spending time with Him, hanging in there week after week, month after month, year after year. Slowly, but surely, as you stay connected to Jesus, more and more of His agape love will flow through you. You watch; you wait; you'll see.

JUNE 30

What is it then? I will pray with the spirit, and I will pray with the understanding also: I will sing with the spirit, and I will sing with the understanding also.
I Corinthians 14:15

'I will,' says Paul. This is where many people have a terrible time with the prayer language or tongues. They say, 'OK, if this is for me and will edify my spirit, I'm open to it.' They might ask for the laying on of hands. They might be in a position where they are sincerely waiting on the Lord. But nothing happens. 'I just want to express my love to the Lord in this unique way, but nothing's happening,' they say in frustration—as though they believe that somehow they're going to go into a trance, their eyes will become glazed, they'll quiver and shake, and their tongue will begin moving against their will.

Paul simply says, 'I will pray in the Spirit. It's a choice I make.'

When we teach our kids or new believers to pray, we don't say, 'Sit there until something happens. If you're really supposed to pray, you'll pray.' No, we set an example for them and give a model to them. Many times, I'll have someone repeat after me, 'Dear Jesus, come into my heart' as a simple prayer of salvation. Does the fact that they're echoing my words make their prayer ineffective or insincere? No. They're just learning how to pray, and that's where they're at in their development.

So too, I suggest that praying in the Spirit is a lot simpler than we make it. It's just saying, 'I will pray right now with words I don't understand, trusting the Lord is inspiring these words and partnering with me in the process.' Praying in the Spirit is not a feeling I feel. It's a decision I make. And once I begin to do this, it's so simple.

I'm not on a tongues-speaking kick by any stretch of the imagination. But it's a beautiful expression for me personally to say, 'I don't know how to pray with understanding about this. I'm frazzled and fried mentally. So I'm going to pray in the Spirit,'—and as I do, my spirit is edified. The prayer language is available to anyone, to *everyone* who simply believes.

JULY 1

But by the grace of God I am what I am...

I Corinthians 15:10

'Who shall I say sent me?' Moses asked God when told he was to lead the Israelites out of bondage.

And God said unto Moses, '*I AM THAT I AM*' (Exodus 3:14). I suggest to you that this phrase was ringing in Paul's mind and resonating in his heart when he said, 'By the grace of God I am what I am'—for in Exodus 34, God went on to explain just who He is...

> *The LORD God, merciful and gracious, longsuffering, and abundant in goodness and truth, Keeping mercy for thousands, forgiving iniquity and transgression and sin, and that will by no means clear the guilty; visiting the iniquity of the fathers upon the children, and upon the children's children, unto the third and to the fourth generation.*
>
> *Exodus 34:6-7*

Because of the injustice which seems to plague our culture, we could have a tendency to think that if God came on the scene today, surely it would be as a God of Justice. Yet while God is indeed just, He chooses instead to identify Himself as merciful and gracious. What a relief this should be to us. Justice means getting what we deserve. And who of us would dare say, 'Lord, give me what I deserve'? Mercy, on the other hand, means being spared judgment which we rightfully deserve—and grace goes even farther than that, for grace means getting blessings we don't deserve.

But God didn't stop there. He went on to say that He is longsuffering. The Hebrew word for longsuffering means l-o-n-g suffering. 'Why aren't You doing something, God?' 'How can You put up with Him?' or, 'Why don't You deal with them?' we cry. God bears with the sin we see in others for the same reason He bears with the sin He sees in us: He is longsuffering. That's His nature. And He's abundant in goodness and truth—lavishing blessings upon us, being completely honest and truthful with us.

God alone is the One who is merciful to thousands, forgiving iniquity and rebellion and sin. And even if generation after generation continues to turn their back on Him, He visits each one, bringing conviction for the purpose of conversion.

'What gives me the right, the authority to correct you?' Paul could have asked the Corinthians. 'There was a time when I thought I had earned that right. After all, I was born into the tribe of Benjamin, circumcised the eighth day, a Pharisee of Pharisees, zealous for the Law, righteous in my behavior. But although I was religious outwardly, I was sinning inwardly. And all of my attempts to earn God's blessing, all of my seeking to manipulate Him to get Him to bless me proved to be a waste (Philippians 3:4-7). Now I know I'm a sinner.

'But because God is who He is—because He is merciful and gracious, longsuffering and forgiving, I am what I am: a trophy of His grace.'

JULY 2

...And his grace which was bestowed upon me was not in vain; but I laboured more abundantly than they all: yet not I, but the grace of God which was with me.

I Corinthians 15:10

When we were new in faith, many of us looked at works—Bible study, prayer, service, and tithing—as ways to get God to respond to us. But as we grow in faith, we come to understand that works are not meant to get God to respond to us. Rather, works are the inevitable response to the goodness and grace He has *already* lavished upon us. When I consider that I'm going to heaven, that my sins are forgiven, that God has given me His Word, that the Holy Spirit lives within me—I have no other choice but to serve Him wholeheartedly.

An understanding of the grace of God results in works. But the works are a response to God—not a means of getting God to respond to them. The fallacy of 'seed faith theology'—in which people are told to give money, offer prayers, or engage in service in order to get something back from God—is that all of those things are the inevitable response of one who understands what God has *already* done on his or her behalf.

'I labor more abundantly than everyone,' Paul says. 'Because God has been so good to me, I can't help it.' So too, if you are one who truly embraces and enjoys the grace of God, you will be more engaged in His service than you were a year ago. You just won't be able to do otherwise.

JULY 3

But if there be no resurrection of the dead, then is Christ not risen: And if Christ be not risen, then is our preaching vain, and your faith is also vain. Yea, and we are found false witnesses of God; because we have testified of God that he raised up Christ: whom he raised not up, if so be that the dead rise not. For if the dead rise not, then is not Christ raised: And if Christ be not raised, your faith is vain; ye are yet in your sins. Then they also which are fallen asleep in Christ are perished.

I Corinthians 15:13-18

'Show us a sign that You are who You claim to be,' they said.

'One sign I'll show you. Destroy this temple, this body, and in three days I will raise it up' Jesus answered (John 2:19).

Houdini claimed that on the 50th anniversary of his death, he would come back from the dead. So on that date, a group of his followers gathered around his grave in San Francisco, waiting for him to return. They waited and waited and waited. Then they went home.

Jesus uniquely, singularly rose again from the dead. Lots of people make all sorts of claims, but our Hero, our Leader, our Lord Jesus Christ delivered. He came through. And had His offering not been acceptable, our Great High Priest would never have emerged from the tomb on Easter Sunday...

As the high priest, dressed in linen, went into the Holy of Holies on the Day of Atonement to sprinkle blood on the mercy seat, the people would wonder and wait—for if the high priest was himself defiled, if the high priest was himself polluted by sin, he would be smitten dead in the Holy of Holies. But if he emerged, his linen garments sprinkled with blood, the people would know the offering took. They would know their sins were forgiven.

What about our Great High Priest, Jesus Christ? Wrapped in linen, He was placed in the tomb. All of heaven wondered. All of history waited. Did the Offering take? Was His blood accepted? Because He emerged from the tomb on that glorious Easter Sunday, we know the Offering took; we know His blood was accepted; we know that we are forgiven.

Whether you're talking to the skeptic on the campus, at work, or in your neighborhood, the issue is singular: did Jesus rise from the dead? If He did, that makes Him unique in history. It validates His claim. And it means our sins are forgiven. The entire argument hinges on the single issue of the Resurrection.

JULY 4

The first man is of the earth, earthy...
I Corinthians 15:47

According to Psalm 103, the Father understands that we are earthy. Therefore, I am personally persuaded that many of us expect more of ourselves than our Father expects of us. We put pressure upon ourselves, set lofty goals, make endless promises. But in reality, we're just dusty and earthy. 'We have this treasure, Jesus Christ, in earthen vessels,' Paul will say in his second letter to the Corinthians (4:7). Jesus is the Treasure. We're just the earthen vessel, the clay pot.

From time to time, many of us try to polish and point our earthen vessels by trying to put on an act of spirituality. In reality, however, all that does is detract from the beauty of the Treasure inside. That is why, in describing how He wanted to be worshipped, the Lord didn't prescribe an altar made of cut stones, polished brass, or beaten gold. It was to be made of earth (Exodus 20:24) in order that nothing would detract from the sacrifice laid upon it.

So too, that is wrong which obstructs people's view of Jesus. Even in preaching, worshipping, or witnessing, anything which points to ourselves is sin. So many people don't witness, teach Sunday school, or serve in other ways because they don't feel polished or articulate enough. Little do they realize that they are the ideal candidates for ministry because people will marvel at the Treasure and not at them.

Whether it be congregationally or personally, the key to ministry is to get out of the way and let people see the beauty of Jesus, the Treasure within.

July 5

...Stand fast in the faith...
I Corinthians 16:13

I look at the massive oak tree and realize it wasn't massive initially. An oak tree is nothing more than just a little nut that refused to give ground. So too, by God's grace, we don't have to give ground. We can be consistent in our time of worship; we can be committed to the study of Scripture; we can be faithful in prayer.

People who are successful in any endeavor have one thing in common: they're part of the 1% who finish what they begin. Whether regarding career, kids, or the things of the Kingdom—most people have great ideas and start well. But they don't finish. They give up. They give ground.

'Father, I have glorified Thee and finished the work Thou gavest me to do,' Jesus said (John 17:4). Finishing the work God gave Him to do wasn't just an idea in His journal or a thought stirring in His mind. It was something Jesus *did*.

Has God called you to teach Sunday school? Do it and stay with it until He leads you in a different direction. Has He called you to have a time of morning worship? Then do so. Has He spoken to you about spending time discipling your kids? Then do it. I believe the Lord wants every one of us to be hugely successful in the things of the Kingdom. His burden is easy, His load light. The only question is, will you give ground—or will you stand fast?

JULY 6

The grace of our Lord Jesus Christ be with you. My love be with you all in Christ Jesus. Amen.

I Corinthians 16:23-24

There could have been those in Corinth who said, 'If you care so much about us, Paul, why did you point out our carnality and rebuke us for our immorality? Why were you so rough on us?'

Yet, under the inspiration of the Spirit, Paul simply says, 'I do love you.'

Because open rebuke is better than secret love (Proverbs 27:5), the rebukes and exhortations which come our way should be embraced as friends. It's much more comfortable for me to ignore a prickly situation or issue. But that's not love. Love says, 'I care more about your excelling and your succeeding than about what you think of me. If you think I'm not a nice guy, that's OK if what I'm saying will provoke you to love and to good works, to think through what you're doing and perhaps repent from the direction you're heading.' Faithful are the wounds of a friend (Proverbs 27:6). But make sure your correction is done in love...

As the disciples sat at the Last Supper, under the table were 24 dirty, stinky feet. To remedy the situation, Jesus didn't give a lecture on foot washing. No, He girded Himself with a towel and washed feet Himself (John 13:4-5).

I have the right and responsibility to give admonition, exhortation, and correction; to openly rebuke and wound if necessary only if I am willing to wash the feet of the people with whom I deal. If I'm not willing to walk with them through their difficulty, stand by them in their trouble, kneel with them in prayer, it would be wiser for me to keep silent.

Paul was one who had the right to correct, admonish, and rebuke the Corinthian Christians because he worked with his hands to support himself, put up with their insults and risked his life to be with them. Thus, it was truly from his heart that Paul said to the church at Corinth, 'My love be with you all in Christ Jesus.'

JULY 7

For we would not, brethren, have you ignorant of our trouble which came to us in Asia, that we were pressed out of measure, above strength, insomuch that we despaired even of life: But we had the sentence of death in ourselves, that we should not trust in ourselves...

II Corinthians 1:8-9

Demetrius the silversmith was angry with Paul. So many people were getting saved in Ephesus that his business was being affected by loss of revenue from the sale of idols. Following his instigation of a riot, soon the entire city was in an uproar (Acts 19). Yet the dark days at Ephesus had a purpose indeed: they caused Paul to rely solely on God.

Like Paul, the tendency of most of us is to try to solve our problems with our own strength. Therefore, as He did with Paul, the Lord brings us to the end of ourselves from time to time—to the point where we feel pressed beyond measure, despairing even of life—in order that we will have no other choice but to call upon Him and find in Him greater strength than we could ever find in our own ability.

He was a go-getter from the very beginning, as evidenced by his grabbing his older twin brother's heel in a failed attempt to be first-born. Throughout his life, Heel-Snatcher, or Jacob, was one who drew from his own cunning and acumen to get ahead—until the day he heard that his brother, from whom he had cheated his birthright and blessing, was headed his way, accompanied by 400 men.

So desperate was Jacob that when an angel appeared to him, he said, 'I have no other heel to snatch; I'm at the end of my resources; I won't let you go until you bless me.' So they wrestled all night. And although Jacob ended up with a blessing when his name was changed from Jacob to Israel, from 'Heel-Snatcher' to 'Governed By God,' he also limped away with a dislocated hip, as though God said, 'With every step you take, you will be reminded that you—who once walked so proudly, who once stood so confidently—came to the end of yourself. And it was the best thing that that ever happened to you, for now, in your brokenness and weakness, you'll be stronger and more useful than you could have ever been in your own energy and cleverness.'

It's a great day when a man finally comes to the end of himself and realizes, 'I don't need to go to another seminar or call another counselor; I don't need to enroll in another program or come up with another creative idea. All I need is You, Lord. I'm going to wrestle with You. I'm going to cling to You. I'm going to depend on You because I need to be governed by You.'

July 8

But I determined this with myself, that I would not come again to you in heaviness. For if I make you sorry, who is he then that maketh me glad, but the same which is made sorry by me?

II Corinthians 2:1-2

Paul was a man who talked to himself. 'When you go to Corinth again, make sure you don't go with a heavy heart,' he said.

I point this out because sometimes spiritual self-talk is absolutely necessary. I believe the Psalmist set the example for us when he said, 'Bless the Lord, O my soul. And all that is within me, bless His holy name' (Psalm 103:1). In other words, 'Get it in gear, soul. Wake up and start praising.'

In I Samuel, we read of an ill-fated military endeavor wherein David and his men left their camp in Ziglag only to return to find their city burned down and their wives and children taken into captivity. As a result, David's men—400 men in number—were so angry with David that they wanted to kill him. It was at this point that David could have descended into real depression. Instead, we read that he encouraged himself in the Lord (I Samuel 30:6).

Do you ever do that? Do you say, 'I'm not going to get down. I'm going to talk to myself about what God has done for me, how good He has been to me, how He's seen me through so many times previously'? I encourage you to encourage yourself in the Lord. Talk to your soul. Speak out the Scriptures. Memorize them or read them aloud. And as they go from your mouth into your ear, let them bless your heart.

Encourage yourself in the Lord when you're driving in your car, when you're walking down the street, when you're feeling kind of blue. David did. And what happened? His countenance changed. He rallied the troops behind him once again. They went after the marauders and captured everything that was lost.

But what would have happened had David remained depressed? I wonder how much is lost and wasted in our own lives because we fail to follow the example of David and Paul, because we don't encourage ourselves in the Lord.

JULY 9

But we all, with open face beholding as in a glass the
glory of the Lord, are changed into the same image
from glory to glory, even as by the Spirit of the Lord.

II Corinthians 3:18

Because there is none righteous, because none seeks after God
(Romans 3:11), we are able to see the Lord not by anything we've
done or haven't done—but simply and completely by His grace.
Because He's lifted the veil from our eyes, we can look into His face.
And in so doing, we are changed.

We are changed not by a program, a practice, or a procedure, but
by a Person. We are changed by looking at Jesus—by spending time
with Him, learning about Him, receiving from Him, offering worship
to Him.

Stay in the Scriptures, gang. Spend time in the Word daily. Come
together for Bible study. Sing songs of adoration—for it's in
worshipping, in studying, in looking at Jesus that you'll become
like Him.

JULY 10

We having the same spirit of faith, according as it is
written, I believed, and therefore have I spoken; we
also believe, and therefore speak.

II Corinthians 4:13

Quoting Psalm 116, Paul says, 'I speak that which I believe—that
the Lord will raise us up, that all things will work out for His glory.'
This same concept is present in the Book of Hebrews.

> *Let your conversation be without covetousness; and*
> *be content with such things as ye have: for he hath*
> *said, I will never leave thee, nor forsake thee. So that*
> *we may boldly say, The Lord is my helper, and I will*
> *not fear what man shall do unto me.*
>
> Hebrews 13:5-6

'He hath said...that we may say...' To speak out words of faith in the time of difficulty is oh, so important in the life of the believer. If all we talk about is our frustration, pain, and sadness, we will faint. But if we speak that which He hath said—that He is with us always (Matthew 28:20), that all things work together for good to those who love God (Romans 8:28), that greater is He that is in us than He that is in the world (I John 4:4)—we will be renewed day by day.

In Hebrews 11, we read that the worlds were framed—as a carpenter frames a house—by the Word of God. So too, we frame the world in which we live by the words we speak. Speak words of grumpiness, doubt, fear, cynicism—and that's the world you and your family will inhabit. But speak words of faith, hope, and joy even when you're going through hard times—and such will be the characteristics of your world. Paul could have been murmuring and complaining, doubting, whimpering, and crying. But that's not what he chose to do. 'Yes, we're going through tough times,' he said, 'but we have the spirit of faith.'

July 11

> *We then, as workers together with him...*
>
> II Corinthians 6:1

According to II Corinthians 5:20, we are ambassadors for Christ, sharing the good news of the Gospel with everyone we meet. But here's the most delightful part—we are workers not just *for* Him, but *with* Him. He doesn't send us on an assignment, wishing us luck as we leave. No, moment by moment He's with us as we talk to, share with, and love people. And He's with them too! This gives me a great deal of confidence in ministry.

If you were hungry, I could share with you my peanut butter and pickle sandwich. But I would not be certain it would minister to you. Maybe you'd like it, but maybe you wouldn't. Thus, it would be with a certain amount of apprehension that I would offer it to you.

There are a number of things we could sell or share about which we'd feel some hesitancy. But when we share Jesus Christ, all hesitancy dissipates—for He is guaranteed. Consequently, to the person who comes to me with a troubled heart, I can say, 'Let me pray with you right now because Jesus is truly right here—and He will give you peace. He'll walk with you through this valley. He'll make Himself known to you in the right way at the right time. I *know* this to be so.'

I've yet to send a person out to seek the Lord who has come back saying, 'It didn't work. I prayed. I read my Bible. I talked to Him. I waited on Him. But it didn't work.' That's because the promise of James 4:8 is that if we draw near to Him, He will draw near to us—not that He might draw near—but that He *will*.

JULY 12

Be ye not unequally yoked together with unbelievers...
II Corinthians 6:14

'I want to be big-hearted and open-minded, so I'm going to marry her or develop a business partnership with him even though he or she isn't a believer.'

'Wait a minute,' says Paul. 'Don't misunderstand. Be big towards your brothers and sisters in the Lord. But be careful you don't err by being yoked in partnership or relationship with an unbeliever.'

> *Come unto me, all ye that labour and are heavy laden,*
> *and I will give you rest. Take my yoke upon you, and*
> *learn of me; for I am meek and lowly in heart: and ye*
> *shall find rest unto your souls. For my yoke is easy,*
> *and my burden is light.*
>
> *Matthew 11:28-30*

The Greek word translated 'easy' means 'good fit.' Because an ill-fitting yoke would cause chafing of the hide or even a dislocation of the animal's shoulder, yokes were custom-designed to ensure a perfect fit. No doubt Jesus knew whereof He spoke in using this analogy, for the Greek word translated 'carpenter,' used concerning Joseph and, by implication, Jesus, is *tekton*, from which we get our word 'technical.' The tekton was not the framer, but rather the finish carpenter, a master craftsman. Jesus and His father, Joseph, were master craftsmen. Thus, there is historical evidence to support the tradition that the specialty in their carpenter shop was yokes.

'Take My yoke upon you,' Jesus says. 'It will fit you perfectly, and the load you're pulling will become light as you link with Me.'

JULY 13

> *Wherefore come out from among them, and be ye*
> *separate, saith the Lord, and touch not the unclean*
> *thing; and I will receive you.*
>
> *II Corinthians 6:17*

Jesus was the Friend of sinners (Luke 7:34). But the important thing to note is that wherever Jesus went, sinners were permanently and radically impacted by Him. Therefore, when you walk into places where worldly stuff is going on, if people start turning to God and repenting from their sin, go for it! If you're truly impacting the place you're in—excellent! But if the place is impacting you, causing your own spirit to sag, get out. Pull away. Back off immediately.

'Oh, but I'm mature in the Lord,' you say. 'So it's OK for me to go into this business venture even though my partners are unbelievers.'

Is it really? I refer you to what happened to one of the greatest men of history...

Jehoshaphat was a uniquely blessed man. Revival broke out around him; blessings flowed from him; good things came to him. And then, as his life is coming to an end, there's a P.S. in his story...

> And after this did Jehoshaphat king of Judah join himself with Ahaziah king of Israel, who did very wickedly: And he joined himself with him to make ships to go to Tarshish...
>
> II Chronicles 20:35-36

A godly Jehoshaphat joined with an ungodly Ahaziah in the shipping business. But the venture sunk.

You might have walked with the Lord for 30 or 40 years or more. Don't be like Jehoshaphat, saying, 'This might not be God's best for me—but I know my ship will come in eventually.' A person might become rich financially by joining with an unbeliever, but what does it profit him if he gain the whole world and lose his soul (Mark 8: 36)? What good is it if it causes him to be only a shell of what he once was spiritually?

What's your legacy, dad? At one time, you were about the things of the Kingdom; you were a servant, a leader, a worker. But now you're known as a business whiz. How tragic. Don't be yoked with unbelievers in any endeavor which will cause you to sink spiritually.

JULY 14

Having therefore these promises, dearly beloved, let
us cleanse ourselves from all filthiness of the flesh...
II Corinthians 7:1

For the Old Testament picture of this New Testament principle, turn to II Kings 5...

In the Old Testament, leprosy is a very appropriate picture of sin, for it begins seemingly insignificantly, but spreads insidiously. When Naaman, a prominent Syrian ruler who had contracted this terrible disease was told by his servant girl that there was a prophet in Israel who could cure him, he sent a message to the king of Israel, who, in turn, sent for Elisha. Expecting Elisha to pronounce some sort of magical incantation over him, Naaman was 'wroth' when Elisha told him to wash in the Jordan River seven times. After all, Naaman thought the Jordan nothing more than a muddy creek compared to the rivers of his own country. Thus, Scripture says he 'turned and went away in a rage.'

But his servants didn't give up so easily. 'If Elisha had asked you to do something difficult, you would have done it,' they said to Naaman. 'Therefore, why not see what happens if you comply with this seemingly simple command?' So Naaman did indeed dip himself into the Jordan seven times—the number of completion—and he came out healed and whole.

Likewise, we who are eaten by the leprosy of sin must dip in the water over and over and over again. What water? Didn't David say in Psalm 119 that a young man shall cleanse his way by taking heed according to the Word? Didn't Jesus say in John 15 that we are clean through the Word which He has spoken unto us? Didn't Paul declare in Ephesians 5 that we are washed by the water which is the Word of God?

Let the Word of God cleanse you and an amazing thing will happen. You may never become a scholar of theology, but as you submerge yourself in Scripture, the leprosy which once gnawed on you will begin to be cleansed from you. To those who are struggling with their flesh and looking for a quick answer, we need to say, 'Plunge into Scripture. Plug into Bible study. And keep at it over and over and over again—for it's God's Word which will cleanse you and wash away the sin which hounds you.'

JULY 15

Nevertheless God, that comforteth those that are cast down, comforted us by the coming of Titus...
II Corinthians 7:6

When Paul was going through the wringer internally, externally, emotionally, and physically, how did God comfort him? Through Titus. This amazes me. You see, Titus was one of Paul's students, one of his disciples. After sending him to Corinth with his first letter, Paul says it was when Titus returned that he was built back up.

I'm afraid my reaction would have been, 'Oh, it's just Titus. Lord, why didn't You send me someone famous or deep? Billy Graham perhaps. But Titus? He's just one of my boys. How can *he* help me?'

I think of Jesus in the Garden of Gethsemane. As He sweat great drops of blood while He prayed with intensity, an angel came and strengthened Him (Luke 22:43). Jesus could have said, 'I'm way above the angels.' Instead, He received the ministry of the angel.

So too, Paul received encouragement from Titus because he recognized an important principle: often the Lord comes to us in the unexpected person at an unexpected time in an unexpected way...

'We know Him,' they said. 'He's the carpenter's son' (Mark 6:3)—not realizing He was the Son of God.

Mary wept at the tomb, mistaking the Lord for a gardener (John 20: 15).

On the road to Emmaus, they thought He was a stranger (Luke 24: 18).

On the Sea of Galilee, they thought He was a ghost (Matthew 14:26).

Don't miss your Titus, gang. It might be your son or daughter. It might be a neighbor or co-worker. It might be someone you would never think had much to offer, but they'll come to you with words of encouragement—if you're wise enough to listen. Many people miss out, waiting for a pastor or a prophet, an author or a musician because they fail to recognize the Lord in the person sitting right next to them.

July 16

Now therefore perform the doing of it; that as there was
a readiness to will, so there may be a performance
also out of that which ye have.

II Corinthians 8:11

'You've expressed the desire to give,' Paul says. 'Now do it.'

Herein lies a great danger for us, for one of the great hazards of Bible study is thinking that by writing something in our notes or agreeing with it in our hearts, we're actually doing whatever it is we're writing down or agreeing with. James likens this to one who looks in a mirror and realizes there should be some changes made but doesn't do anything about it (James 1:23-24).

'Happy are ye if ye *do* these things,' Jesus said (John 13:17). If you're basically unhappy, melancholy, depressed, discouraged, or defeated, the reason could very well be that there is something the Lord has told you to do with which you agree theoretically, but which you have failed to work out practically.

Her physical condition rendered her ceremonially unclean for twelve years. That is, her husband would divorce her; the community would shun her; she would not be allowed to worship in the temple. But then the Rabbi from Galilee walked through her city. Thinking if she could even touch the hem of His garment, she might be healed, she did just that—causing Jesus to call her something He never called any other women when He said, 'Daughter, your faith has made you whole' (Matthew 9:22). What faith? Just a simple touch.

Forget the big plans, the high hopes, the visions of grandeur. Just do something now. Open your heart. Share with the person who's struggling financially. Write a letter of encouragement. Pray for the person who's hurting. Do something. Do anything. Just do it. The blessing is not in agreeing—it's in *doing*.

July 17

> *The God and Father of our Lord Jesus Christ, which is blessed for evermore, knoweth that I lie not. In Damascus the governor under Aretas the king kept the city of the Damascenes with a garrison, desirous to apprehend me: And through a window in a basket was I let down by the wall, and escaped his hands.*
>
> II Corinthians 11:31-33

We find the story to which Paul alludes in Acts 9...

As he headed towards Damascus in order to persecute Christians, the Lord confronted Paul, and he was converted immediately. Shortly thereafter, God said of him, 'He is a chosen vessel unto Me to bear My name before the Gentiles and kings and the children of Israel' (Acts 9:15). 'Paul will talk to kings and impact some Jews, but he'll be a minister to Me among the Gentiles primarily.'

Yet such a heart did Paul have for the Jews that he said he would be damned for their sake if it meant they would be saved (Romans 9:3). So he headed straight for the synagogues as if to say, 'I can do You a whole lot of good, Lord. I was trained to be a Pharisee. I know how they think.' And it made sense logically. Paul seemed to have the gifts, the background, and the testimony to impact the Jews radically. But they didn't buy what he was saying, so he left Damascus and spent three years in the Arabian wilderness being tutored by Jesus Himself (Galatians 1:17)—after which time he headed once again to the Jews.

He proved to them Biblically and persuasively that Jesus is indeed the Christ. The result? They wanted to kill him (Acts 9:23). And his heart must have sunk. He went to Jerusalem next. And when he got there heartsick, let down, wondering what was happening, he joined himself to the disciples. But even they were afraid of him, so he spoke boldly to the Grecians—those Jews who had adopted Gentile customs—as if to compromise with the Lord. What did they do? They decided to kill him (Acts 9:29).

At this point, the believers sent him out of the country. He went to Tarsus for seven to ten years where he ministered in obscurity. He must have been thinking, 'I don't get it.' But the Lord had plans for Paul. Barnabas sought him out, saying, 'Let's go minister in the north to the Gentiles.'

'Great!' said Paul. And at last he began ministering to those he was supposed to, the world was turned upside down, and the fruit remains to this day.

That is why he said, 'I'm going to glory in what was the hardest thing in my life—when I was let down, when things weren't working out, when I was wondering where the Lord was. The greatest glory in my whole life was when the doors I thought would open up were shut tight—because it was then that God had His way.'

'Use me, Lord,' we cry. 'I would make such a great worship leader.' Yet as the weeks turn into months and the months into years, we wonder, 'What's happening?'

'Don't worry,' Paul would say to us. 'I look back now and see that the day I was denied the ministry in which I thought I would do so well as the most important turning point in my life outside the turning point of my salvation.'

If you're let down, understand this: if you're walking with the Lord to any degree, you're going to look back and say, 'I am so glad He said no.' Time will always prove the Lord to be right. That is why Paul could say, 'If I must glory, I will glory in the biggest disappointment of my life. Yes, I was heartsick at the time, but now I see the incredible wisdom of God.'

JULY 18

And he said unto me, My grace is sufficient for thee:
for my strength is made perfect in weakness.
II Corinthians 12:9

Like Paul, we ask for help from the Lord. As far as our Father is concerned, however, the purpose of prayer is not that He might give help to us, but that He might give *Himself* to us.

We want something.
The Father says, 'It's Some*one*.'

'It's Me you need. You want Me to take away the pain, to solve the problem, to get you out of the situation—but that's not what you need. You need Me. And the very problem you're seeking to get away from, the very situation you desire to get out of is the very one which is making you talk to Me, spend time with Me, depend on Me. You'll be stronger when you're weak because you'll have no other choice than to draw strength from Me. You'll do better when you're weak because you'll have to rely on Me.'

July 19

In reproaches, in necessities, in persecutions, in distresses for Christ's sake: for when I am weak, then am I strong.

II Corinthians 12:10

'If you only knew what power there is in an accepted sorrow,' wrote Madame Guyon 400 years ago. Understand this, dear saint, it is not wrong to pray to the Father when there's a thorn jabbing at you or to share with the Father the desires that are mounting within you. You desire a certain thing to open up, to work out, to be taken away. There's no problem with communicating this to the Father. Whether it's a physical thorn in the flesh—sickness, disease, or bodily difficulty—or whether it's an emotional thorn in the flesh, we are to pray not once, not twice, but without ceasing (I Thessalonians 5:17).

Life is not a playground, gang. It's a battlefield. And the sooner we understand this, the wiser we'll be. This is not heaven. If you're seeking to have heaven here now—no thorns in your flesh, no problems poking you, no disappointments coming to you—your life will be hellish because this is not heaven. It is when I finally realize that, like Paul, for me to live is Christ and to die is gain, that life becomes extremely meaningful and completely enjoyable. We're here for a short season. There will be thorns in our flesh. There will be things poking us and disappointing us. Oh, what power there is, though, in an accepted sorrow.

Pray without ceasing until the Lord either takes away the difficulty, gives you the healing, develops the relationship, or opens the job— until He either does that which you're asking or lets you know, as He did with Paul, that His grace is sufficient for you to bear the pain or the disappointment.

Never forget that God is not as interested in your present comfort as He is in your eternal state. Trust Him when He says, 'This thorn is necessary to draw you close to Me that you might give your all in service to Me, that you might depend wholly upon Me.' For it is then you will hear from Him the words your soul longs to hear: 'Well done, good and faithful servant. Enter into the *joy* of the Lord' (Matthew 25:21).

Pray. For as you grab the lever of prayer with the hand of faith, one of two things will happen: blessings, healing, the working of God will come down upon you—or else the lever will yank you up into heaven where you'll hear your Father say, 'Now that I've got your attention, I don't want you healed because it is in your weakness that My strength will flow through you.'

Brothers and sisters, pray 3 times, 30 times, 300 times until you either get the answer you're asking for or you hear the Father say, 'No, and here's why...' Don't settle for anything less.

If you pray this way, I believe you'll experience successful prayer 100% of the time. Talk to the Father about your thorns and your difficulties and keep praying until the answer comes your way or until, like Paul, you have understanding and revelation and can say, 'That's a closed issue. I don't need to talk about that anymore. I get it, Father. Your grace is sufficient for me.'

JULY 20

And I will very gladly spend and be spent for you; though the more abundantly I love you, the less I be loved.

II Corinthians 12:15

'Others come and smite you in the face, take your money, pounce on you—and yet you respect them,' says Paul. 'Me? I give my all for you, yet the more I give to you, the less I'm loved by you.'

Why is it that the more you give to some people, the less they respect and love you? If someone is haughty and arrogant, sometimes people will be in awe of him. But if someone says, 'I'm willing to spend all I have on your behalf,' people think he must not be very special.

Don't be depressed, surprised, or discouraged when the more you love people, the less they love you—for this provides you a great opportunity to give simply for the sake of giving in true agape love. When you give to someone and he gives back to you, when you're nice to someone and she's nice to you—that's wonderful. But the highest form of giving is when you give and nothing is given back. Your reward will be great in heaven, and your personality will be shaped more closely into the image of Jesus Christ.

JULY 21

Finally, brethren, farewell. Be perfect, be of good comfort, be of one mind, live in peace; and the God of love and peace shall be with you. Greet one another with an holy kiss. All the saints salute you. The grace of the Lord Jesus Christ, and the love of God, and the communion of the Holy Ghost, be with you all. Amen.

II Corinthians 13:11-14

No doubt, the hearts of the Corinthians would be encouraged and inspired by these warm words of Paul. Mine is. But there is one phrase which troubles me greatly. And I bet it troubled the Corinthians as well—for in the midst of Paul's beautiful benediction and heartwarming affirmation are words which cause within me a real consternation: be perfect. Why couldn't Paul have said, 'Be happy,' or 'Be good,' or 'Be all that you can be'? Why did he have to say, 'Be perfect'?

If you have a newer translation, perhaps your Bible renders this phrase, 'Be mature.' Other paraphrases read, 'Grow up.' And while these are both close to the meaning, linguistically the word Paul uses encompasses more than maturity or growth. It literally means, 'Be perfect.' We can seek to sidestep it. We can try to get around it, but it means just what it says.

The implications are amazing, for if the Scriptures tell you and me that we are to be perfect, to do what's right, it must mean that in every situation, in every day we live, there is right and there is wrong. This should be obvious to us, but there's a point in the history of Israel when the Lord sent the prophet Isaiah to indict the people concerning this very issue.

> Woe unto them that call evil good, and good evil; that
> put darkness for light, and light for darkness; that put
> bitter for sweet, and sweet for bitter.
>
> Isaiah 5:20

At this juncture in their history, the people of Israel were confused in their understanding of right and wrong. They were entirely mixed up in their morality. So the prophet Isaiah thunders, 'Woe to those in your society who say that light is dark and dark is light, who are all mixed up in their morals and ethics.' And we see the same thing in our own culture. Yet even as people argue for traditional family values, we still miss the mark. Why? Because values are subjective. For example, I value my Volkswagen van. But you and I could argue indefinitely about what the value is because of the subjective nature of values. No, the issue is not values. The issue is perfection.

What is perfect? The Law of the LORD is perfect (Psalm 19:7). Given to us by God rather than generated within the mind of man, the Law of God is non-negotiable.

'Be ye perfect,' Jesus said, 'even as your Father in heaven is perfect.' But then He went on to say, 'Unless your righteousness exceeds that of the scribes and Pharisees, you'll not enter into the Kingdom of heaven' (Matthew 5:20).

There are two ways to go about trying to be perfect. You can steel yourself morally and ethically by erecting rules and regulations around yourself. Then you'll be like a man in a bathysphere—those big balls made out of cast iron with walls six inches thick—exploring the deepest trenches of the Pacific Ocean. Yet as you sit cramped and confined within your bathysphere, what will you see? Little fish with extremely thin skin swimming around totally free. How can these fish survive such depths? The answer is simple: the pressure within them is equal to the pressure outside of them.

There are those in the Moral Majority and Religious Right who say, 'We're going to construct iron plates of rules and regulations around us.' But there's a better way. Christ *in* us is the hope of glory (Colossians 1:27). It's not the Law outside of us, but the Lawgiver, the Lover of our Soul, Christ Jesus *in* us who will whisper to us, 'Why are you going in there? Why are you watching that? Why are you thinking those thoughts? Let Me show you a better way of thinking, of speaking, of acting, of living.'

'I will write My will in your heart,' God declared (Jeremiah 31:33). And He does so through His Spirit who dwells within us.

My bathysphere has sprung a leak or two along the way. So has yours. But when Jesus Christ died for our sin, He paid the price for the leaks we've sprung, for every mistake we've made. Thus, it is through Him and Him alone that we can be perfect by being perfectly forgiven.

JULY 22

...Immediately I conferred not with flesh and blood:
Neither went I up to Jerusalem to them which were
apostles before me; but I went into Arabia...

Galatians 1:16-17

In religious circles today, it's cool to have a D.D.—a Doctorate of Divinity. Paul had a D.D.—a Doctorate of the Desert. He was in good company: Moses, John the Baptist, and Jesus all spent time in the desert.

So too, maybe for you these are dry, difficult days. It could be that God wants to reveal Jesus Christ to you in a fresh way, but for that to happen, He may do to you what He did to John the apostle when He sent him to Patmos...

At about 100 years of age, John was exiled to Patmos, a rocky, barren, seemingly God-forsaken island. It was a tough situation, and no doubt John questioned what was going on. 'I'm old,' he could have said. 'I've trusted in the Lord; I'm linked to Him; why this isolation?'

But then he saw Jesus Christ. John started writing, and 22 chapters later, the Book of Revelation was completed.

When was revelation given to John?
When he was isolated on an island.

Perhaps you're at a point where you're saying, 'Who can I talk to?' or, 'What counsel can I receive?'—when in reality, the Lord may have you at this season on an island of isolation in order to give you a revelation of Jesus Christ. Don't bemoan your condition.

Don't bewail your situation. Worship the Lord. Draw close to Him. Be still—and you will see Him in ways you never could have had you been anywhere else.

JULY 23

...For by the works of the law shall no flesh be justified.

Galatians 2:16

Are you trying to earn God's favor through morning devotions or Wednesday night Bible study attendance, through memorizing verses or witnessing, through not going here and not doing that? If you are, you're making a big mistake. You are justified by faith and faith alone—not only when you were born again, not only when you were saved ten years ago—but today, right now. God's blessing will be upon the life of any man, woman, teenager, or older person who simply says, 'I'm not going to try and earn Your blessing, Lord. I can't. But I hear You declaring, Father, that You want to bless me by Your grace through my belief in Your Son. And I welcome such blessing.'

Dear brother, precious sister—the blessings of God are not based upon what you do or don't do. It's not, 'OK, God, I didn't see that movie. Aren't You proud of me? And because I didn't, here's what I'm expecting You to do for me...'

No. The blessings of God are based upon one thing singularly: faith in His grace. We can receive His blessing for one reason: the sin which cut His blessing off and separated us from the Father has been washed away by the blood of Jesus Christ. Therefore, if I choose to sin, it's not that God will withhold His blessing in order to punish me. No, the blood of Jesus Christ has cleansed me from all sin—past, present, and future (I John 1:7,9). If I choose to sin, I destroy myself.

Balak, king of the Moabites, hired Balaam the prophet to curse the people of Israel (Numbers 22). But no matter how Balaam tried, he could only pronounce blessing upon them. 'I'm paying you good money to curse these people,' Balak said. 'Let's build another altar, and you can try again.' So again, Balaam opened his mouth, but only blessing came out. After a third altar, a third try, and a third failure, Balak was desperate.

'I can't help it,' explained Balaam. 'I'm trying to curse them, but they're God's people. They deserve to be cursed, but God's for them.' Seeing his fee slip through his fingers, however, Balaam came up with a new plan. 'I can't curse them,' he told Balak, 'but they can curse themselves. Here's what you do: get your foxiest ladies and send them into the Israelite camp. As they bat their eyelashes and swish their skirts, have them invite the Israelite guys into their tents, then have them pull out their little idols—their Ashtaroths—and say, "This is the way we worship in this country. Don't you want to worship with us?"'

'Good plan,' Balak said. So he got his girls and sent them into the camp of Israel. They enticed the guys into their tents, and just as planned, the Moabite women pulled out their idols. Sure enough, the Israelites took the bait—and ended up cursing themselves, the end result being a plague which wiped out 24,000 of them (Numbers 25:9).

So too today. God says 'Blessings upon you. You're justified by the hearing of faith because you believe in the work of My Son.' As far as God is concerned, the sin which would bar me from 'the spout where the blessings come out,' was taken away by the blood of Jesus Christ. I cannot be cursed.

But I can curse myself and so can you. Watch your step, young person. Listen up, 45-year-old man. 'Oh, it's OK to see that film,' you say. 'It's only got a few scenes that are slightly compromising,' or 'It's OK to hear that music. There are only a few questionable words.' Watch out. You're cursing yourself. We live in a culture where the advice of Balaam is being worked out unlike any other time in human history. Be very careful. You'll get drawn into tents you never thought you would enter, and you'll be wiped out in the process.

JULY 24

*This only would I learn of you, Received ye the Spirit
by the works of the law, or by the hearing of faith?*
Galatians 3:2

This verse speaks not only of being born again, but also of receiving the fullness, baptism, or 'coming upon' of the Spirit to empower your life. After Jesus was crucified and raised again, He appeared to the disciples in the upper room and said, 'Receive ye the Holy Ghost'—and as He breathed on them, they indeed received the Spirit (John 20:22).

At that point, the disciples were saved. But then Jesus said, 'Go to Jerusalem and wait for the promise of the Father (Acts 1:4). You shall receive power when the Holy Ghost comes upon you and you shall then be My witnesses in Jerusalem, Judaea, Samaria, and the uttermost parts of the earth' (Acts 1:8).

So they went to Jerusalem and waited. On the tenth day, as they were in the upper room, they heard the sound of a mighty rushing wind and saw cloven tongues of fire hovering over their heads. The Spirit came upon them, they began to praise the Lord in other tongues, they were energized to boldly proclaim the Gospel—and the world has never been the same.

Such is what the Lord wants for you and me. When you became a Christian, the Holy Spirit came *in* you. But has the Holy Spirit come *upon* you? I know you have the Holy Spirit, but does the Holy Spirit have you? 'Have you received the Holy Spirit since you believed?' Paul asked the people of Ephesus (Acts 19:2). So too, I ask you: 'Have you received the Holy Spirit since you believed?'

In years past, many of us were part of churches or traditions which said, 'Here's the way to receive the power of the Spirit: get rid of all of the sin in your life. Give up your drinking. Smash your TV. Stop smoking. Get it together. Then the Holy Spirit will come upon you to empower you and use you.' Consequently, many people spent months, years, even decades trying to clean up their acts in order to earn the power of the Holy Spirit.

Others of us waited day after day, week after week, in what used to be called 'tarrying meetings.' 'We're going to wait for the Holy Spirit to come upon us,' we said. 'And if we praise loud enough, pray hard enough, wait long enough, the Lord will give us the Holy Ghost, and we'll be changed. We'll impact people radically.'

Paul would say, 'No way.' How do you receive the Holy Spirit? Whether you're talking about the indwelling of the Spirit through salvation or the empowering of the Spirit through baptism, it's the same way: not by works of the Law, but by *faith*—just by hearing the Word.

'That's it?' you ask. 'You mean I don't have to clean up my act, get it together, stand on my head, or fast 30 days?'

No. We receive the Spirit not by works, but by the hearing of faith. Therefore, by *faith* I can take that which was provided for me and say, 'Thank You, Lord. Even as I sit in this pew, I ask of You and receive from You the power of the Holy Spirit upon my life right now.'

'Too simple,' you say.

Talk to Paul. He said, 'Don't let anyone complicate this thing. You receive the Spirit simply by the hearing of faith.'

July 25

He therefore that ministereth to you the Spirit, and
worketh miracles among you, doeth he it by the works
of the law, or by the hearing of faith?

Galatians 3:5

In the days when the healing evangelists were crisscrossing the country and drawing huge crowds under big-tops, many thousands of people were truly touched and definitely impacted by one of the biggest faith healers of all: A.A. Allen. He had the biggest meetings and the most powerful impact in the healing arena—until he died in San Francisco in a cheap motel room of cirrhosis of the liver. He was a complete alcoholic. How could this be?

It is because the miracles wrought and the Spirit given are not by the works of the Law, but simply by the hearing of faith. Folks, A. A. Allen understood that what he did was centered not upon his great faith in God, but upon God's great faithfulness to him. And once you understand that simple truth, it will affect everything you do in ministry.

For years, I was under the impression that the key to ministry, to being used by God, to seeing folks saved or filled with the Spirit, was my faith. Therefore, the greater my faith, the more God would do. Not true. The key was not my faith in God at all—but His faithfulness to people.

Consequently, last Monday night at Caveman Park in Grants Pass, with a couple hundred high-school kids, I gave an invitation at the end of my teaching, and I just expected kids to respond—not because of the persuasiveness of my message, but because I know the goodness of God. He wants to save people. He cares about every single kid there. It wasn't because of my presentation or preparation that I expected them to respond. No, it was because I knew God was eager to respond to any of those kids who wanted to come to Him. So when I said, 'Which of you wants to receive the coming upon of the Spirit right now?' most of them raised their hands.

'Uh-oh,' you may have thought had you witnessed the scene. 'What are you going to do now, Jon? What if you pray and nothing happens? What if they don't speak in tongues? Worse yet, what if they *do*?'

Folks, it's not my job to be concerned about those things. I just have total confidence in the great faithfulness of God to touch any boy, any girl, any man, or any woman anytime, anywhere who is hungering and thirsting for righteousness. When this is understood, it is so incredibly freeing. But until it's understood, Satan will whisper in your ear,

'You don't have the technique down.'
'You don't know enough verses yet.'
'You haven't prayed hard enough.'
'You haven't worshipped long enough.'

Precious people, Satan will paralyze you until you understand that every area of ministry is based not upon your faith, but upon God's faithfulness. If you believe this, you'll find yourself talking to people and expecting them to respond in some way.

If it's dependent upon me, my knees knock, my forehead breaks out in beads of sweat, my mouth gets dry, my lips become sealed. I am paralyzed by fear because I know I haven't done enough. But once I understand that the one who ministers the Spirit, the one who works miracles doesn't do it by the works of the Law, I am free!

JULY 26

But that no man is justified by the law in the sight of God, it is evident: for, The just shall live by faith.
Galatians 3:11

The words, 'the just shall live by faith' are first seen in Habakkuk 2:4 when, in response to his complaints concerning the prophesied

Babylonian invasion, the Lord told Habakkuk to look to Him rather than at the circumstances.

They are seen again in Romans 1:17 where Paul stresses *justification* and in Hebrews 11 where the emphasis is on *faith*. Here in Galatians, the accent is on *live*. Want to be happy, fruitful, excited, and set free in your Christian life? The *just* shall *live*—really live—by *faith*.

Martin Luther beat his body with whips, crawled for miles on his knees, fasted for weeks at a time in order to get close to God. But nothing worked. And then one day he read this verse—and he understood that the Christian experience is not 'Do, do, do'—it's 'DONE!' Jesus did it *all*.

Dear saints, get rid of the burden of trying to be spiritual. Get rid of the notion that since you had morning devotions ten times in a row, God owes you a blessing. It doesn't work that way. You are justified by faith *alone*.

'Then I don't have to have morning devotions?' you ask.
No, you don't.
'I can sleep in?'
Yeah, you can.
'I don't have to pray or study the Word?'
Nope.

You don't *have* to do any of those things. You *get* to. You *get* to check in with God morning-by-morning, moment-by-moment. You *get* to spend time late at night or before the sun rises seeking the face of the Lord. It's not *got* to, it's *get* to—and that makes all the difference in the world, for once you're free from the 'got to's,' you invariably do more than you ever did before.

James said, 'Faith without works is dead' (James 2:20) because true faith will always bring about lots of works.

When you fell in love with your husband or wife, you didn't have to be told to call her; you didn't have to be reminded to hold his hand; you didn't have to be urged to communicate. When you're in love, you long to be in touch—and that's what the Father wants from you and me. 'Love Me,' He says. And the more I realize that He loves me through His grace and mercy being poured out upon me, the more I have no choice but to love Him in return. So I do more under love than I ever would do under the Law.

Think about that first letter your girlfriend wrote you, guys. As you stuck it in your pocket, did you say, 'Boy, one of these days I really need to read this letter. I'll set my alarm 15 minutes earlier tonight and read it first thing in the morning'? And then as you rolled out of bed half an hour after the alarm went off, did you say, 'I really want to read this letter, but I don't have time now. Maybe tonight. No, *Home Improvement* is on. Can't miss that. I'll get to it tomorrow'?

No! It doesn't work that way. When you received that letter, you ripped it open, read it, analyzed it, parsed the verbs, researched it, read between the lines—you couldn't put it down!

The same thing happens when you understand grace and mercy. You say, 'You bless me, Lord, when I don't pray. You love me when I'm not lovable. You take care of me when I fail to walk with You. You're faithful to me day after week after year. I want to find out more about You.' That's what it means for the just to *live* by faith.

July 27

Christ hath redeemed us from the curse of the law,
being made a curse for us...

Galatians 3:13

When man sinned, God said to Adam, 'From this point on, you will

Labor for bread,
   Live by the sweat of your brow,
      And work through thorns and thistles.'

Then came Jesus, the Last Adam.

In the Upper Room,
   His broken body became our bread.
In the Garden of Gethsemane,
   His sweat mingled with blood.
On Calvary,
   The thorns of the earth were embedded in His brow.

'I've absorbed it all,' Jesus said, as He who knew no sin became sin for us, as He Himself became the curse. This is what Paul is driving home.

What Jesus did is so incredible, so wonderful, how could we think that, through our own efforts, we could add anything to His work on our behalf?

JULY 28

> *For if the inheritance be of the law, it is no more of promise: but God gave it to Abraham by promise.*
>
> *Galatians 3:18*

It was when Abraham had no children that God told him his offspring would number as the stars of the sky, as the sand on the seashore. But Scripture records that Abraham believed God anyway. 'OK, Lord,' Abraham replied, 'I don't know how You're going to do it, but if You want to bless me in that way, it's fine with me.'

And God said, 'That's the faith that will justify you, Abraham—just believing in Me.'

Some time went by. Again, the Lord appeared to Abraham. 'I am your shield and your great reward,' He said.

'That's great, Lord,' answered Abraham, 'but I still don't have any kids. The years are going by, and I'm not getting any younger.'

'Abraham,' said the Lord, 'let's cut a covenant.'

In Abraham's day, when two parties wanted to seal an agreement, they would cut an animal in half and meet each other in the middle, thereby saying, 'We're dead serious about this.'

So Abraham got a bullock, cut it in half, laid it out, and sat there waiting for God to show up. He waited, and waited, and waited, wondering where God was. When birds started swarming around the carcass, with stick in hand, Abraham stood up and shooed them away. Time passed, Abraham's eyes grew heavy. His head started bobbing, and then slumping, and finally he was out. Sometime later, he awoke, looked at the bullock, and saw it had been barbecued. God had come when Abraham was asleep and had moved all the way through the carcass.

God didn't meet Abraham halfway. He did the whole thing, saying, 'Abraham, this promise I'm giving you is not based upon your agreeing with Me and doing your part. No, I'm going to do it *all*, and I'll even do it while you're asleep.'

God still does it all, precious people. Your salvation, the blessings which are poured upon you, the work of the Spirit which flows through you in ministry—it's *all* God.

'Don't I have any part to play?' you ask. Yes. Your part is to shoo away the birds of unbelief that will invariably come and pick at the promises of God's Word. Whatever God said He will do is an accomplished fact—yet vultures of doubt and buzzards of cynicism will come and say, 'God's not going to use you. He's not going to bless you. You haven't been praying enough.' Peck, peck, peck.

Your part is to chase away those birds by saying, 'Lord, You told us You would supply all our needs according to Your riches. You told us You would never leave us or forsake us. You told us You're preparing a place in heaven for us. You told us You would give the Holy Ghost to us. Thank You, Lord.'

July 29

> *But when the fulness of time was come, God sent forth his Son, made of a woman, made under the law, To redeem them that were under the law...that we might receive the adoption of sons.*
>
> *Galatians 4:4-5*

The Greek word for 'adoption' is *huiothesia*. 'Huios' meaning *son*, 'thesis' meaning *position*. Huiothesia means *taking the position of a son*. The Son of God took our position on the Cross of Calvary, paying for our sins, in order that we might in turn take the position as sons of God.

Understand this: adoption is not the method of entry *into* God's family. As Jesus told Nicodemus in John 3, we enter into God's family only by being born again. Rather, adoption speaks of our privilege and standing *within* God's family. The moment we were born again, we were placed in an adopted state as heirs, as sons of God.

We think of adoption in terms of adopting a little baby. But that's not the biblical concept of adoption. Biblical adoption refers to a full-grown adult. It would be like, before retiring from Ford Motor Company and having no sons, but wanting his name to continue, Henry Ford approaching a 24-year-old Harvard student and saying, 'Would you let me adopt you? If you will, you'll have a place on the Board of Directors, a salary of $2.5 million a year, a summer house in Hawaii, a winter house in Tahiti, a private jet, and your own yacht.'

So too, the moment you were born again, you assumed the position of an adopted son—heir to the riches of the Father. Too often people say, 'I really can't be used by the Lord because I've only walked with Him five years,' or, 'I can't get involved in intercessory prayer because I'm just a new Christian.' Wrong. As far as the privileges and responsibilities of the Kingdom go, you were adopted as a mature son with as much right to be blessed and used by the Lord as Billy Graham.

JULY 30

Tell me, ye that desire to be under the law, do ye not hear the law? For it is written, that Abraham had two sons, the one by a bondmaid, the other by a freewoman. But he who was of the bondwoman was born after the flesh; but he of the freewoman was by promise.

Galatians 4:21-23

To validate his argument, Paul appealed to Abraham, father of the Jewish race, to whom God said, 'I'm going to bring you into a new land. I'm going to give you a new name. I'm going to make you great. And from you will come forth a people as innumerable as the stars in the heaven or the sand on the seashore.'

Abraham believed God—but when he was 86-years-old, with the promise yet to be fulfilled, his wife, said, 'Honey, I realize God spoke to you, but let's be practical. You're 86. I'm 76. This promise isn't going to come to pass the way we thought it would. Therefore, take my slave girl, Hagar, have relations with her, and the child you produce will be the promised seed from which will come the nation God promised you.'

Folks, when God gives a promise, almost invariably there is a gap of time between the giving of the promise and the fulfillment of the promise. And it is in that gap of time that we get impatient. 'Time is running out,' we say. 'I've got to make something happen.'

Abraham agreed to Sarah's plan, the result of which was the conception and birth of a baby boy named Ishmael. Thirteen years went by. Then God spoke to Abraham again, saying, 'I'm still going to give you a child.'

'Let Ishmael live,' said Abraham. 'He'll do.'

'No,' said God. 'Ishmael is not the fulfillment of My promise. He's only your fleshly attempt to help Me out.'

As I look back over my life, I see that every time I got impatient and tried to help God or take things into my own hands, the result has always been trouble—Ishmael. Now, because God is so good, the promise still comes because He's faithful to His Word. But the problem is that now I have a bunch of Ishmaels to deal with. You see, to this day, blood is shed daily in the ongoing struggle between the Arabs and the Jews—the children of Ishmael and the children of Israel. So too, in my own life, whenever Ishmael is born as a result of my own fleshly efforts, strife, anxiety, and tension are also birthed in my life.

Push God, rush God, help God out—and you'll have an Ishmael on your hands. Abraham was a great man, and yet this friend of God, this father of faith, this incredible saint had a problem which God recorded as a lesson for each of us today: he was impatient.

'Impatient?' you say. 'He waited how many years for God to keep His promise?'

It was at least 12 years between the time Abraham was given the promise and the time he went into Hagar. But it could have been as many as 18 years. Some of us think, 'I've been waiting 18 days, 18 weeks, 18 months. When is God going to fulfill His promise to me?' Abraham waited 18 *years* before he said, 'I better help God.' But it was a disaster nonetheless.

JULY 31

Paul, an apostle of Jesus Christ by the will of God...
Ephesians 1:1

'Make your calling and election sure,' Peter declared (II Peter 1:10). Paul was one who knew his calling. He was called by the will of God to be an apostle, prepared for it from the earliest days of his life. Growing up the son of a rabbi, seated at the feet of Gamaliel—the foremost rabbinical scholar of the day—Paul eventually became a member of the Sanhedrin, the Jewish Supreme Court. And all of his studying, all of his efforts to be righteous in his own energy, all of his attempts to keep the Law blamelessly would be preparatory to make him the minister of the Gospel of Grace.

Not only did Paul know his calling—he also knew his Bible. And with this knowledge came the absolute frustration of trying to live under legalism and religiosity. Consequently, all of his life experiences were preparing him to be an apostle of Jesus Christ. The same is true for you.

You see, God wants to place each one of us in the spot for which He has prepared us from the beginning. God's will is not something which is heavy or difficult. No, God's will fits perfectly with the make-up of your personality and with what He's taken you through in life experientially.

God sees where He wants you to serve Him—whether that be on a construction site, a classroom, or a courtroom; as a butcher, baker, or banker. We often make a mistake in thinking that what we're doing is second best, that if we were really serious about our faith, we'd be in 'full-time ministry.' Wrong. The Lord stations His men and women ingeniously where He sees they can minister most effectively so that the people around them will be impacted eternally.

What has God prepared and trained *you* to do? Be content to do what God has called you to do—to serve where He has placed you—for yours is just as holy and high a calling as that of any preacher or apostle.

AUGUST 1

Blessed be the God and Father of our Lord Jesus Christ, who hath blessed us with all spiritual blessings in heavenly places in Christ.

Ephesians 1:3

'We're blessed with all spiritual blessings in heavenly places,' Paul writes jubilantly from his prison cell, 'and they're all in Christ'—not *from* Christ, but *in* Christ. The blessings we crave are not promises we pray for, but a Person we walk with.

'Oh, Lord,' we say, 'I need some bread.'
 'I *am* the Bread,' Jesus answers (John 6:35).
'Show me the way,' we cry.
 'I *am* the Way,' Jesus declares (John 14:6).
'Tell me the truth,' we pray.
 'I *am* the Truth,' Jesus proclaims (John 14:6).

We think we need help in this area or deliverance from that thing. We think we need satisfaction in a profession or blessing in a relationship, little knowing that our heart's desire will only be truly fulfilled in Jesus. How do I know? Because II Corinthians 1 ends by saying, 'Yea, all the promises of God are in Him yea and amen.' All the promises of God are fulfilled in *Him*, in Jesus.

Two nights ago, with Tammy away at a pastors' wives' conference and the kids tucked in, I grabbed my Bible and had the best time reading Isaiah 54 as I walked the streets of Jacksonville. God spoke to me through each phrase as I stopped under the streetlights to read another verse and marvel how it related to me. I returned home awed at how the Lord walked with me in the evening hour.

Do I tell you this to impress you? No. I say it because you can find the same thing tonight. Turn off the TV. Put down the *TIME* magazine. Grab your Bible, go for a walk, and I promise God will meet you.

AUGUST 2

Having predestinated us...
Ephesians 1:5

Is there a pre-determination concerning salvation? Yes. But guess what? God is never seen anywhere at any time in the Bible predestining someone to go to hell. He only predestines people to go to heaven.

> *He that overcometh, the same shall be clothed in*
> *white raiment; and I will not blot out his name out of*
> *the book of life, but I will confess his name before my*
> *Father, and before his angels.*
> *Revelation 3:5*

The implication of this passage is enormous, for it seems to suggest that every man's name is written in the book of life—until he makes it clear that he has no interest *in* the Lord, that he doesn't want to walk *with* the Lord, that he wants to turn his back *on* the Lord. Only then is his name blotted out.

Thus, when the book of life is opened at the Great White Throne Judgment, when all of the unbelievers are brought before God and discover their names absent from its pages, it's not that their names were never in the book. It's that their names were blotted out because they chose not to accept God's plan of salvation for their lives.

> *For whom he did foreknow, he also did predestinate*
> *to be conformed to the image of his Son, that he might*
> *be the firstborn among many brethren.*
> *Romans 8:29*

Before the world was even spoken into existence, God saw the people who would respond to His love—not those who would initiate a search for Him, for none seeks after Him (Romans 3:11)—but those who would be inclined to respond to Him.

Whom He foreknew, He predestinated, saying, 'I can see that Mitch is going to respond when I make Myself known to him, when the Gospel is shared with him. Therefore, I predestine Mitch to be part of My eternal Kingdom.'

'Well,' you say, 'then why was someone who God knew wouldn't respond to Him allowed to live in the first place?'

The answer is that if a person was not allowed to play his life out to the fullest extent, he could protest at the Great White Throne.

'I got rid of you early because I could see that you weren't going to respond to Me,' God would say.
'Oh, but I would have,' the unbeliever would protest.
'No, you wouldn't,' God would say.
'Yes, I would have,' the unbeliever would insist.

And there would be a perpetual argument. So even though it is His desire that none should perish, but that all should come to repentance (II Peter 3:9), God lets Joe Schmo live his 70 years to prove that righteous and true are His judgments (Revelation 16:7).

Then why does hell exist? Jesus gave us the singular reason: hell exists for Satan and his demons (Matthew 25:41). It was never God's intent to allow anyone on earth to spend eternity in hell. In fact, the only way anyone can get there is over the dead body of His Son.

AUGUST 3

...According to the good pleasure of his will, To the praise of the glory of his grace...

Ephesians 1:5-6

Here's why God adopted you; here's why He predestined you; here's why He chose you; here's why He's blessed you in Christ in heavenly places: because it's His good pleasure to the praise of the glory of His grace. Period.

Like Israel, we are called a chosen people (I Peter 2:9). Why are we chosen? According to the verse before us, we are chosen to the praise of the glory of His grace. That is, we are chosen to showcase God's grace. This means that in the ages to come, millions of angels, living creatures, and all of creation will look at you and me who have been chosen, who have been adopted, who have been elevated to be with Christ in heavenly places—and they will say, 'Look at the people God chose to be joint heirs with His Son. They're just a bunch of rag-tag renegades. Truly His grace is unbelievable, unfathomable, incomparable!'

That's why Paul said, 'Look around you. There are not many wise, many strong, many noble among you' (I Corinthians 1:26).

When I was in high school, I thought the key to an effective ministry was to get the quarterback and the cheerleader saved, to go for the head honchos, the big guns, the beautiful people. But that's not what Jesus did. He turned the world upside down with the street people, the outcasts, and the forgotten folks.

In other words, He used people just like us.

AUGUST 4

...Wherein he hath made us accepted in the beloved.
Ephesians 1:6

We are accepted because we're in the Beloved—we're in Christ. It doesn't matter how you feel about yourself. You don't have to take your spiritual temperature hour by hour.

You don't have to wonder, 'Am I hot? Am I cold? How am I doing?' You won't have to go through the kind of introspection which will inevitably set you up for spiritual depression if you understand the simple principle that you are embraced not because of *who* you are, but because of *where* you are.

Where are you? You're in Christ. And once you accept this truth, you will enjoy your relationship with the Father in a brand new way. You'll throw away your spiritual thermometer; you'll quit analyzing how you're doing; and you'll rejoice that you are simply, totally, wonderfully in Christ.

AUGUST 5

That in the dispensation of the fulness of times he might gather together in one all things in Christ, both which are in heaven, and which are on earth; even in him.

Ephesians 1:10

What is the big picture? What is the mystery? It is that in due time, *everything* in heaven and earth will be gathered together in Christ, around Christ, and for Christ.

Benjamin, my seven-year-old, and I went to Pappy's for a pepperoni pizza. 'This is the kind of pizza the Ninja Turtles eat,' Ben declared. 'They like it so much, they even steal it.'

'They do?' I said. 'Well, that reminds me of a story....'

And I proceeded to tell Ben the sad story of how Achan stole from Jericho (Joshua 7). When I finished, Benny understood that stealing leads to problems and pain. And suddenly, sitting down over a pizza at Pappy's had meaning and substance and depth in a way it wouldn't have had the moment not been brought together in Christ, talking about the things of the Lord.

Oh, you've found this to be true. Whether it's talking to your kids or planting flowers in your garden, listening to a co-worker or practicing with a teammate—whenever you're focused on Christ and bringing the moment under the authority of Christ, you're right in the middle of the flow of what God says life is all about.

Isn't God gracious to make His will known to us? After all, He could have said, 'There's a mystery to life. Figure it out. Good luck.' But He didn't. I'm so thankful I can live wisely and prudently because He's made known to me the mystery of His will: that everything is in Christ and for Christ.

Are you full of joy tonight? Are you at peace? Are you content? Do you have rest? If so, you understand the mystery of His will. Are you bitter, angry, frustrated, or upset? Then you don't. On any given day, the extent to which you understand the mystery of His will will be the extent to which peace reigns in your heart.

Whenever I am uptight or pressured, I know it's because I've chosen not to remember that *everything* is flowing to the glorious day when it will *all* be gathered together in Christ.

AUGUST 6

...Being predestinated according to the purpose of him who worketh all things after the counsel of his own will.

Ephesians 1:11

'Who hath counseled the Lord?' asked Isaiah (40:13). The answer? Most of us.

'Now, Lord,' we say, 'I don't know if You're seeing this right. I don't know if You understand the severity of the situation I'm in. Lord, did You see what he just did? Did You hear what she just said?'—as if we expect the Lord to say, 'No. Thanks for filling Me in! What should I do about it?'

God works everything after the counsel of His *own* will. And although we might be tempted to ask what right the Lord has to do this, Paul asks the much more logical question when he says, 'Who are you—a lump of clay—to question the plan of the Father?' (Romans 9:20).

I'm sure Jeremiah was confused when, after preaching 40 long years to the people of Judah, no one responded. So it was that at a certain point in his ministry, the Lord said to him, 'Jeremiah, take a break. Go to the house of the potter and there you will learn a lesson.'

When Jeremiah did indeed go to the house of the potter, he watched him place a lump of clay upon the wheel and position his foot upon the pedal. As the wheel began to spin round and round, the potter began to put pressure on the clay, skillfully shaping and molding it into something of beauty.

There are times when I feel as though I'm spinning my wheels, going in circles, or feeling pressured. 'Where are You, Father?' I cry. 'Don't You care about me? How could You allow this to happen in my life?' But then the Lord brings me back to the very simple realization that the Hands which put pressure on my life and the Foot which spins the wheel have holes in them where nails pierced them as the Master Potter hung on the Cross to die in my place.

That's why Communion is so very important in the life of the believer. Somehow all of the questions and confusion I so often feel as I analyze my situation and question my circumstances are solved immediately when I remember Jesus' unbelievable, undeniable love for me.

AUGUST 7

That the God of our Lord Jesus Christ, the Father of glory, may give unto you the spirit of wisdom and revelation in the knowledge of him.

Ephesians 1:17

All of us crave wisdom and revelation. Each of us longs for instruction and insight in knowing how we should walk, what we should do, where we should go. But notice what Paul tells us. It is profoundly simple and simply profound, for he says that the wisdom and revelation you and I so desperately desire is found solely in the knowledge of *Him*.

Peter and John found this to be true. The singular explanation for their ability to boldly and intelligently address the multitude was the acknowledgement that they had been with Jesus (Acts 4:13).

When people ask, 'What should I do? What is God's will in this situation?' the answer is very simple: the wisdom you need, the revelation you seek is found in knowing Jesus.

How do we know Jesus? By spending time in the Gospels. You may be working your way through Ezekiel or chewing on Romans—but make sure that you daily take in something from Matthew, Mark, Luke, or John. I believe a real key to understanding God's will for your life is to continually focus on Jesus. There's only one Isaiah, only one Hebrews—but there are four Gospels. Could it be that in this God is saying, 'I don't want you to miss this. Whatever else you're learning, the key to it all is My Son'?

Just as Jesus said on the Emmaus Road, all Scripture points to Him (Luke 24:27). If you're spending time with Him in the Gospels, the rest of the Word will all become clear.

AUGUST 8

...That ye may know what is the hope of his calling...
Ephesians 1:18

Throughout Scripture, the word 'hope' always refers to that which is coming, to that which is ahead. I'm convinced the single greatest problem carnal Christians have is that they don't know the hope of His calling. They don't know the reality of heaven. Consequently, they are constantly striving for material things and are continually chasing carnal pursuits. They remain in bondage, depressed, and discouraged because they don't see the big picture of eternity.

If you're not happy at this moment, neither will you be with a change of location, salary, or ministry. You'll not be happy until you know the hope of His calling. That's why Jesus said, 'Let not your hearts be troubled... I go to prepare a place for you' (John 14:1-2). The key to overcoming a troubled, perplexed, stressed heart is to focus on the hope of His calling, on what's ahead, on heaven.

'But heaven seems so far away,' you say. 'For years, I've been hearing Jesus could come at any time. But where is He?'

'Beloved,' Peter said, 'be not ignorant of this one thing: one day is with the Lord as a thousand years, and a thousand years as one day' (II Peter 3:8).

A day is as a thousand years. Maybe you're saying, 'Is that ever true! Will this day *ever* end?' If you are in a strained marriage, a single person aware of your loneliness, or if you're physically afflicted, a day can indeed seem like a thousand years.

'Lord, where are You?' you cry. 'I've been talking to You. I have total trust in You. But where *are* You?'

This day is as a thousand years because in your day of difficulty and dilemma, pressure and pain, sadness and sorrow, you have the unique opportunity to share the fellowship of the Lord's suffering and to pray for others in a way you never would have been able to otherwise. We want to get out of the trial, solve the problem, move on.

The Lord, however, says, 'Not so fast. I want this day to be as a thousand years for you. The discoveries you'll make, the understanding you will glean, the gifts of praise, the expression of even frustrated prayer will affect you for the next zillion years. Because My coming is near, and your heavenly account is pretty small, I'm giving you an opportunity to make some huge investments in the few days that remain before you go to heaven.'

You for whom this day has seemed as a thousand years—rejoice. Savor each moment. Extract each minute. Take every opportunity in this long, long day you're in to thank the Father for the opportunity to store up treasure which will make you rich for eternity.

AUGUST 9

...And what the riches of the glory of his inheritance in the saints.

                                        Ephesians 1:18

As saints, we're God's inheritance, His treasure, His prize.

Us?
Yes.
Me?
Yep.

In Jesus' day, men would bury their treasure in a field for safekeeping. But if a man died before he could tell someone where his treasure was buried, it would be left in the field until someone stumbled upon it.

Such is the case in Matthew 13. One day a man is walking through a field. He trips over something, brushes the dirt from it, and discovers it's a treasure. So what does he do? He does everything he can to buy the field in which the treasure is buried. Because he wants the field? No, because he's after the treasure.

Jesus said that's the way the Kingdom is. The field is the world. God the Father gave the world to Adam. But when Adam sinned, he inadvertently handed it over to Satan. That's why there is rape and famine, pollution, corruption, and death on our planet.

But Jesus came to buy the world back. Why? Because He wants to hang out on the Columbia River? No. He's not interested in the world. He bought the world to get the treasure. He bought the world to get *you*.

AUGUST 10

Far above all principality, and power, and might, and dominion, and every name that is named, not only in this world, but also in that which is to come: and hath put all things under his feet...

Ephesians 2:19-22

Principality, power, might, and dominion are all words that describe various categories of demonic entities and angelic beings. Jesus has power over them all, and the same power that caused Him to be resurrected is in you. Whatever you're struggling with, whatever I'm wrestling through is infinitesimal compared to what it took to raise Christ into heaven. Therefore, if I'm in bondage, it's not because I need more power but because I've failed to utilize the power already in me.

We say, 'I'm addicted.'
God says, 'You're free.'

We say, 'I'm wounded.'
God says, 'You're as whole as you need to be.'

We say, 'I need counseling. I need drugs. I need a program.'
God says, 'You have Me.'

How does this work out practically? All things are under Jesus' feet. What things? Dominions, powers, addictions, problems, pornography, profanity, gossip, depression, meanness, temper, sadness, laziness—whatever it is you can't get over.

'But my problem is so overwhelming,' you say.

It couldn't be any more overwhelming than the waves threatening to drown the disciples. Yet even the waves which rolled over their heads were under Jesus' feet and provided the very foundation He walked upon to reach them (Matthew 14:25).

Nothing is over Jesus' head. All things are under His feet. Jesus is in absolute control of every situation, be it financial, physical, relational, vocational, or parental. Whatever might seem to be rolling your way, ready to sink your boat, and wipe you out is already under His feet—and might be the very path He chooses upon which to walk to you.

AUGUST 11

For this cause I Paul, the prisoner of Jesus Christ for you Gentiles...

Ephesians 3:1

Paul penned this epistle seemingly as a prisoner of Rome. Yet he gives us a different perspective of his situation when he writes, 'Indeed I'm a prisoner. But I'm a prisoner for a cause.' What cause?

The incredible revelation as seen in Chapter 2, that Jews and Gentiles are brought together in Jesus Christ into a new entity. 'We're in this thing together,' said Paul.

Not only was Paul a prisoner for a cause, He was a prisoner of Christ. 'I'm not a prisoner of Nero,' he declared. 'I'm not a prisoner of the Roman Empire. I'm a prisoner of Jesus Christ. And He has brought me to this place.'

I hate to say it, but I'm glad Paul was in prison—because our Bible is a whole lot richer and the Body much more complete as a result. You see, while he was in prison, Paul wrote the letters we value so greatly.

In addition, the guards to whom he was chained as a prisoner began getting saved one by one and were returning to Caesar's palace as born-again believers. That is why in his letter to the Philippians, Paul says, 'The saints in Caesar's palace, your new brothers in Christ, greet you' (Philippians 4:22).

Why do I point this out? Because I think happy will be the one who realizes that wherever he is has been ordained by the Lord to bring about good things if he will have eyes to see and patience to wait. Whenever I complain about my circumstances or situation, I am really complaining about my Father, for it is He who sets our course and determines our days.

Paul never lost this perspective. That is why He could say, 'I'm a prisoner of Jesus Christ, for it is He who has captivated my heart and brought me to this place.'

August 12

Wherefore I desire that ye faint not at my tribulations for you, which is your glory.

Ephesians 3:13

'Don't lose heart over my troubles,' says Paul. 'They're for *you*.' How could that be?

In his tribulation, in his confinement, Paul was a living demonstration of what it means to have Christ living in him, the hope of glory.

A.W. Tozer was right when he said that before God can use a man greatly, He must allow him to be hurt deeply. Why? Because the old adage is true: people don't care how much we know until they know how much we care. And what makes us care in our service to people, our interactions with people? Paul gives the answer in II Corinthians 1 when he writes

> *Blessed be God, even the Father of our Lord Jesus Christ, the Father of mercies, and the God of all comfort; Who comforteth us in all our tribulation, that we may be able to comfort them which are in any trouble, by the comfort wherewith we ourselves are comforted of God. For as the sufferings of Christ abound in us, so our consolation also aboundeth by Christ.*
>
> *II Corinthians 1:3-5*

In other words, the degree of the crushing, the tribulation, the difficulty in which you find yourself will be the degree of consolation you will receive. And consolation comes to us in order that we may in turn comfort others with the comfort we have found in Him.

This passage is so important, gang. God allows us to go through crushing trials even as Paul did in order that we can explore and experience His presence and His comfort—and then share it with others.

In our darkest times, we only truly receive from those who have gone through similar difficulties. When the one who has walked the same path we're walking says, 'I found consolation in Christ,' his words are like water to the desert of our soul because he's not simply telling us a theory—he's telling us what he has experienced personally and practically.

That's why, in talking about his own ministry here in Ephesians 3, Paul says, 'Don't faint. Don't lose heart because of our tribulation, it's for you. God meets us and comforts us in the dungeon of difficulty, in the prison of tribulation so that we can comfort *you*.'

Not only does God use tribulation to comfort the saints—He uses it to convince the sinner. You see, many unbelievers have been witnessed to hundreds of times by sincere Christians. Yet they remain unmoved because they are unknowingly waiting to see the mystery of Christ in the life of a believer. How will this happen? Here in Ephesians 3, Paul links the answer to his own difficulty.

Innumerable as grasshoppers, the Midianites were an intimidating enemy indeed. Nevertheless, God instructed Gideon to take only 300 men to do battle against them. After choosing his 300 men, Gideon gave each one a trumpet, a jar, and a torch—and led them up in the hills surrounding the valley wherein the Midianites slept. Then, following his lead, Gideon's men blew their trumpets and broke their earthen vessels—each of which contained a lit torch.

Hearing the commotion, the Midianites woke up and, seeing the torches—each of which they assumed represented at least a division of soldiers—they grabbed their swords and in their confusion began swinging wildly, destroying each other in the process. Thus, Gideon's men had front-row seats as they observed what happens when light comes pouring forth from a broken vessel.

We have this treasure—the Light of the world, Jesus Christ—in earthen vessels, declares Paul (II Corinthians 4:7). When is He seen? Not when things are comfy and cushy and easy. Not when things are hunky dory. The world is not impressed with that. The enemy is not beaten back by that. The world wants to *see* the mystery of Christ in us—not just hear about it. How do they see it?

They see it when we're broken. They see it, Wife, when your husband walks out on you unexpectedly—and yet you keep worshipping the Lord faithfully. They see it, Dad, when the doctor says, 'It's malignant'—and yet you remain strong in your faith. When the business goes belly-up, when your teenager breaks your heart, when you get cut from the team, when you don't make the squad people get to see the light in the earthen vessel as the vessel is broken. They get to see Christ in you, the hope of glory. And in seeing this mystery, they are drawn to the Master.

August 13

For this cause I bow my knees unto the Father of our Lord Jesus Christ, Of whom the whole family in heaven and earth is named, That he would grant you, according to the riches of his glory, to be strengthened with might by his Spirit in the inner man.
Ephesians 3:14-16

'While I'm in prison, I'm praying for you that the Holy Spirit might strengthen you in the inner man,' says Paul.

Do you care about your kids, Mom and Dad? Pray for them.

Do you care about your church, saint? Pray for us.

Do you care about your community? Pray that the Holy Spirit will work in the inner man.

So many have knowledge in their heads, but it hasn't dropped 18 inches into their hearts. How does that happen?

Through prayer. Paul says, 'I bow my knee—I assume the posture of intensity—and I pray. I can give you all of the head theology in Chapters 1, 2, and the first part of 3. But my prayer is that it will make its way to your *heart*.'

AUGUST 14

...That ye, being rooted and grounded in love, May be able to comprehend with all saints what is the breadth, and length, and depth, and height; And to know the love of Christ, which passeth knowledge, that ye might be filled with all the fulness of God.

Ephesians 3:17-19

How can you know something which passes knowledge? How can you be filled with the fullness of God when God cannot even be contained in the Universe?

I suggest to you the answer lies in this phrase, 'being rooted and grounded in love.' What is rooted? What is grounded? What is love? The Tree of Calvary was rooted. The Cross was grounded. Therefore, the only way I can truly know the love which passes knowledge is when I focus my eyes upon the Cross of Calvary and see what is the breadth and the length and the depth and the height of the love of God...

I see the breadth of His love as Jesus stretched out His arms on the Cross.

To what lengths did He go? Because He was slain before the foundation of the world (Revelation 13:8), His sufferings are elongated beyond anything we can comprehend, for He had to die for every one of our sins. Thus, the length to which He went to accomplish this is staggering.

How deep did He go? Listen as He cried out on the Cross, 'My God, My God, why hast Thou forsaken Me?' He cries out in the depths of despair, from the depth of hell paying for your sin, for my sin.

What is the height of His love? Look up and see Him on the Cross, praying, 'Father, forgive them, for they know not what they do.'

The only way I can truly know that which passes knowledge is to consider the height and depth and length and breadth of the Cross— that which was rooted and grounded on the hill called Calvary. And I am reminded of it each time I partake of the Lord's Table.

Do not forsake the Lord's Table, dear saint, for it is there you will know that which cannot be known. It is there you will be filled with the fullness of God. It is there you will be rooted and grounded in the mystery of God's love as you consider the Cross.

August 15

I therefore, the prisoner of the Lord, beseech you...
Ephesians 4:1

The word 'therefore' being such a pivotal word in Scripture, whenever you come across it in the Word, it's good to stop and ask what it is there for. In this case, as Paul begins the second half of his letter, launching into the practical aspects of our life in Christ, he refers to the doctrinal foundation he laid in Chapters 1-3. In other words, before telling us how we are to walk, he reminds us we must first understand where we sit.

In Chapters 1-3, Paul told us we were adopted into God's family, elected before the foundation of the world, redeemed by the blood of the Lamb, sealed with the Holy Spirit—all while we were dead in our sin. And this is where so many Christians stumble. They try and walk before they sit. Sermons are preached; seminars are given; books are published on the way husbands should love their wives and the way wives should submit to their husbands; or the way we should live in purity; or what we should do as a Church Body—all without acknowledging what God has already done for us, all without factoring in the fact that there's nothing we can do to make God love us any more than He loves us right now.

I have found that most Christians believe they are the initiators in spiritual life, feeling that if they can just pray enough, do enough, be enough, God will love them and bless them. So they try to walk worthy—but sooner or later, they fail and throw in the towel.

Our Christian walk is not something we do to try to earn God's favor or merit His love. Rather, it is a response to how He loves us, what He's done for us, how good He's been to us. 'We love Him,' the Apostle John said, 'because He first loved us' (I John 4:19). He is the Initiator, we are the responders. We don't love Him *so* He'll love us. We love Him *because* He first loved us.

AUGUST 16

But ye have not so learned Christ; If so be that ye have heard him, and have been taught by him, as the truth is in Jesus.

Ephesians 4:20-21

The world embraces greediness, uncleanness, and empty-headedness. 'But you,' said Paul, 'have not learned Christ that way.' Notice Paul doesn't say, 'You haven't learned *about* Christ that way.' He says, 'You haven't learned Christ that way.'

I can learn about Abraham Lincoln. I can read books about him, and I can go to Disneyland and 'Meet Mr. Lincoln' 15 times in a row.

That's the way some people learn about Jesus. They read Matthew, Mark, Luke, and John 15 times in a row and think they know Him. But in reality, they only know *about* Him.

To learn Christ implies communion and intimacy with Him. How does this happen practically? As you spend time studying John's Gospel, for example, read a verse or two, then say to the Lord, 'That convicts me,' or, 'That confuses me,' or, 'That reminds me,' or, 'That blesses me,'—for in so doing, you will be communing *with* Him personally rather than merely learning *about* Him academically.

So whether you go for a walk, lock yourself in your bathroom, or drive to a secluded spot—find a place you can talk to the Lord as you read about Him. It will make all the difference in the world, for then you will truly learn Christ.

AUGUST 17

And that ye put on the new man, which after God is created in righteousness and true holiness.

Ephesians 4:24

Notice the order here: first you put off the old, then you're renewed in your mind. In other words, you decide you're no longer going to walk like those who are involved in sin. And as you begin to put on a whole new way of talking, living, and behaving—your new lifestyle eventually becomes who you are. It's not deception. It's a decision. People who are like Christ have made a conscious decision to put on the new man, to put on Christ— and they become what they have chosen to put on.

If I merely sit here and wait for something to happen—for my personality to change, for my heart to feel loving, for my soul to feel kind—I'll wait forever. I've got to make a choice. I must choose to be compassionate. I must choose to be loving. And as I do, I become compassionate; I become loving.

AUGUST 18

And be not drunk with wine, wherein is excess; but be filled with the Spirit; Speaking to yourselves in psalms and hymns and spiritual songs, singing and making melody in your heart to the Lord; Giving thanks always for all things unto God and the Father in the name of our Lord Jesus Christ.

Ephesians 5:18-20

When I feel things aren't going very well, I'm tempted to lose heart. And when this happens, I know there's only one thing to do: speak to myself in psalms and hymns and spiritual songs.

No wonder David was discouraged. He and his men returned from fighting the Amalekites only to discover that their town had been burned by their enemies, their wives and kids taken hostage.

'This is your fault, David,' said his men. 'You took us away from here.' And so angry were they that they wanted to kill him.

So what did David do? He encouraged himself in the Lord (I Samuel 30:6). He sang songs. He wrote psalms. He began to praise and worship. As a result, he rallied his men once again and they recovered all that was lost.

Had David remained in his depressed state, not only would he have been rendered ineffective, but the women and children would have remained captive. And so will you until you begin to worship. God's will is that you be free—and nothing will free you from the tyranny of your own situation like worship. You will be profoundly blessed and amazingly productive whenever you give thanks to God for *all* things in the name of our Lord Jesus Christ.

AUGUST 19

Not with eyeservice, as menpleasers; but as the servants of Christ, doing the will of God from the heart; With good will doing service, as to the Lord, and not to men.

Ephesians 6:6-7

You are to do what's asked of you enthusiastically. The word 'enthusiasm' comes from the Greek phrase, *en theos*, or 'full of God.'

Eugene Ormandy, Conductor of the Philadelphia Philharmonic, dislocated his right shoulder because he conducted with such enthusiasm. We know so little of this kind of service. We don't separate our shoulders. We barely wrinkle our ties. That's why we don't ascend to the level God would have us enjoy in so many arenas.

David was a man who went above and beyond the call of duty, bounding over walls (Psalm 18:29), expending great energy. And the men around him developed that same mentality. Hiding out in the cave at Adullam one day, David mused, 'I would give anything for a drink of water from the well at Bethlehem.'

Hours later, as the sun began to set, three of his men—Adino, Eleazar, and Shammah—approached him. Their clothes were tattered, their flesh bruised and bleeding.

'Where did you guys go?' David must have asked.

And in my mind's eye, I can see a tear running down his dusty cheek as they handed him a skin of water, drawn from the well of Bethlehem (II Samuel 23). The most precious gift David ever received was from three of his 'employees' who had risked their lives to please him. And it was Adino, Eleazar, and Shammah who remained chiefs of his mighty men once he became king.

Who becomes a mighty man on the job, in the Church, for the Kingdom? The one who hears the heart of his employer. The world says, 'Skate by. Leave early. Cover up.'

But God, who sees all, says, 'I'm looking for men and women who, with good cheer, enthusiasm, and singleness of heart respect those in position over them with fear and trembling.' Such a one will go far in the things of God.

AUGUST 20

Put on the whole armor of God, that ye may be able to stand against the wiles of the devil.

Ephesians 6:11

The first step to being strong is to realize that life is not an encounter group. Life is not a bonding meeting. Life is not a playground. Life is a battleground. And the reason so many in the Church are weak is because they're not armed for battle.

If the men who stormed the beaches of Normandy on D-Day did so dressed in their jammies, something would have been terribly wrong. Yet I believe we live in a day of 'jammy Christianity.' 'Let's put on our jammies and talk about how we feel,' we say. 'Let's have a slumber party, and we'll all bond.'

No. Paul tells us to put on our armor, to take advantage of the equipment God has given us to navigate life and negotiate the war which surrounds us.

Dear saint, you can stand against the wiles of the devil—the cunning, clever attacks of Satan—only to the degree that you're protected with the *whole* armor of God.

AUGUST 21

Peace be to the brethren, and love with faith, from God the Father and the Lord Jesus Christ. Grace be with all them that love our Lord Jesus Christ in sincerity. Amen.

Ephesians 6:23-24

The way to be strong is to wear the armor. I know some who almost physically put on the armor of God every morning. 'I'm going to be conscious of truth in my inner life today,' they say. 'And I'm going to make sure my heart is right. I'm going to tell everyone I meet today something of the Good News of the Gospel. And should I be barraged with fiery darts, I'll run to the protection of the congregation. I'll be consciously looking for the Lord's return today. And I'll carry my Bible with me in order that I might meditate upon it to have an exacting word for someone in need.'

While all of that is wonderful for some, I have found that the majority of us are more like my son Benjamin...

Benjamin, my first-grader, is in such a hurry to get out the door and off to school in the morning, he thinks he can't be bothered with getting dressed. His solution—until we told him otherwise—was to go to bed wearing the clothes he would wear the next day

Maybe, like me, you find it overwhelming to go through the practice of putting on your armor a piece at a time. I suggest, like Benjamin, you make it a whole lot simpler: just put on Jesus...

He is the Truth (John 14:6).
He is our Breastplate of righteousness (Romans 13:14).
He guides our feet in peace (Luke 1:79).
He is our Shield of faith (Hebrews 12:2).
He is the Captain of our salvation (Hebrews 2:10).
He is the Word made flesh (John 1:14).

It's all wrapped up in *Him*—which is why when we love Him in sincerity, we experience His peace in our hearts and His grace in our lives.

AUGUST 22

Being confident of this very thing, that he which hath begun a good work in you will perform it until the day of Jesus Christ.

Philippians 1:6

Ten years have passed since the day Paul first came across Lydia and the rest of the women praying by the riverbank. And here, in a Roman prison, thinking about what the Lord had done in and through them, Paul's heart is filled with confidence concerning the Philippian church.

I believe if Paul were alive today, he would exhibit the same confidence. Oh, I am aware of those who say, 'What's wrong with the Church? Why isn't the Church on fire?' But to those who say that there needs to be revival, I say, 'Don't you see it?' To those who call for radical renewal, I say, 'Don't you get it? Look around and see what God is doing. It will blow your mind. It will warm your heart. It will cause you to applaud the Father for His faithfulness and goodness. What He's done for us personally and corporately blows me away totally.'

Why is it the tendency among so many Christians to think that the Lord is always asking for more, more, more—that if they pray one hour, they should have prayed two; that if they witnessed to three people this month, they should have witnessed to four? It's my conviction that many, many, many Christians expect more out of themselves than God ever does.

How quick we are to beat up ourselves and other Christians. Yet if we would only open our eyes and see what the Lord is doing in the person sitting right next to us, we'd see a miracle—for the fact that God would mature and develop, build and use people like us is nothing short of miraculous.

Like Paul, I thank God upon every remembrance of you. He's doing an awesome work in your lives. He's taking you through deep waters and tough times—and you're coming out the other side stronger than ever.

'Fear not, little flock, for it is the Father's good pleasure to give you the Kingdom,' Jesus said (Luke 12:32). He's pleased *with* you. He's done a great and marvelous work *through* you. And I'm confident that He who began a good work *in* you shall complete it until the day of Christ Jesus—when He comes back to take us all to heaven.

AUGUST 23

For God is my record, how greatly I long after you all
in the bowels of Jesus Christ.

Philippians 1:8

Rather than referring to the heart, Paul's culture referred to the intestines as the seat of deepest emotions. 'I long for you greatly,' said Paul, 'not just superficially, but deep within me.'

What gave Paul this kind of love? What caused him to pen this epistle rather than pout about his own situation? I believe it was because Paul utilized his prison time to pray. He cared *about* the Philippians because he prayed *for* them.

Who's on *your* nerves? Who's robbing you of joy? Maybe it's your boss or husband, a coach or teacher, a colleague or neighbor. Pray for them, for as you do, a couple of things will happen. First of all, because God answers prayer, they'll change. But secondly—and much more importantly—*you'll* begin to change...

In Exodus 28, we read that on the ephod, which the high priest wore, was a breastplate. And upon the breastplate were gems representing each of the twelve tribes of Israel. Thus, the people of Israel—those who were often stubborn, backslidden, unappreciative, and rebellious—were to be as gems on the heart of the high priest.

But that's only half the story. You see, inscribed on the shoulders of the high priest's ephod were the names of the tribes. In other words, the high priest could not carry the gemstones of the tribes on his heart if the names of the tribes were not on his shoulders. Spiritually, the shoulder speaks of bearing burdens. Thus, as the high priest bore the burden of intercessory prayer *for* the people, he would experience a change in his heart *toward* the people. He would view them not as dirt clods or pieces of coal—but as gems.

Gang, pray for the people who bug you. Pray God's blessing upon them. Pray for God's work to be flowing through them. Pray good things to happen to them. Hold them up on the shoulders of intercession, and you will find that they will become gems in your heart. You cannot be angry or bitter towards someone for whom you're praying. That's why prayer is so important—not only because others will change, but because we will.

AUGUST 24

But I would ye should understand, brethren, that the
things which happened unto me have fallen out rather
unto the furtherance of the gospel.

Philippians 1:12

Just as God used a sling in David's hand, a pitcher in Gideon's hand, and a rod in the hand of Moses, He used chains on Paul's hands. That's not surprising, for chains are what open the door to speak to people who would not otherwise give us the time of day.

You see, it's when a wife hangs in there with her difficult husband; it's when an employee refuses to talk behind his boss's back; it's when a high-schooler willingly submits to his parents that people take note, thereby opening opportunity for the wife, the employee, the high-schooler to share the reason why.

I'm convinced that the troubles, challenges, and problems we face are custom-designed to do one thing: to allow us to draw others *to* Jesus Christ and to encourage them *in* Jesus Christ.

'But my burden is too heavy,' you say.

Listen, God will not tempt you above what you are able (I Corinthians 10:13). God doesn't play favorites—and if He has put you in a certain imprisonment, it's because He has prepared you for it and given you everything you'll need to go through it.

AUGUST 25

For I know that this shall turn to my salvation through your prayer, and the supply of the Spirit of Jesus Christ, According to my earnest expectation and my hope, that in nothing I shall be ashamed, but that with all boldness, as always, so now also Christ shall be magnified in my body, whether it be by life, or by death.

Philippians 1:19-20

Christ was magnified through Paul's difficulty. 'Why does Christ have to be magnified?' you ask. 'Isn't He big enough already?'

Think with me...

Our sun is so big that, if hollowed out, it could hold 1.3 million earths. The sun, however, is dwarfed by the star Antares, which could hold 64 suns. But Antares is a pipsqueak compared to Hercules, which could hold 110 million Antares. Yet Hercules is a speck compared to Epsilon, the largest known star, which could hold 3 million Hercules.

These objects are *huge*, folks! Why then do they seem so small when we look at them in the night sky? Because we are so far away. Therefore, we use a telescope to magnify them and bring them closer to us.

People are far away from Jesus. What will make Him clear to them? Seeing Him walk with us and provide for us through the telescope of our difficulties. If this be true—if Christ is magnified in our hard times—the most logical thing for us to do in such times is to do what Paul did: rejoice.

AUGUST 26

Let nothing be done through strife or vainglory; but in lowliness of mind let each esteem other better than themselves. Look not every man on his own things, but every man also on the things of others.

Philippians 2:3-4

This is the key: let each one of you esteem others as being better than yourself. How does that happen? By simply realizing that every single person around you, that every single person you meet is better than you in some way or at some thing than you are. And once we look into their lives and explore who they are, we must conclude, 'It's a privilege to know you. I have no right to look down on you. You're better than me.'

My natural, carnal mind doesn't work this way. My carnal mind wants to find fault with the person next to me so I can feel better about myself. But Paul says just the opposite: go around school tomorrow and look at every other student as being better than you—and treat them accordingly. And as you begin to develop the mindset that you're privileged to be with everyone around you, the result will be joy. But it can't be done apart from dependence upon the Lord day by day, moment by moment. It's a challenge—and yet it's something we can *choose* to do.

I believe verse 4 is really the key to verse 3. I will esteem others as better than myself to the degree that I listen to their stories and explore who they are—for if we knew the secret hurts and pains and suffering of even our chiefest enemy, we would find all of our animosity evaporating. If we looked *into* people instead of down *on* people, we would be filled with compassion *for* people.

AUGUST 27

But made himself of no reputation...
Philippians 2:7

This phrase in Greek is 'kenosis,' or literally, 'he emptied himself.' Jesus emptied Himself. Of what? Of His divinity? No. When Jesus came as a Man, He was still God. Then of what did He empty Himself? He emptied Himself of His Divine powers.

The implications of the doctrine of kenosis are huge because it means that everything Jesus did—the miracles He ministered, the prayers He prayed, the teachings He gave—were not done in His own power. Jesus healed and prayed and taught through the power of the Holy Spirit as He followed the Father's directives.

Because I didn't know this for probably 20+ years, when I read that Jesus walked on water, I thought, 'Big deal. He's Jesus'; when I read that He overcame temptation, I thought, 'Big deal. He's Jesus'; when I read that He spent the night in prayer, I thought, 'Big deal. He's Jesus.' Thus, the miracles and stories of the Gospels were irrelevant to me as far as they related to being an example or model for me.

I didn't understand kenosis. I didn't grasp Philippians 2. I didn't comprehend that when Jesus came to earth, He emptied Himself of His Divine abilities—which means everything Jesus did, He did as a man just like me. Before He did anything, Jesus had to be obedient to the Father, to pray, to put Himself on the line, to be empowered by the Spirit—or nothing would happen. That's why He said, 'Of my own self, I can do nothing' (John 5:30)—and neither can you.

When a man who is serious about loving and serving God understands the kenosis of Philippians 2, he'll never look at Jesus the same way. He'll see that Jesus' life is truly a model for anyone willing to be directed by the Father and empowered by the Spirit.

AUGUST 28

Wherefore, my beloved, as ye have always obeyed,
not as in my presence only, but now much more in my
absence, work out your own salvation...

Philippians 2:12

In addition to having a mind submitted to the will of the Father, Paul says that another key to joy is to work out your salvation. Notice he doesn't say, 'Work *for* your salvation,' or 'Work *on* your salvation.' He says, 'Work *out* your salvation.'

What does it mean to work out one's salvation? It's like going to the YMCA—it means you exercise it and strengthen it.

Notice also that Paul says we are to work out our *own* salvation...

What if Peter had said that day, 'Hey guys, look at me. I'm walking on water. You all should walk on water. Come on, guys. Get it together. Step out. Follow me. You can do it. Test your faith'?

We've all heard sermons along those lines, and I understand the intention, but they're terribly flawed. Peter walked on water not because he had faith. Peter walked on water because Jesus said, 'Come.' Jesus didn't tell James or John, Andrew or Bartholomew to come. The language is clear that His command was given to Peter singularly (Matthew 14).

Work out your *own* salvation. What's God working in *your* heart? What's He calling *you* to do?

In the course of a single evening, I read two outstanding books by two good Christian brothers. One said Christians should move into the city in order to minister to the multitudes. The other said Christians should move out of the city, as did the desert fathers. Unable to reconcile the two, I was troubled until the Lord spoke to my heart saying, 'Jon, what have I called *you* to do? What have

I placed on *your* heart? I am the One who cared for the poor, and this brother is showing that side of Me. I'm also the One who moved to a solitary place and communed with the Father, and the other brother is showing that side. Let every brother reflect that which I have made clear to *him*.'

AUGUST 29

For it is God which worketh in you both to will and to do of his good pleasure.

Philippians 2:13

It's God who gives us the desires and the abilities to do what He wants us to do.

Although he was only 17-years-old when he had a vision of the sun, moon, and stars bowing before him, Joseph knew it spoke of a position of authority he would assume over his brothers. And sure enough, as prime minister of Egypt, his brothers did indeed bow before him, asking help from him (Genesis 42:6). Joseph's dream came to pass— but not before he was thrown in a pit and tossed into prison.

Here's where a lot of us blow it. 'I have a vision,' we say. 'It's in me to be a mother, so why aren't I married?' or 'It's in me to be a missionary, so why isn't it happening?' or 'It's in me to work with kids, so why aren't the doors opening?'

Understand this, dear brother and precious sister, concerning another man who had to go through hard times before his vision was fulfilled: Scripture says it was not until he *patiently endured* that Abraham obtained the promise (Hebrews 6:15). You might land in a pit or two. You might go through a prison or three—but know this: God will fulfill that which He has placed in your heart if you patiently endure and don't give up.

I'm slowly but surely learning that what I really want, that what I truly desire is His will. Why? Because I've demanded my will too many times and gotten it only to be disappointed. Other times, I've watched the Lord work in ways I wasn't anticipating and seen that what came of it was wonderful.

AUGUST 30

But I trust in the Lord that I also myself shall come shortly. Yet I supposed it necessary to send to you Epaphroditus, my brother, and companion in labour, and fellowsoldier, but your messenger, and he that ministered to my wants. For he longed after you all, and was full of heaviness, because that ye had heard that he had been sick. For indeed he was sick nigh unto death...

Philippians 2:24-27

Epaphroditus was the man the Philippians sent to encourage and to bring financial assistance to Paul. 'I'm sending him back your way,' said Paul, 'because he was concerned that you might be worried about his condition, having heard he had been sick.'

What? Epaphroditus was sick when he was with Paul—Paul, the one whose sweatbands were used to bring healing to people; Paul, the one who laid his hands on people and they recovered; Paul, the one who was known for moving in the miraculous. Why didn't Paul heal Epaphroditus immediately? For the same reason he didn't heal Trophimus (II Timothy 4:20), or Timothy (I Timothy 5:23), or even himself (II Corinthians 12:7).

Ultimately, everyone will be healed, for by Jesus' stripes, we are *all* healed (Isaiah 53:5). The only question is timing. When they ask for healing, some are healed immediately. Others, five years later.

Others, not until they get to heaven. Healing has nothing to do with a person's spirituality or faith. It has everything to do with God's sovereignty.

Three times Paul prayed for deliverance, only to hear the Lord say, 'No, Paul. When you are weak, then My strength is manifested. My grace is sufficient for you' (II Corinthians 12:9). Thus, I encourage those who are afflicted to follow Paul's model, to pray 3 times, 30 times, or 300 times—until they receive what they're asking for or until they have a peace in their heart which says, 'This is what the Lord has for me, and I can embrace it.'

AUGUST 31

That I may know him, and the power of his resurrection, and the fellowship of his sufferings, being made conformable unto his death.

Philippians 3:10

When do you really know the Lord? When you realize He's alive. When do you really understand He's alive? When you go through tough times—the fellowship of suffering. When I'm cruising along on 'Easy Street', I don't know Jesus the way I often discover Him when I'm going through difficulties or problems, heartaches or setbacks, tragedy or pain.

Here in Philippians, this book of rejoicing, Paul says, 'Don't despise the difficulty, the tragedy, the tough time, the setback, the heartache—for those are the times you will understand that Jesus is truly risen. When the day is dark, the waters deep, the outlook grim—you'll see Jesus.'

'Sure, I want to know the Lord,' people say. 'I just don't want to go through tough times. Of course I want to know His power—but I don't want to deal with the fellowship which comes through suffering.'

Yet the only way you can know the Lord intimately is through the power of His resurrection. And the best way to experience the power of His resurrection is through hard times...

'How many men did we throw in the fire?' asked Nebuchadnezzar. 'Three, your highness.'
'Well, how is it that I see four, and the fourth is like the son of God?'

So clearly did Shadrach, Meshach, and Abed-nego see Jesus in the fire of suffering that they chose to remain in the fiery furnace with Him rather than to walk free without Him (Daniel 3:26).

We know the Lord by realizing He's with us in times of suffering and by choosing to say, 'Lord, I'll die to myself in order to have fellowship with You. As long as I try to protect myself, I'll not know You in the way I want to. So Lord, I choose to conform myself to Your death. Do what You want in my life.'

When Jesus started talking about the Cross, Peter's response was, 'Be it far from Thee, Lord. It's not going to happen' (Matthew 16:22).

And Peter's is a cry we utter as well. 'Not the Cross,' we say. 'Not death or bankruptcy, break-ups or leukemia. We want Cadillacs, miraculous healings, and holy laughter—that's our kind of Christianity, Lord.'

We're just like Peter. But when, to one degree or another, we experience the fellowship of suffering, we begin to say, 'I now choose death in order that I might know Jesus better.'

Christians are the only people who can truly choose to rejoice and be happy when things on the outside seem so bleak because we're the only ones who know there will be a fellowship in suffering which will manifest the power of Jesus and His resurrection, and which will, in turn, allow the degree of intimacy with God which will make us deeply happy and truly blessed.

SEPTEMBER 1

For our conversation is in heaven; from whence also
we look for the Saviour, the Lord Jesus Christ.
                                        Philippians 3:20

Newer versions translate the word 'conversation' as 'lifestyle'
or 'citizenship.' Why? Because a person's citizenship—be he
English, French, or Australian—can be readily identified through
his conversation, through the way he speaks. The same is true
spiritually, for Scripture declares that out of the abundance
of the heart, the mouth speaks (Matthew 12:34). What is your
conversation, your lifestyle, your citizenship? It will be revealed in
the heat of battle...

After civil war had broken out between the men from Gilead and the
men from Ephraim, Jephthah, leader of the Gileadites, ordered his
men to seal the passes lest the Ephraimites get away.

'But how will we identify them?' asked his men. 'They're our
brothers.'
'Tell them to say the word 'river,' or 'shibboleth,' said Jephthah.

Why? Because the men from Ephraim could not pronounce the
sound of 'sh.' Thus, instead of 'shibboleth,' they said 'sibboleth'—
and were immediately betrayed by their speech (Judges 12).

The same holds true for you and me. In the heat of battle, how do we
talk? When the accountant says, 'You're bankrupt'; when the doctor
says, 'It's cancer'; when your boyfriend says, 'Goodbye', what do we
say? Our speech, our conversation will reveal whether we're men
and women who live for the material, the temporal, the earthly—or
whether we are those who live for heaven singularly.

SEPTEMBER 2

Who shall change our vile body, that it may be fashioned like unto his glorious body, according to the working whereby he is able even to subdue all things unto himself.

Philippians 3:21

Not only will our bodies be changed to be like His, but all things will be subdued, or 'put in order.' At last! All things will be subdued, re-ordered, made right...

According to a recent Gallup poll, if Michael Jordan ran for the US Senate in Illinois, he would win by 70%. No one knows what he thinks. No one cares where he stands. None of that matters because, after all, he's Michael Jordan. And we want him to be our leader.

Why? Because he can bounce a rubber ball filled with air and jump a few inches higher than the other guys who are also bouncing a rubber ball filled with air. And because he can jump a little higher, he can jump up and drop the rubber ball through a metal hoop.

Wow! Awesome! No wonder we want him to be our leader!

Our culture is topsy-turvy, gang—and the only answer is heaven, for in heaven people will not be abuzz about Michael Jordan—they'll be talking about Pearl Good...

Pearl Good cleaned houses to make enough money to be able to travel to wherever Billy Graham would be speaking, get a cheap motel room and, unbeknownst to him, pray around the clock for the Crusade. If you want a trading card that's going to be worth something in eternity, forget Michael Jordan's—get Pearl Good's!

We're all mixed-up, folks. Our society is confused. Our values are wrong. Do I despair over this? No, because everything will be made right in heaven.

To the person complaining about cultural chaos, heaven is the answer. To the person who says life is unfair, heaven is the answer.

To the Pearl Goods of the earth, heaven is the answer.

Heaven will:
   Solve every problem,
      Answer every question,
         Right every wrong.

We're going to be there soon, gang...and I can't wait!

SEPTEMBER 3

Therefore, my brethren dearly beloved and longed for, my joy and crown, so stand fast in the Lord, my dearly beloved.

Philippians 4:1

Whenever you come to the word, 'therefore' in Scripture, it's wise to stop and ask what it's there for. Here at the outset of Chapter 4, Paul refers to the end of Chapter 3, wherein he tells us we don't have to be hopeless as we watch our culture crumble, for when Jesus returns, He'll put all things in order.

In light of the fact that the Lord's return is at hand, Paul tells the church at Philippi to stand fast, to stand confidently, to stand firmly in Him.

More and more, I'm convinced that heaven is the whole deal—just realizing that we're soon going to be there and that we have a single job to do: to grab as many people as we can and say, 'Come along with us to heaven.'

I think we worry far too much about what we're doing or how we're feeling. We analyze ourselves endlessly. We scrutinize our situations continually. We ponder our circumstances tirelessly. But in reality, the joy, the crown lies in sharing with people who don't know Jesus, in praying for folks who will be cut off from Him unless they open their heart to Him. I believe the reason Paul could talk so much about joy in this epistle—even while he was in chains—was because he was thinking about the people he knew would be in heaven with him eternally because he had shared with them personally.

SEPTEMBER 4

And I intreat thee also, true yokefellow, help those women which laboured with me in the gospel, with Clement also, and with other my fellowlabourers, whose names are in the book of life.

Philippians 4:3

After ministering in various areas, the disciples returned to Jesus excited about what they had seen. 'Lord,' they said, 'even the demons are subject unto us as we share in Your name. It's amazing what's happening!'

But what did Jesus say?

He said, 'Don't rejoice in what you've seen. Rather, rejoice that your names are written in the book of life' (Luke 10:20).

We should be full of ecstasy and elated continually not because we cast out a demon or saw a healing or were used in ministry. We should be amazed constantly over one thing primarily: the fact that we're saved.

Hell is real, gang. We don't understand it. It's still sort of fuzzy to us. But Jesus knew the reality of hell, even as He knew the reality of heaven.

That is why He said to His disciples, 'Here's what you should be excited about: because your name is written in the book of life, you're not going to hell. You're going to heaven where you will live with Me forever.'

The knowledge that we're headed for heaven should keep a smile on our faces every day of our lives. Heaven alone should keep praise flowing from our lips perpetually.

'I don't feel good,' we groan.
Who cares? We're not going to hell!

'I'm not appreciated at work,' we cry.
Who cares? We're going to live eternally.

'I won the lottery!' we shout.
So what? That's nothing compared to heaven!

SEPTEMBER 5

And the peace of God, which passeth all understanding, shall keep your hearts and minds through Christ Jesus.

Philippians 4:7

The older I get, the more I'm learning that prayer is not a monologue. It's a dialogue. I'm discovering more and more that the real need in my life is not for God to hear from me, but for me to hear from Him. And I find that as I walk, drive, or get on my knees, if I will pray a phrase or two and then just rest and be quiet, the Lord will bring specific Scriptures to my mind or will write His will upon my heart concerning how I am to pray.

But if I pray sentence after paragraph after page and then say, 'OK, that wraps it up for prayer time today'—I really miss it. Oh, I know that even that kind of prayer has power. Any prayer is better than no prayer. But I suggest that if you learn to pause and listen in prayer, the Lord will show you how to believe on behalf of another and how to pray specifically concerning any given situation.

SEPTEMBER 6

Finally, brethren, whatsoever things are true, whatsoever things are honest, whatsoever things are just, whatsoever things are pure, whatsoever things are lovely, whatsoever things are of good report; if there be any virtue, and if there be any praise, think on these things.

Philippians 4:8

The theme of Paul's epistle to the Philippians is that the key to experiencing joy in your heart is to have the right thoughts in your mind. How are we to think? We're to think on things that are true, honest, just, pure, lovely, of good report, virtuous, and praiseworthy.

Even spiritual men and women become discouraged. You can see it in their eyes. And they wonder why. It's because they've been thinking thoughts which are not true and honest, lovely and pure. They stared at David Letterman before they went to bed. And they wonder why they wake up grumpy.

If you are prone to depression, do not watch late night TV. You'll wake up cynical about life and with a tainted, twisted perspective. Instead, fill your mind with the goodness of God and the wealth of His Word, and, like Paul, you'll awake with a song in your soul.

SEPTEMBER 7

Not because I desire a gift: but I desire fruit that may abound to your account.

Philippians 4:17

A difficult area for ministers is to address the subject of finances because it can appear to be self-serving. Nevertheless, Paul hits this issue head-on by saying, 'It's not that I want a gift. It's that I want you to have fruit.'

When the person gets to heaven who gave the tithe which is the Lord's and offerings which are above and beyond that, I guarantee he's not going to say, 'Phooey, I tithed faithfully. If I hadn't tithed, I could have had a new patio set. And if I had only saved that extra hundred dollars from that offering, I could have had a new barbeque.'

No. For the next zillion years, he'll never regret what he gave to the Lord today. The old adage is true: you can't take it with you—but you can send it ahead. Read the book of Ezra. See the listing of the names verse after verse, page after page, recording the exact amounts people gave for the building of the temple. Why would God 'waste' so many verses about what people were giving to that project? I believe it's because in it He is saying, 'I notice what people give to Me and record it forever.'

SEPTEMBER 8

But my God shall supply all your need according to his riches in glory by Christ Jesus.

Philippians 4:19

A favorite of 'Precious Promise' collections, this verse is indeed a powerful promise. But notice to whom it's given. Taken in context,

Paul is saying, 'Know this, you who are faithful in giving: God will supply all of your need.'

'Can I borrow your boat?' Jesus asked.
'Sure,' said the fishermen.

So Jesus pushed out a little ways into the Sea of Galilee, and, using the water as a natural amphitheater, He preached to the multitude gathered on the shore.

'Thanks for letting Me use your boat,' He said to the fishermen when He was finished. 'Go ahead and take it out now.'

They did—and when they cast their nets into the water, so great was the haul that it almost sunk their boat (Luke 5:3-6).

If we give, God will supply all of our needs because we just can't out-give Him. Develop a life of tithing—and you'll be just as amazed as were those fishermen by the Lord's provision in your life.

SEPTEMBER 9

Paul, an apostle of Jesus Christ by the will of God, and Timotheus our brother, To the saints and faithful brethren in Christ which are at Colosse: Grace be unto you, and peace, from God our Father and the Lord Jesus Christ. We give thanks to God and the Father of our Lord Jesus Christ, praying always for you.

Colossians 1:1-3

Although Paul had never been to Colosse, what he heard about the believers there caused his heart to rejoice and to respond by praying continual blessing upon them.

I encourage you to do the same thing. When you hear something good about someone, pray for him. My tendency is to pray for those I hear are hurting or backsliding. That is needed indeed, but it's also vital to pray for people who are doing well because the enemy will inevitably launch an attack against them in order to destroy their witness and tear down their testimony.

Be like Paul. When you hear or see someone doing well, thank the Lord for him and intercede on his behalf.

SEPTEMBER 10

As ye also learned of Epaphras our dear fellowservant, who is for you a faithful minister of Christ; Who also declared unto us your love in the Spirit.

Colossians 1:7-8

I like Epaphras. He goes around speaking good things. He says, 'I have good news about great things happening with those guys in Colosse.'

I want to be like Epaphras—talking about how great someone is behind his or her back, for not only does this please the Lord, but it has an impact on me as well.

How? To a very real degree, you are whom I say you are when you're not around. You see, if all of you leave here tonight and, on your way home, talk about what an idiot I am, I will become that person to you the next time we meet. Talk negatively about me, and, even if those things are not totally true, that's what I will become in your sight.

On the other hand, if you speak well of a person behind his back, that is the way you will tend to view him. The next time you see him, you will approach him with an entirely different mindset than if you had come down on him.

The power of words is awesome. For that reason, we must be very careful. Gossip good stuff. That's what Epaphras did.

SEPTEMBER 11

For this cause we also, since the day we heard it, do not cease to pray for you, and to desire that ye might be filled with the knowledge of his will in all wisdom and spiritual understanding; That ye might walk worthy of the Lord unto all pleasing, being fruitful in every good work, and increasing in the knowledge of God; Strengthened with all might, according to his glorious power, unto all patience and longsuffering with joyfulness; Giving thanks unto the Father, which hath made us meet to be partakers of the inheritance of the saints in light: Who hath delivered us from the power of darkness, and hath translated us into the kingdom of his dear Son.

Colossians 1:9-13

You who desire to be prayer warriors, carefully consider this prayer. Notice how Paul prays for things we don't even think about. We pray, 'Oh, Lord, help him to get over his arthritis, or be happy in her relationship, or get the new car.'

But what does Paul pray? Under the inspiration of the Spirit, Paul prays that the Colossians would,

Know the will of God and walk worthy of Him;

Be fruitful and strengthened with His might;
Be patient and full of joy.

Those are the important issues. *Those* are the issues of eternity. So if you want to know how to pray for your kids, grandchildren, parents, or husband—listen to Paul pray.

SEPTEMBER 12

In whom we have redemption through his blood, even the forgiveness of sins: Who is the image of the invisible God...

Colossians 1:14-15

People have lots of ideas about what God is like...

The Hindu says, 'God must be loving, benevolent, and gentle. Therefore, He must be a cow.'

The American Indian, watching an eagle soar effortlessly and majestically upon the wind currents says, 'God is an eagle.'

The ancient Egyptian sees the awesome power of the sun and says, 'God is Ra. God is the sun.'

Each culture speaks a partial truth, but all miss the total picture because all of humanity is blind. So what did God do? He came and dwelt among us in the Person of Jesus Christ. Therefore, when I want to know what God is like, I don't have to try and figure out His nature. I can study the life of Jesus, for He alone reveals God in totality. He alone is the 'image of the invisible God.'

SEPTEMBER 13

For by him were all things created, that are in heaven, and that are in earth, visible and invisible, whether they be thrones, or dominions, or principalities, or powers: all things were created by him, and for him.

Colossians 1:16

This, gang, is the secret of life. Jesus is not the created one, He is the Creator. 'This is the day the Lord hath made,' we sing. What does that mean? It means this day is made for Him, and the only way it will work is if I live for Him because, in so doing, I will be fulfilling the only reason it was created.

'I don't like that,' you might say. 'I don't like the implications or the restrictions.'

And the Lord would say to you, 'Tough. That's the way life works. And when you live your life to know Me, you'll find your life working. But if you don't, you're sure to crash...'

I could say, 'I'd like to see the valley tonight. So I'll just rev up my Montero, drive up a mountain, hit the accelerator, and fly over the valley. It'll be great!' But the fact is, my Montero was not made to fly.

So too, people say, 'I'm going to fly high and live for myself.' But they crash because they weren't made for any other purpose than to glorify God. *That's* why they exist. *All* things were made by and for Jesus. And that includes us.

SEPTEMBER 14

And he is before all things, and by him all things consist.

Colossians 1:17

There's an interesting law of science called Coulomb's Law of Electricity which very simply says like charges repel. If you have a magnet in your right hand and a magnet in your left hand, and you push the positive ends towards each other, they push away. Opposite charges attract; like charges repel. But here's a great mystery: in the nucleus of the atom, protons are packed together which are *all* positive-charged particles.

What keeps these positive-charged protons from repelling like the magnets? What holds them together? Science doesn't know. You can study quantum physics and learn lots of hypotheses and theories, yet to this day, it's a mystery to scientists—but not to believers, for Scripture tells us the real answer. It is Jesus Christ who holds all things together. And the day is coming when, suddenly, He will let go...

But the day of the Lord will come as a thief in the night; in the which the heavens shall pass away with a great noise, and the elements shall melt with fervent heat, the earth also and the works that are therein shall be burned up.

II Peter 3:10

This was written, of course, before man knew anything about nuclear physics or about things being dissolved instantaneously. But now we know if the 'atomic glue' which holds the atom together were to suddenly disappear, everything would dissolve in zillion-degree 'fervent heat' accompanied by a 'great noise' so powerful and quick it wouldn't even be heard.

For, behold, I create new heavens and a new earth:
and the former shall not be remembered, nor come
into mind.

Isaiah 65:17

Everything will vaporize and evaporate as if it never existed. Not only that, but in heaven, even the memory will be taken away. Think about that next time you're hammering, painting, fixing your house. Of course, we should be good stewards of the things with which God has blessed us, but we must have the right perspective, always remembering that the things of this earth are temporary.

By *Him* all things are held together—not just physically, but in my life personally. My emotions, my family, my mental stability—He holds it all together. I forget that sometimes. Things fall apart, and I fly off the handle whenever I take myself out of His custody and say, 'Lord, that's MY thing. That's MY situation, MY problem, MY challenge. I'LL dealt with it!'

No. By *Him* all things are held together. By *Him* all things consist.

SEPTEMBER 15

For it pleased the Father that in him should all fulness
dwell.

Colossians 1:19

All fullness is in Jesus. Therefore, the closer I am to Jesus, the fuller I will be as a man. Conversely, the further I pull away from Jesus, the emptier I'll feel inside. All of creation centers around Jesus, is held together by Jesus, points to Jesus, and finds its fulfillment in Jesus. It's all about Jesus.

Some people compartmentalize their Christianity like a Swanson's TV Dinner. They've got their recreation section, their relationship section, their financial section, their hobby section, and their Christian section. So on Sunday they concentrate on church; Monday through Friday on money; evenings on relationships, and Saturday on sports and hobbies.

But ultimately, they find it frustrating and ineffective because God intended our lives not to be TV dinners, but chicken pot pies—all stirred together so that when we're skiing, we're praising God for the beauty around us; when we're at work, we're praying, 'Lord, help me use this as a point of ministry'; when we're with family, we're seeking not a break *from* service, but an opportunity *for* service. It's all mixed together.

If you continue to 'TV-Dinner' it, you're going to be depressed and discouraged. But it won't be because God is punishing you. It will simply be the result of your failure to understand that Jesus holds all things *together*, that in Him all fullness dwells.

SEPTEMBER 16

Whereof I am made a minister, according to the dispensation of God which is given to me for you, to fulfil the word of God; Even the mystery which hath been hid from ages and from generations, but now is made manifest to his saints: To whom God would make known what is the riches of the glory of this mystery among the Gentiles; which is Christ in you, the hope of glory.

Colossians 1:25-27

The mystery is Christ living in you, not just telling you what to do...

I spent hours upon hours watching the same film loop over and over. I was attending Biola University, where I threw the discus. The film loop was of Jay Silvester's world record discus throw. My teammates and I watched the way Silvester pivoted his feet. We watched the way he led with his hips. We watched the way he kept his arm behind him until the chest broke through the 'glass wall' before it came through and released the platter. Truly, it was a thing of beauty! But although I watched the film thousands of times, and although I tried an equal number of times to duplicate what Jay Silvester did, I never came close.

So too, a lot of Christians are looking at the film loops. They study the Scriptures by the hour, which is wonderful, but it will ultimately lead to frustration until they understand the mystery. You see, if Jay Silvester could have left the film loop and taken up residence within my body, I would have pivoted perfectly, landed my feet just right, led with my hip, and tossed the discus for a world record.

'*This* is the mystery,' writes Paul. '*This* is what I'm coming to share with you. It's not you being like Christ. It's Christ *in* you, showing you how to pray, what to do, and how to spend your time as He writes His will on your heart' (Jeremiah 31).

It's not imitation.
It's impartation.
It's Christ *in* us—the hope of glory!

September 17

Whereunto I also labour, striving according to his working, which worketh in me mightily.
Colossians 1:29

Mom and dad, that which you will most effectively communicate to your kids is that which works in you. Sunday school teacher, youth worker, home group leader—what will ultimately be fruitful in your ministry is that which has personally been worked through and lived out by you. So many ministries lack power because they are based on sharing concepts which are true but which lack impact because they haven't been worked out in the life of the teacher.

Gang, I'll tell you what to share with your kids, neighbors, friends, or third-grade Sunday school class: share what works in *your* life because it's not how much you know, it's how *well* you know what you know.

Has what you're teaching been worked out through your life? Has it become a part of you? If you share only what you've heard from others, your teaching will be dry. However, if, like Paul, you share that which 'worketh in you mightily,' your teaching will be anointed because it will truly be Christ *in* you ministering the hope of glory.

SEPTEMBER 18

> *In whom are hid all the treasures of wisdom and knowledge.*
>
> Colossians 2:3

All wisdom, all knowledge is in—not from—Jesus. Whoever desires wisdom to navigate life successfully must come to the realization that there is nothing more, nothing less, nothing else than Jesus. All treasures of wisdom are in Him.

William Randolph Hearst, the billionaire publisher, became rather eccentric in his later years. One day, looking through a book of famous artwork, a painting caught his eye. 'I want this painting for my collection,' he said to his aides. But after making some inquiries, his aides reported that they were unable to locate the particular work.

'If you value your jobs,' Hearst barked, 'do whatever it takes to find that treasure, and secure it for me immediately.'

Three and a half months later, the aides returned to Hearst. 'Did you find the treasure?' he asked.
'Yes,' they replied. 'After much searching and painstaking research, we found it.'
'Did you purchase it?' he asked.
'No.'
'Why not?' Hearst demanded.
'Because we found it in your warehouse.'

So too, Paul says to the Colossians, 'You already have all the wisdom and knowledge you will ever need to get through life successfully. It's all in Christ. When you got Him, you got it all.'

September 19

And this I say, lest any man should beguile you with enticing words. For though I be absent in the flesh, yet am I with you in the spirit, joying and beholding your order, and the stedfastness of your faith in Christ.
Colossians 2:4-5

In the days of the Roman Empire, a certain wealthy senator became estranged from his son. When he died unexpectedly, his will was opened. 'Because my son does not appreciate what I've done, I leave all of my worldly possessions to my loyal slave, Marcellus,' the will read. 'However, because I am a man of grace, I bequeath to my son one of my possessions of his choosing.'

'Sorry,' said the testator to the son. 'You can only take one of your dad's possessions. Which will it be?'
'I take Marcellus,' said the son.

Brilliant!

That's the idea. When you take Jesus Christ, you get all the treasures of wisdom and knowledge. When you open your heart to Him, you find everything you need. It's all in Him.

Why is this understanding so important?—because it is the only way to keep from being sucked into 'enticing words,' cults and other dead-end pursuits of pseudo-spirituality.

That's what was happening in Colosse. People were coming on the scene saying, 'Hey, what Paul is preaching is fine, but there's much more.'

'No,' Paul says, 'Be steadfast in your faith in Christ. All of the treasures of wisdom and knowledge are hid in *Him*.'

SEPTEMBER 20

As ye have therefore received Christ Jesus the Lord,
so walk ye in him.

Colossians 2:6

Over and over the Scriptures tell us:

> To walk in light (Ephesians 5:8),
> To walk in love (Ephesians 5:2),
> To walk in wisdom (Colossians 4:5).

And here we are told to walk in simplicity. The Christian life is not a run, not a leap, but a walk. To grow in Christ, to advance in our faith, to claim new ground for the Kingdom, we gotta keep walking.

The banks of a certain river in Arizona called the Rio Rivera are lined with a substance called 'near quicksand.' It's almost quicksand—but not quite. If you keep walking on this near-quicksand, you won't have a problem. But if you stop, you'll start sinking and get sucked in.

So too, the Christian experience is a walk. If we don't keep moving, we'll start sinking. And the way to keep moving is not to seek some deeper truth. The way to keep moving is to walk in simplicity. We received Christ simply, totally, completely by faith. And that's the way we are to walk.

SEPTEMBER 21

Blotting out the handwriting of ordinances that was against us, which was contrary to us, and took it out of the way, nailing it to his cross.

Colossians 2:14

The sins which have plagued you are written on a list. Santa Claus makes a list and checks it twice in order to find out who's naughty and nice. Our Father, on the other hand, makes a list and checks it once. Then He nails it to the Cross, where the blood of His Son covers it completely. The list of our sins, shortcomings, and stupidity is blotted out in totality by the blood of the Son of God.

Many Christians aren't healthy because they fail to understand this foundational and profoundly simple principle. They know they're forgiven, but they can't believe the one who hurt them is.

'You can't ignore the abuse, the trauma, the anxiety which has been inflicted upon you,' they are told. 'It must be dealt with.'

Wait a minute! It wasn't ignored, and it *has* been dealt with by Jesus' blood on the Cross. He hung on the Cross of Calvary dying for the very sin which bugs us in others. Therefore, for us to say, 'We gotta dig it up and talk it through,' makes a mockery of what Christ did on Calvary.

'It is *finished*,' Jesus declared. It's done. It's paid for. So be forgiven and forgive one another.

SEPTEMBER 22

And having spoiled principalities and powers, he made a shew of them openly, triumphing over them in it.

Colossians 2:15

When a Roman general conquered an enemy, he would return to Rome in a triumphal procession. The general would ride in the lead chariot, followed by his soldiers. Behind the soldiers walked the conquered men, chained and often naked, to the derisive jeers of the crowds which lined the streets. Paul borrows this image in this verse.

The only toehold or handgrip a demon has on someone is his sin. But if the sin has been washed away by the blood of the Son, the demon has nothing upon which to cling.

Once forgiveness is understood and blood is appropriated, the powers of darkness are rendered powerless.

That's why Peter tells us that when Jesus died, He went into the lower parts of the earth and told the demonic spirits they no longer had authority over us (I Peter 3:19).

If I understand and rejoice in the blood of Christ, demonic powers are nakedly impotent. But they are squatters nonetheless. They won't leave until I say, 'Hey, you gotta go! I'm not going to listen to this depression you're whispering in my ear this morning. I'm not going to buy it because of the blood of Jesus Christ.'

That's what is meant by pleading the blood. It's not a phrase you use, it's an understanding you have. Wherever I plead the blood of Christ, Satan doesn't have influence over me. Let this sink in, gang, and you will really be set free.

SEPTEMBER 23

If ye then be risen with Christ, seek those things
which are above...

                                      Colossians 3:1

The only people who are truly happy on earth are those whose hearts are in heaven.

Peter John came into the kitchen this morning whistling and smiling. 'Sixteen more days, Dad,' he said. Sixteen more days until graduation, and he's through with high school. He sees the finish line. Consequently, it causes him to go through the last couple weeks of school whistling.

I am thoroughly convinced from watching people and studying the Word that the people who are truly content are those who constantly realize that this world is not where it's at. On the other hand, those who try to find happiness here are perpetually frustrated. The possessions they purchase are never quite what they were supposed to be. The relationships they form are never as satisfying as they thought they would be. The dreams they pursue are never as fulfilling as they hoped they would be. Nothing is ever quite right until we realize, 'Hey, it's not here!'

I believe this is why the Lord constantly tells us in the Word to set our hearts on things *above*. People are bogged down, with stomachs churning, brows furrowing, and hearts breaking because they are taking life on earth far too seriously. When a person finally understands heaven is where it's at, he is free to enjoy life. It doesn't matter where he lives, what he does vocationally, what kind of car he drives, bike he rides, or skates he gets around on. All of that is irrelevant because he sees the finish line—he realizes that graduation is only sixteen days away. Set your heart on things above. It's a central message not only of Paul's but also throughout all of Scripture. Live for heaven, and you'll enjoy life.

SEPTEMBER 24

Set your affection on things above, not on things on the earth.

Colossians 3:2

Set your heart on things above. Live for heaven, and you'll enjoy life. How does that happen? Many ways, but I'll suggest three...

Number One: your treasure. Jesus said, 'Wherever your treasure is, there will your heart be also' (Matthew 6:21).

For one week, I had a crush on Denise Fuller and wanted to take her to our church youth group's spring banquet. In order to pay for it, however, I had to sell my one share of American Motors stock which I had bought for twelve bucks. Now, I was really into my one share of stock—so much so that, although I was a big San Francisco Giants fan, before I checked out the box scores to see how Mays, Cepeda, and McCovey were doing each day, I turned to the stock page to check on American Motors' progress. But when this banquet came up, I sold my one share of stock. And guess what. Once I sold my share, I never turned to the stock page again. I just lost interest.

When Jesus tells us to lay up treasure in heaven (Matthew 6: 20), it's not God's way of raising money. Knowing that where our treasure is, our heart will follow, it's His way of raising our hearts and minds out of this world and up into heaven. You see, if you invest your treasure in American Motors, that's where your heart will be. If you put your treasure in your house or hobby, your heart will be there as well. Your heart follows your treasure—so one of the ways we get our hearts on things above is by investing in the Kingdom.

Secondly, we live for heaven through our trials. I am convinced God will send a trial a day our way just to keep us homesick for heaven. If He didn't, we would become bound up in this earth and would miss out eternally on what He has in store for us.

A third way the Lord gets me to set my heart and mind on things above is by transfers—when the people we love precede us into heaven. This process is very important because when you have transferred friends, parents, and spouses in heaven, your heart longs to be there all the more keenly.

Treasures, trials, and transfers—three ways our hearts can be constantly set on things above.

SEPTEMBER 25

And let the peace of God rule in your hearts, to the which also ye are called in one body; and be ye thankful.

Colossians 3:15

The word translated 'rule' is a Greek word which describes an official at an athletic event, similar to a present-day umpire. When people ask, 'Should I move? Should I take that job? Should I marry him?' I often answer with a question: what's your heart telling you? If you're walking with the Lord, the peace of God will be an umpire in your heart calling 'Safe!' or 'Out!'

Women, when he asks you to marry him, don't say yes if there isn't a deep sense of peace in your heart. 'You just have cold feet,' he'll say. But I suggest it is much more than cold feet. It is God working deep within your soul.

Don't move, gang, without the peace of God umpiring and ruling in your heart.

SEPTEMBER 26

And whatsoever ye do, do it heartily, as to the Lord, and not unto men.

Colossians 3:23

The man God uses is a man who knows how to work...

It was when Moses was tending his father-in-law's sheep that God appeared to Him in the burning bush (Exodus 3).

It was when Elisha was plowing with 12 yoke of oxen that Elijah cast the mantle of ministry upon him (I Kings 19:19).

It was when Peter and Andrew were casting their nets that Jesus called them to be fishers of men (Matthew 4:19).

It was when Saul was laboring for the high priest on his way to Damascus that Jesus appeared to him and turned his life around (Acts 9).

Many people who want to be missionaries, ministers, or youth pastors are just sitting 'waiting on God.' But they will still be sitting at age 30, 40, 50, 60, and 70. The answer is to work. Whatever you're doing, do it heartily to the Lord—for it is then that God will tap you on the shoulder and give you tasks that are even more significant for the Kingdom.

SEPTEMBER 27

...And watch in the same with thanksgiving.
Colossians 4:2

One morning, during an eclipse in the Middle Ages, people woke expecting day to dawn. When it didn't, they were terrified. 'Oh, no!' they cried. 'The sun didn't rise today.' When the sun did at last appear, the people cheered, clapped, and blessed God for the sunshine which they had previously taken for granted.

How good it would be for us to wake up and say, 'Thank You for a new day, Father. I'm alive. The sun is out. There's air to breathe. I'm not a slug.'

Personally, I don't think there's anything more abhorrent than grumpy believers. Don't they realize how *good* God has been to them?

They're going to heaven.
They have the Scriptures.
The Spirit indwells them.

Therefore, I don't think there's a single excuse for a rational person to be grumpy. Thanksgiving should flow from our lips constantly.

SEPTEMBER 28

Withal praying also for us, that God would open unto us a door of utterance, to speak the mystery of Christ, for which I am also in bonds: That I may make it manifest, as I ought to speak.

Colossians 4:3-4

Intriguing. Paul says, 'Pray for me, pray for us—not that we'll get out of here, but that the Word will go forth from here.' I think if I were Paul, I would have said, 'Please pray for me that I'll get outta here. I'm tired of being in prison.' Not so Paul. He says, 'My desire is that God's Word will go forth from here, that those around me will really see that Christ lives in me.' Truly, this is the way to pray.

A few months ago, I saw a billboard which said: Pray... it works. And I thought, 'True—but what if it doesn't work?' Most of the time we pray small prayers like, 'Get me outta here.' And when they don't work, we stop praying instead of learning what prayer really is. Prayer is not to get God to see things my way, but rather to get me to see things His way.

This *Associated Press* story caught my eye: walking into her house to answer the phone, Cindy Hartman of Conway, Arkansas, was confronted by a burglar who, after ripping the phone out of the wall, ordered her into the closet. Hartman dropped to her knees and asked the burglar if she could pray for him. 'I want you to know that God loves you and I forgive you,' she said. The burglar looked at her and apologized for what he had done. Then he yelled out the door to a woman in a pickup truck, 'We gotta unload all this. She's a Christian lady. We can't do this to her!' Hartman remained on her knees, and the burglar returned the furniture he had already taken from her home. Then he took the bullets out of his gun, handed her the gun, and walked out the door.

Fascinating story. You see, Cindy Hartman could have prayed, 'Get me out of here,' but instead she prayed like Paul. 'Could I pray for you?' she asked the burglar. *That's* in harmony with the heart of God. How do I know? Because of what Jesus said on the Cross. He didn't say, 'Get Me out of here,' He said, 'Father, forgive them. They don't understand what's going on' (Luke 23:34).

How I want to be more like Paul. I've got so much to learn in this arena—but I see the principle and the rightness of what Paul is modeling here as he prays not to get out of prison, but that he'll have boldness and wisdom in any situation.

SEPTEMBER 29

Walk in wisdom toward them that are without, redeeming the time.

Colossians 4:5

Somehow, we think we're going to live a long time, but James was right when he said life is a vapor, a puff of steam (4:14). Life goes by so fast. Make it count.

How?

Redeem it. Find ways in which you can say, 'I don't want to waste this time because I don't have a lot of time left!'

According to USA Today, the average American will spend six months of his life waiting at red lights. People say, 'I just don't have time to pray'—but what if they decided that at every red light they would pray for people in the Fellowship, for people in the Rogue Valley who don't know Jesus, for people in the world who have never heard His name?

What if they decided to keep an open Bible on the seat next to them in order to read a verse or two during every red light? People say they don't have time to read, to pray, to memorize, to study. Yes they do. I'm not even talking about getting up at 3 a.m. I'm talking about just using the time they're at stoplights.

Oh, that we would redeem the time!

SEPTEMBER 30

Aristarchus my fellowprisoner saluteth you, and Marcus, sister's son to Barnabas...

Colossians 4:10

Remember the story in Acts 12? Setting off on their first missionary journey, Paul and Barnabas take John Mark, Barnabas' nephew, with them. Then somewhere in the early part of the journey, John Mark freaks out and runs home. At the outset of their second missionary trip, Barnabas says, 'I'll get John Mark, and we'll be on our way.'

'Hold on,' Paul says. 'John Mark flipped out and failed us last time. He's not coming again.'
'Yes he is,' said Barnabas, son of Comfort.
'No way,' said Paul. 'There's work to do. We can't have this guy tag along with us. He just doesn't have what it takes.'
'I'm taking John Mark,' said Barnabas
'Fine,' said Paul. 'Go your way. I'll take Silas, and we'll go in a different direction.'

And they parted company.

Years later, we see that Barnabas' work was successful with John Mark, for here in Colossians Paul salutes him.

So too, you who feel like you 'missed the mark,' that God opened a door for you to do something, but you failed—take heart. I don't care how badly you messed up, He's not through with you.

You think you're a failure? Consider this man. He had less than three years of formal education and failed in business in '31. He was defeated for State Legislature in '32, and failed again in business in '34. Finally elected to the State Legislature in '35, he ran for Speaker and lost in a landslide. He was defeated again for Elector in '40 and for Congress in '43. Elected in '46, he was tossed out of office two years later, defeated in a reelection attempt in '48. Failing in business once again, he ran for Senate, but was defeated in '55. He ran for Vice President in '56, was crushed, and was defeated for Senate another time in '58. And then in '60, 1860, Abraham Lincoln won—and went on to become perhaps the greatest political leader in American history.

Could it be that the wit, wisdom, and understanding of human nature which he exhibited so powerfully came as a result of the setbacks, failures, and defeats Lincoln had experienced previously?

Don't despair, precious people. John Mark blew it badly, but came through ultimately. So can you.

OCTOBER 1

Luke, the beloved physician, and Demas, greet you.
Colossians 4:14

In the book of Philemon, which preceded the book of Colossians by a couple of years, Demas is called a fellowservant (verse 24). Approximately six years after this, there's a third mention of Demas, where right before Paul dies, he says, 'Demas has forsaken us, having loved this present world' (II Timothy 4:10). So Demas went from being a fellowservant to one who turned his back on the Lord because he loved the world.

How did this happen? Here's how: the Christian life is like a steam locomotive. When you're first saved and on fire, you stoke the boiler with the Word. You come to church, you're involved in ministry, and you're moving along in your faith. But there can come a time when you start to think, 'Hey, I'm cruising along fine. I don't need to feed the fire so fervently. I don't need to study Scripture so consistently. I don't need to have devotions daily. I don't need to go to church regularly because, look, I'm really moving!'

But here's the deal, gang. Once the fire stops being fed, the engine starts slowing down, although imperceptibly at first. Yes, the train keeps moving down the tracks for a time, and everything appears to be going fine, but little by little the engine goes slower and slower until finally it stops dead in its tracks.

You might be able to go weeks, months, even years on the momentum you gained in the early days—but if you don't continue to feed the fire, eventually you'll stop altogether. And, like Demas, you'll say, 'What happened? How did I end up *here*?'

OCTOBER 2

We give thanks to God always for you all, making mention of you in our prayers; Remembering without ceasing your work of faith, and labour of love, and patience of hope in our Lord Jesus Christ, in the sight of God and our Father.

I Thessalonians 1:2-3

I believe a mature believer will possess the same three characteristics Paul saw in the Thessalonian church...

First, a mature believer demonstrates the work of faith.

'Master, what must we do to do the *works* of God?' the disciples asked in John 6.
'This is the *work* of God,' Jesus answered, 'that you believe on Him whom the Father has sent.'

When a believer says, 'We believe in Jesus Christ and marvel at what He did on the Cross'—*that* is the work of faith.

Secondly, a mature believer labors in love—which is only logical because whenever a person begins to comprehend how much the Lord has done for him, he can't help but love others.

During his visit to the Boys' Town orphanage in the 1940s, a reporter for *Life* Magazine observed a ten-year-old boy carrying a much older boy on his back.

'Isn't he heavy?' asked the reporter.
'He ain't heavy,' said the younger boy. 'He's my brother'—giving rise to the song which would later be written about this true story.

It's not a burdensome obligation, but a labor of love which says, 'God's been so good to me that I can't help but carry someone else.'

Thirdly, a mature believer patiently hopes for the return of the Lord. The night before Jesus' crucifixion, after telling His disciples He would be betrayed, Jesus arose from supper, girded Himself with a towel, and began to wash their feet. Why? Scripture says it was because He knew from whence He came and where He was going (John 13:3).

Knowing we're going to heaven is a key ingredient of maturity because heaven alone allows us to see the big picture and puts everything in perspective.

OCTOBER 3

For neither at any time used we flattering words, as
ye know, nor a cloke of covetousness; God is witness:
Nor of men sought we glory, neither of you, nor yet of
others, when we might have been burdensome, as the
apostles of Christ.

I Thessalonians 2:5-6

Whether it be in the business world, the sports world, or the arena of ministry, don't covet someone else's position. Don't say, 'I want that cloke; I want that spot, so I'll use whatever flattery or treachery it takes to get it.'

I am reminded of the account in I Kings 22...

'Listen Joe,' said King Ahab of Israel to King Jehoshaphat of Judah, 'I've got a problem with the Syrians. So let's form an alliance and battle them together at Ramoth Gilead.'

Jehoshaphat agreed and, upon his arrival at Ramoth Gilead, found Ahab waiting for him. According to the Septuagint, Ahab suggested Jehoshaphat wear his royal robes. Jehoshaphat agreed, and off they went into battle. Unbeknownst to Jehoshaphat, however, the Syrian army had been instructed to spare everyone save the king of Israel. Consequently, imagine Jehoshaphat's surprise when, cloaked in the king of Israel's robes, he found the entire Syrian army heading straight for him.

'Wait a minute! I didn't ask for this,' you'll say as the arrows of criticism fly towards you. Oh, but you did when you coveted that position on the team, that space in the office, that spot behind the pulpit.

That's why Paul didn't come to the Thessalonians with flattery and manipulation. Instead, he came with simplicity and honesty.

OCTOBER 4

For what is our hope, or joy, or crown of rejoicing? Are not even ye in the presence of our Lord Jesus Christ at his coming? For ye are our glory and joy.
                        I Thessalonians 2:19-20

'Yes, we've been beaten up in the city,' writes Paul. 'Yes, we've been chased down by envious Jews. Yes, we're going through real persecution. But you know what? It's all worth it because you're getting saved.'

The greatest joy in the world comes from seeing someone:

> For whom you've been praying,
>   With whom you've been sharing,
>   To whom you've been witnessing,
>   Receive Christ.

Jesus tells us when one person is saved, all of heaven rejoices (Luke 15:7). Truly, joy and evangelism go hand in hand. Thus, my prayer is that we would never lose sight of the privilege, priority, and pure joy of sharing the Good News with people who don't know Jesus.

OCTOBER 5

That no man should be moved by these afflictions: for yourselves know that we are appointed thereunto.

I Thessalonians 3:3

'Don't feel bad about our situation,' Paul is saying. 'Don't be surprised to hear people are chasing us around Greece, throwing rocks at us, trying to destroy us. Appointments with trouble are already in our Daytimers. We told you this would happen. It's all part of the program.'

'Welcome this man,' the Lord told Ananias concerning Paul, 'for I'm going to show him he must suffer greatly for the sake of the Kingdom' (Acts 9:16). This prophecy, given at the very outset of Paul's ministry, would indeed prove to be true.

'Blessed be the Father of mercies, the God of comfort,' Paul would later write to the Corinthians, 'Who comforts us in our troubles that we may be able to comfort others with the comfort we ourselves have received' (II Corinthians 1:4).

A.W. Tozer was right when he said, 'Before God can use a person greatly, He must allow that person to be hurt deeply.'

This isn't because God is mean, but because He knows we can't comfort others unless we've been comforted ourselves.

October 6

For verily, when we were with you, we told you before
that we should suffer tribulation; even as it came to
pass, and ye know.

I Thessalonians 3:4

Trials not only enable us to comfort others, but they purify our own faith as well. That's why Peter said, 'Don't think it strange concerning the fiery trials which come your way. These fiery trials are sent to test and purify your faith' (I Peter 4:12).

What happens when you are in a fiery trial? Shadrach, Meshach, and Abed-nego will tell you: Jesus shows up (Daniel 3:25). That's why James tells us to count it all joy when we fall into trials (James 1:2).

'Whoopee! A trial! How wonderful!' Crazy? Not really, because if you have this mindset in your difficult times, you will see Jesus in a way that will,

Blow your mind,
  Warm your heart,
    And bless your socks off!

Trials don't make or break us, gang. They simply reveal what's inside...

When I hit a bump, the tea which splashes out of the mug on my dashboard was there before the bump. The bump doesn't put the tea in; it just shows what was already in the cup.

'I'm angry because of what he or she did to me.' No. The anger was already there. The bump just brought it out. Truly, the only way a man can really know how he's doing is through bumpy, discouraging, heartbreaking times, for they alone reveal the heart.

OCTOBER 7

Now God himself and our Father, and our Lord Jesus
Christ, direct our way unto you. And the Lord make
you to increase and abound in love one toward
another, and toward all men, even as we do toward
you.

I Thessalonians 3:11-12

There come points in my walk when I say, 'You know, I'm doing pretty good.' I get comfortable as apathy begins to creep into my heart. And the Spirit, speaking through Paul, would give this exhortation to me: 'Jon, the Lord make you to *increase*. I rejoice in what's happening in your life, but may your love for Me grow to an ever-deepening measure.'

'Moab hath been at ease and settled in his lees. Therefore I will pour him out from vessel to vessel,' saith the Lord (Jeremiah 48:11).

The reference is to the way wine was made in Jeremiah's day whereby the winemaker would pick grapes, put them in a vat, stomp on them to get the juice flowing, and then pour the juice into a vessel, wherein the wine sat until the lees, or dregs, settled to the bottom.

The winemaker would then pour the wine into another vessel, leaving the dregs behind, where it would sit while more dregs settled. This process was repeated up to six times, until the end result was wine without any dregs—wine which was pure and sparkling.

'I was just getting comfy,' we cry, 'when my:
  Boss said, "You're through,"
    Girlfriend said, "Goodbye,"
      Coach said, "On the bench."'

'Great!' the Lord says. 'I want to refine and use you as the wine of My Spirit flows through you. But for that to happen, there will be regular seasons where you are poured. Otherwise you'll become cloudy and dull, as you settle in your lees—and I love you too much for that.'

October 8

Paul, and Silvanus, and Timotheus, unto the church of the Thessalonians in God our Father and the Lord Jesus Christ: Grace unto you, and peace, from God our Father and the Lord Jesus Christ. We are bound to thank God always for you, brethren, as it is meet, because that your faith groweth exceedingly, and the charity of every one of you all toward each other aboundeth.

II Thessalonians 1:1-3

In the first verse of his first letter to the Thessalonians, Paul had commended their work of faith, labor of love, and patience of hope. Here, in his second letter, he commends only their faith and love.

Why?

No longer living for the Second Coming of Christ, they had lost their hope.

Of faith, hope, and love, the greatest is love (I Corinthians 13:13)—however, all three elements are essential because it is faith and hope which allow us to love.

How?

Hung up by my past sins, I'd be too *ashamed* to love. But faith tells me my past sins and failures were totally cleansed by the blood of Jesus. Worried about the future, I'd be too *afraid* to love. But hope tells me He's coming again, so there's no need to fear the future.

OCTOBER 9

Which is a manifest token of the righteous judgment of
God, that ye may be counted worthy of the kingdom of
God, for which ye also suffer.

II Thessalonians 1:5

'The fact that you are persecuted and put down is proof that you're a part of the Kingdom,' declares Paul. He would say the same thing to Timothy by writing, 'Yea, all those who live godly in Christ Jesus shall suffer persecution' (II Timothy 3:12).

Hmm. So often I pray to avoid pressures, problems, and persecutions, when, in reality, it is those very things which would have produced Christ-like qualities within me. There is really no other way.

If you want to be like Jesus, hard times are inevitable.

'I want to shine like a diamond in the Kingdom,' we say. You know what a diamond is? It's a chunk of worthless coal which has undergone tremendous amounts of pressure over many, many years. So if you say in your heart, 'I want to reflect Jesus,' know this: there is no other way that will happen than to go through fiery trials over great lengths of time—which is why Peter talks about our faith being purified by fiery trials (I Peter 4:12), and why James says, 'Count it all joy when you go through these trials' (James 1:2).

Although I know this in theory, I still find myself praying, 'Lord, I don't want to deal with this. Lord, I don't want to go through that. Lord, do I have to go *there*? Lord, get me out of here!' In reality, such prayers are unwise because they can actually hinder the work the Lord was doing in me through those very difficulties.

Consequently, I am praying less and less, 'Lord, help me Yourself,' and more and more, 'Lord, help Yourself to me. I am tired of directing You. Put me wherever *You* see I'll be happy and most fruitful. *You* know best.'

OCTOBER 10

When he shall come to be glorified in his saints, and to be admired in all them that believe (because our testimony among you was believed) in that day. Wherefore also we pray always for you, that our God would count you worthy of this calling, and fulfil all the good pleasure of his goodness, and the work of faith with power: That the name of our Lord Jesus Christ may be glorified in you, and ye in him, according to the grace of our God and the Lord Jesus Christ.

II Thessalonians 1:10-12

When Jesus comes, He will be glorified not *among* His saints—but *in* them.

I venture to guess that none of us bought the latest *Ladies Home Journal* expecting to see our names on the Ten Most Admired People list. Nor did we buy the latest edition of *Who's Who in America*, eager to see our names inside.

You see, this is not our day. This is the 'day of man' (Job 10:5)—'man' referring to fallen humanity. But when Jesus returns, He will be glorified and admired in all who believe. This means we'll see Jesus in each other. 'Wow, I thought you were a lightweight,' we'll say; or, 'I thought you were weird; or, 'I thought you were callous, cruel, pompous, or vain. But now look at you! I see *Jesus* in you!'

Oh, to have such a mindset this side of eternity—to join Paul in 'knowing no man after the flesh' (II Corinthians 5:16), but instead seeing Jesus glorified in His saints even now.

OCTOBER 11

Who opposeth and exalteth himself above all that is called God, or that is worshipped; so that he as God sitteth in the temple of God...

II Thessalonians 2:4

'Little children,' wrote John, 'it is the last time: and as ye have heard that antichrist shall come, even now are there many antichrists; whereby we know that it is the last time' (I John 2:18).

The word 'anti' does not only mean 'against.' It also means 'in place of.' Thus, the spirit of antichrist can be in the temple of my own body. I'm not talking about demons, but about the mindset which leads me to say,

'I don't need to rely on Christ.
    I don't need to pray about my kids today.
        I don't need to pray about how to use my time.'

And what will be the result? The same thing which will follow the physical antichrist: I will experience 'famine, wars, and rumors of wars' (Matthew 24:4-8). I'll have problems in my marriage, my family, my ministry.

That's why people often go through unnecessary tribulation. They could have been 'raptured to heaven' by spending time seeking the Lord in the morning. They could have been 'caught up in the clouds to meet Him in the air' and thus gained a heavenly perspective on the day before them. But instead they chose to captain their own ship, plot their own course, and rely on their own wisdom instead of Christ's.

Oh, none of us here are antichrist in the sense that we're against Him. But each of us here is vulnerable to the subtle thinking which takes the place of Christ whereby we make our own decisions and call our own shots. The spirit of antichrist can pollute any of us. Let's be wise and say, 'My temple is dedicated to only One: Jesus Christ. *He* will reign in my heart. *He* will rule my life.'

October 12

Therefore, brethren, stand fast, and hold the traditions which ye have been taught, whether by word, or our epistle.

II Thessalonians 2:15

Newer translations correctly render the word 'traditions' as 'ordinances.' There are those who say, 'Baptism is no longer necessary. The Lord's Table is optional. There's no need to pray the Lord's Prayer. Meeting together for Bible study is helpful, but not crucial.'

Jesus was baptized in water. So was Peter. So was John. So was D.L. Moody, C.H. Spurgeon, and Billy Graham. I may not have the boldness of D.L. Moody, the fervency of C.H. Spurgeon, or the anointing of Billy Graham—but I can stand exactly where they stood in the waters of baptism.

I can sit where the greatest Christians have sat throughout the ages and have the same meal they had as I partake of Communion.

I can't preach like R. A. Torrey or Charles Finney—but I pray exactly as they did when I pray, 'Our Father which art in heaven...'

I don't have the power of the early Church, but I do exactly as they did every time I meet with fellow believers to study the Word (Acts 2:42).

We have a glorious heritage, gang. And Paul would say to us, even as he said to the Thessalonians, 'Don't minimize the traditions. Hold on to them. Your faith will be the richer, your walk will be the surer for it.'

OCTOBER 13

Paul, an apostle of Jesus Christ, by the commandment
of God our Saviour, and Lord Jesus Christ, which is
our hope.

I Timothy 1:1

Paul often referred to himself as 'an apostle by the will of God' (I Corinthians 1:1, II Corinthians 1:1, Ephesians 1:1, Colossians 1:1). In this case, however, he says, 'It's not just His will for me, it's His *command* that I am to be an apostle—one who is sent out, one who shares truth.'

The things that we have been commanded to do can sometimes become wearying when we find ourselves in situations we weren't anticipating—like prison. After all, it was from a Roman prison cell that Paul wrote to Timothy. And in this, I am reminded of another who found himself a prisoner...

'Oh, Lord, I cannot speak. I am but a child,' Jeremiah protested when called to minister.

'Before you were born, I knew you and ordained you to be a prophet,' the Lord replied. 'I will put My words on your lips—and you shall go.'

So Jeremiah did. And what happened? He eventually ended up in a dungeon.

'OK, Lord,' he said. 'Yes, You commanded me. Yes, You anointed me. But people aren't responding. No one is getting saved.'

So Jeremiah decided to quit prophesying, to quit sharing—until he realized that the Word of God was like fire in his bones and that he could not keep quiet (Jeremiah 20:9).

Maybe like Jeremiah, or perhaps like Paul, you feel imprisoned and are tempted to throw in the towel, to quit sharing the Gospel with people since none seem to respond. But if you do, the Word of God will burn in your heart as surely as it did in Jeremiah's, and, like Paul, you will realize you have no choice in the matter, for you are under the command of God.

OCTOBER 14

O Timothy, keep that which is committed to thy trust, avoiding profane and vain babblings, and oppositions of science falsely so called: Which some professing have erred concerning the faith. Grace be with thee. Amen.

I Timothy 6:20-21

After telling us that professionally, we're to be good workers, and financially, we are to be content and generous, Paul moves to his third and final exhortation concerning the Church and her ministry to the world when he says that intellectually, we are to be true to the Word.

If you want to navigate life now and eternally without being embarrassed, study the Scriptures, and do what they tell you to do. Without exception, the times of which I'm ashamed are the times I didn't do what the Word said to do. When I violated the Word, when I did my own thing, when I chose to ignore a command or a principle, it always ended in error and shame.

May the Lord continue to help us walk wisely in these dark and treacherous days. May the Lord give us a heart to continue to study the Word—not academically only, but with a determination to obey it practically.

OCTOBER 15

Thou therefore endure hardness, as a good soldier of
Jesus Christ. No man that warreth entangleth himself
with the affairs of this life; that he may please him
who hath chosen him to be a soldier.

II Timothy 2:3-4

Knowing they would be mowed down by Nazi machine guns, the first soldiers off the landing craft at Omaha Beach charged valiantly. Those who miraculously made it to shore safely began to climb the cliffs, knowing they were most likely climbing to their deaths.

What would cause a man to hit the beach or to climb a cliff knowing he would be gunned down in the process? Subsequent studies have shown that the heroes of D-Day did so out of respect and appreciation for their commanding officer and fellow soldiers.

The concept of fighting for one's country is sometimes too big, too abstract. But risking one's life for one's commander or for the soldiers right beside him makes the goal worthwhile.

Paul didn't give Timothy ten theological reasons why he should serve the Lord. Rather, he gave him only one: to please the Commanding Officer and fellow Soldier who had laid down His life for him.

OCTOBER 16

If we believe not, yet he abideth faithful: he cannot
deny himself.

II Timothy 2:13

You travel with me halfway across the country to Yellowstone National Park. There we are, standing by the fence waiting for Old

Faithful to erupt—as it does every 92 minutes. But after about 30 minutes, you become bored and you see a goose which you follow into the woods. I remain by the fence and see the spectacle of Old Faithful's geyser. You, on the other hand, miss out because you're on a wild goose chase. Finally you say, 'This is dumb. I'm going back to position myself close to Old Faithful again.'

Now, when Old Faithful sees you coming, it doesn't say, 'Well, well, well. Look who's finally decided to show up. There's no way I will erupt for you. You've been on a wild goose chase.' No, Old Faithful erupts regularly, faithfully, no matter where you are or aren't.

Paul is saying that God is, in the best sense of the word, Old Faithful, because His blessings are continually flowing. If I go off on a wild goose chase, I won't be blessed—not because the blessings aren't there, but because I've moved away. But once I realize I'm in the woods on some crazy excursion and return to the geyser of the goodness of God's grace, I find that God is faithful still.

For years, I thought God had to be primed—through praise, prayer, and devotion. And I thought if I could just pump the handle of His blessings hard enough, blessing would start coming my way. But then I realized His grace is there any time I choose to come back to my senses and come back to Him.

God cannot deny Himself, gang. He's not faithful one day, and frustrated the next. He's not generous one day, but stingy the next. He is continually and completely *faithful*.

OCTOBER 17

This know also, that in the last days perilous times
shall come.

II Timothy 3:1

Knowing his death was imminent, I believe Paul nonetheless thought the Rapture would happen either in his lifetime or shortly thereafter. So do I. I believe the Rapture will happen in my lifetime.

'Well,' you say, 'if Paul thought the Rapture would happen in *his* lifetime, and it didn't—and if men of God throughout the ages have felt as though they were living in the last days and the Rapture would happen in *their* lifetimes, and it didn't—doesn't it seem foolish to think the Rapture will happen in *your* lifetime?'

Not at all. Throughout the history of the Church, the greatest men and women of the faith have all lived their lives believing that the Lord's coming was nigh. And even though the Lord didn't come when they thought He would, looking for His return impacted their lives in such a way that they left their mark on history and will be rewarded greatly in eternity (II Timothy 4:8). Luther, Calvin, Spurgeon, Finney, Moody, Torrey all felt the Lord's coming was close at hand. Put me in their company any day!

I choose to live my life looking for the Lord's coming. And if I am wrong, even if He doesn't come back for another 500 years, I would rather go through the days I have left looking for the sudden appearing of Jesus Christ because I know the effect it has upon the life of any man or woman who believes He could come today: one's heart does not get troubled as easily; one is not prone to sin so readily.

If you want to live a zealous, exciting, fulfilling, pure Christian life, live it looking for the Lord's coming (I John 3:3).

OCTOBER 18

In hope of eternal life, which God, that cannot lie, promised before the world began.

Titus 1:2

Paul's intent is that people do better, go further in the glorious hope of eternal life. 'And this is eternal life,' Jesus prayed in His High Priestly prayer, 'that they may know You, the only true God, and Jesus Christ whom You have sent' (John 17:3).

We usually think of eternal life as existing someday far away in heaven. But that's only part of it. According to Jesus' prayer, eternal life is knowing the Lord here and now in our hearts. Thus, the farther I get from the Lord, the more hellish things become. But the days in which I spend time with the Lord, I experience something of heaven on earth. The closer I walk to the Lord, the more heavenly my days will be.

It was after Enoch fathered his son, Methuselah, that Scripture records he began to walk with God (Genesis 5). Kids will make one walk with God—especially a kid like Methuselah. Living to the age of 969, he must have been home for 500 years!

'Enoch walked with God and he was not, for God took him' (Genesis 5:24). I can almost hear the Lord saying, 'You know, Enoch, this walk we've enjoyed together has been so wonderful. You've walked with Me so closely that now we're closer to My house than yours. Come on Home.'

'This is eternal life,' Jesus prayed, 'that they may know You, Father— not out there geographically, but here and now intimately.'

OCTOBER 19

...Zealous of good works. These things speak, and exhort, and rebuke with all authority. Let no man despise thee.

Titus 2:14-15

Telling his contemporaries as well as those younger and older than him the truth would probably not have been easy for Titus. And it may not always be easy for you. But if you're a boss, a Bible study teacher, a parent, or a coach, there are times when you need to speak the truth, as hard as it may be.

Then said I, Ah, Lord GOD! Behold, I cannot speak: for I am a child. But the LORD said unto me, Say not, I am a child: for thou shalt go to all that I shall send thee, and whatsoever I command thee thou shalt speak. Be not afraid of their faces: for I am with thee to deliver thee, saith the LORD. See, I have this day set thee over the nations and over the kingdoms, to root out, and to pull down, and to destroy, and to throw down, to build, and to plant.

Jeremiah 1:6-8, 10

That's what moms and dads, pastors and grandparents, bosses and coaches have to do sometimes. We're called to pull down in order that we may build up.

Purge me with hyssop, and I shall be clean: wash me, and I shall be whiter than snow. Make me to hear joy and gladness; that the bones which thou hast broken may rejoice.

Psalm 51:7-9

As a shepherd, David understood the meaning of broken bones. You see, when a lamb would stubbornly and rebelliously continue to wander away from the flock, the shepherd would break its legs and place the lamb on his shoulder where it would remain until its bones were healed. When the lamb could walk again, so bonded was he with the shepherd, he would never stray again.

Like sheep, we all go astray (Isaiah 53:6). Therefore, in His love, the Good Shepherd breaks a bone or two and carries me while I whine and cry and wonder what He's doing. But as the days and weeks and months go by, I find myself closer to Him than I had ever been previously, and all I can say is, 'Thank You, Lord.'

Part of shepherding means breaking a bone or two. Thus, Titus would have to speak words that could cause tears to flow or bones to snap. But he could do so with authority, knowing it was an opportunity for the wounded sheep to one day walk with its Shepherd more intimately.

OCTOBER 20

I thank my God, making mention of thee always in
my prayers, Hearing of thy love and faith, which thou
hast toward the Lord Jesus, and toward all saints.
Philemon 4-5

There's lots of talk today about preventive medicine—keeping people healthy rather than merely taking care of them when they're sick. Paul here models not preventive medicine, but preventive ministry when he says to Philemon, 'Hearing that your family's walking with the Lord and that there's a church in your house causes me to pray for you constantly.'

We generally only pray for people when we hear they're sick or struggling, going through tough trials or facing hard times. And pray we must. But in addition to that, I suggest we pray like Paul. I suggest we pray for those who are doing well that they might do even better.

It's when the enemy sees people doing well that he decides to launch an attack against them. Why? He knows he's lost their souls, but if he can pull them down in depression or discouragement, he knows they'll be unable to impact others whose souls he's not yet lost. Satan doesn't spend his time on the lost. You will never read in the New Testament where Satan himself is warring against an unbeliever. He saves himself totally and exclusively for those who are in Christ, for those who are walking with God. In every instance where you see Satan in the New Testament, you will always see him coming against believers in order to minimize their effectiveness for the Kingdom.

This makes it all the more important for us to pray for those doing well, for they are sure targets of the enemy.

OCTOBER 21

I beseech thee for my son Onesimus, whom I have begotten in my bonds.

Philemon 10

While he was chained to a Roman guard, Paul came into contact with a man named Onesimus who was a fugitive in the city of Rome, a runaway slave who had stolen goods from his master. It is possible that Paul somehow bumped into Onesimus in the marketplace and began to dialogue with him. It is also possible that Onesimus was apprehended and chained to the same guard as Paul. We are not exactly sure how the paths of Onesimus and Paul crossed, but cross they did.

Onesimus found there was no freedom in freedom itself, for although he was free from his master, he was still a slave to his own conscience, to his own sin. But Onesimus was to discover that although there is slavery in freedom—there is also freedom in slavery.

How?

Jesus calls all who are weary and heavy laden to voluntarily, willingly take His yoke upon them. And all who do, find freedom in their labor for Him. That's why Paul said, 'I am a bondslave—a slave by choice (Romans 1:1). Marriage proves this point, for it is, in a sense, slavery. And it can either be glorious or miserable, depending on with whom you are linked!

The question in this life is not whether or not you're yoked, but to *whom* are you yoked? If we are yoked to Jesus, we are yoked to the quintessentially excellent Master, to the One who loves us so much, to the One who's so good for us and so good to us.

OCTOBER 22

Thou hast loved righteousness, and hated iniquity; therefore God, even thy God, hath anointed thee with the oil of gladness above thy fellows.

Hebrews 1:9

'Because You've loved righteousness and hated iniquity,' said the Father to the Son, 'You are anointed with the oil of gladness above all others.'

Did you know that gladness is directly proportional to holiness? Happiness and holiness go hand in hand. That is why crowds flocked around Jesus. Wasn't He the Man of sorrows (Isaiah 53:3)? Certainly. But there was also a gladness and joy about Him unlike that of any other human being in history. Jesus was immensely attractive to the crowds because holiness and happiness are directly proportional.

Some folks don't see this until they're 40 or 50 or 60-years-old. And some never see it at all. They think holiness is drudgery. They think if they're righteous, they won't be happy, that they'll just have to endure the pain of Christianity. But nothing is further from the truth.

To the extent you choose to be holy is the extent to which you will be happy. Conversely, to the extent you compromise holiness is the extent to which you diminish happiness. It's just that simple.

OCTOBER 23

While it is said, To day if ye will hear his voice, harden not your hearts, as in the provocation. For some, when they had heard, did provoke: howbeit not all that came out of Egypt by Moses.
Hebrews 3:15-16

How were the children of Israel delivered from Egypt? By blood and water—the blood which they applied to the doorposts before Passover, and the water of the Red Sea which drowned the chariots pursuing them.

So too, we are delivered from 'Egypt'—from damnation and destruction—by the blood and water which flowed from Jesus' side on the Cross of Calvary. Yet, like the children of Israel, although they are delivered from Egypt, too many Christians spend their whole lives wandering between Egypt and the land of abundance. Year after year, they trudge through life thinking, 'Well, this is as good as it can get until I die and go to heaven, the Promised Land.'

That's not what God intended for us, gang. He intended to take us out of Egypt, through the wilderness quickly, and into the Promised Land of the Spirit-filled, abundant life. You see, the Promised Land in Bible typology is not a picture of heaven. It's a picture of life in the Spirit. How do I know?

Because while there are no giants in heaven, no battles, no war, the Spirit-filled life is filled with many giants to wrestle, battles to wage, wars to win.

Only Joshua and Caleb realized that giants, battles, and wars notwithstanding, God would indeed give them the Promised Land. And thus, they did not provoke God.

OCTOBER 24

But with whom was he grieved forty years? was it not with them that had sinned, whose carcases fell in the wilderness? And to whom sware he that they should not enter into his rest, but to them that believed not?

Hebrews 3:17-18

To whom did God say, 'You shall not enter into the rest, the Promised Land, the abundance of milk and honey'? I would have thought it would have been to those who worshipped idols, to those who didn't have morning devotions, to immoral men, or to those who didn't offer sacrifices. Yet, in reality, the only thing which kept the children of Israel from the Promised Land was their lack of faith.

This is critically important theology, for the singular sin which kept them from blessing was simply thinking God's promise was just too good to be true. Precious people, you can live the abundant, Spirit-filled, successful, exciting, thrilling Christian life if, instead of saying, 'God can't bless me because I haven't been to Bible study,' or, 'I've been yelling at my husband,' or, 'I haven't had morning devotions regularly,' you say, 'I'm a spiritual grasshopper, Lord. But if You want to bring me into this great land of blessing, I'll gladly go in!'

The sin of Hebrews 3 is singular. It's not fornication, as destructive as that sin may be. It's not idolatry, as sad as that sin is. It's just not believing how good God is.

Recently home from Bible School, Peter John shared with me how passionate he and his friends are about seeing their generation brought into the Kingdom. 'So I get up early in the morning and pray and spend time in the Word. I do so good for about three or four days,' he said. 'But then I get tired. I sleep in. I miss my devotional time. And I don't go to prayer meeting.' With tears running down his cheeks, this football-playing son of mine said, 'Dad, I want to do so well, and I'm not.'

'Peter,' I said, 'when you learn the lesson which took me years and years to understand, you'll be on your way. And that lesson is simply this: blessing, anointing, ministry, fruitfulness, and victory are not about you.'

'It's not about the work you do for the Lord; it's about the work He did for you. It's not about your prayer to the Lord; it's about His intercession for you. It's not about your faith in the Lord; it's about His being faithful when you falter. It's all about *Him* being the Hero, the Prayer Warrior, the Victor, the Friend, and the Faithful One.'

OCTOBER 25

So we see that they could not enter in because of unbelief.

Hebrews 3:19

Gang, the key not only to ministry, but to every area of spirituality is found in John 10...

Of John the Baptist, Jesus said, 'This is the greatest man who ever lived.' Yet Scripture also records John did no mighty miracles (John 10:41). So what made John the greatest man who ever lived? One thing: He wasn't talking about power in prayer; he wasn't teaching victory through discipline; he simply said, 'Behold the Lamb. Check Him out. Follow *Him*.'

Happy is the day when a woman grasps the fact that spiritual life has nothing to do with her and everything to do with God. Happy is the day when a man finally realizes all he has to say is, 'I don't know why You put up with a grasshopper like me, but Lord, if You want to allow me to be in ministry, if You want to give me a family, if You want to bless me in countless ways—that's OK with me!'

Don't let anyone sell you a bill of goods saying, 'The reason I'm so successful is because I pray night and day. And the reason you will never be part of the chosen few is because you don't.'

Any man, *any* woman can leave here tonight to be used mightily and blessed exceedingly beyond anything they could ask or even think if they would just learn to say, 'I believe You, Lord.'

Contrary to what many teach, the deceitfulness of sin is always saying, 'I've got to do more. I've got to be bigger, stronger, better in my spiritual walk so that I can battle the giants ahead of me.'

No, God says *that*'s the sin which will keep you out.

Dear saint, it's all about God's work for you, not your work for Him.

Fix your eyes on Jesus.
  Be blown away by Him.
    Behold the Lamb!

OCTOBER 26

For unto us was the gospel preached, as well as unto them; but the word preached did not profit them, not being mixed with faith in them that heard it.

Hebrews 4:2

What does it mean to mix the Gospel with faith?

We see the answer in Acts 12...

When Herod put Peter in prison, Scripture records that the Church got together and prayed fervently. God sent an angel to Peter as he slept between two guards.

'Arise,' said the angel—and the chains fell off Peter's wrists and legs. So Peter got up and followed the angel into the city even though Scripture tells us he thought it was nothing more than a vision. Walking through the streets of the city, however, he realized it was no dream.

Now, had Peter not stood up and stepped out, had he not started moving, but instead said, 'This is a neat thought, an interesting insight,' had he not mixed the angel's command with faith—even though the chains were off and the door was opened, he would have remained in jail.

What about us? God gives a promise to us, and we say, 'It's a vision. It sheds some esoteric light on theology—but it can't really mean I can step out. So I'll just stay in my prison, wait for my execution, and be comforted with this thought.' No! Get up! Step out! Go for it! And you might discover its reality. Listen folks, the Word being mixed with faith means we stand up and start moving...

You pray for your teenage son, 'Lord, revive him. Bless him. Help him.' Get up and expect him to do well. Start treating him like he *is* doing well, and you'll find the promise is true. But if you stay in your cell, theorizing and saying, 'I need to study deeper on this matter,' you'll never enter the Land of Promise regarding your situation.

How much faith does it take? Look at the believers in Acts 12...

Knock. Knock. Knock. 'It's Peter.'
'No, it can't be Peter. Lord, we pray that You would free Peter.'
Knock. Knock. Knock. 'It's Peter.'
'No, it can't be Peter. Lord, we pray that You would free Peter...'

How much faith did they have? About a mustard seed's worth. But Jesus said that's all it takes to move a mountain. I'm convinced that if you have only enough faith to pray, that's enough to start things happening, to start doors opening. It doesn't take much. The promises, the blessings, the good things of God happen when you take the Word and mix it with faith.

OCTOBER 27

...Seeing ye are dull of hearing.
Hebrews 5:11

The term translated 'dull of hearing' is the word for 'ignorant' in Greek. But the ignorance spoken of is not due to never hearing. Rather, the ignorance spoken of is the result of ignoring. In other words, when truth was shared, the response was, 'Big deal. I don't care what you say. I have my own perspective.'

There are those who say, 'I'm just not getting anything out of Bible study. I go to church, but nothing registers with me. I read the Bible, but it just seems like ink on paper.' Why? It could very well be because they are those who are dull of hearing. Why? Because God spoke to them a week ago, a month ago, a year ago concerning something they were to do. But they ignored it. Why, then, would God keep speaking to them if they refused to do those things He already made clear to them?

It is a loving Father who says, 'Jon, I'm going to make it real simple: when you do step 1, I'll take you to step 2. When you do what I ask, when you incorporate what I show you—then I'll take you further down the road. But I'm not going to keep on heaping instruction and insight upon you if you're only going to ignore what I've already told you.'

Dear saint, what's the last thing God told you to do? Have you done it?

OCTOBER 28

And they shall not teach every man his neighbour,
and every man his brother, saying, Know the Lord: for
all shall know me, from the least to the greatest.

Hebrews 8:11

Our brothers and sisters in the 1st century Church were the most radical Christians in all of history. They sold all of their possessions; they spread throughout the world; they lived for the Kingdom. But you know what? They didn't get together like this and study Hebrews because Hebrews wasn't yet written. They didn't study the theological implications of Romans because Romans wasn't written. They didn't scrutinize the teachings of Jesus as recorded in John's Gospel because John's Gospel wasn't written.

They didn't have the written New Testament—but they did understand the reality of the New Covenant. They obeyed what the Lord was writing in their hearts—and they turned the world upside down (Acts 17:6). Then, when the New Testament was written and began to circulate through the Church, it was a confirmation of what they were already doing because it was the same Lord who had been writing His will for them upon their hearts.

Today, sad to say, many don't understand the New Covenant. Our Trinity is God the Father, God the Son, and God the Holy Bible. We've lost touch with how the Holy Spirit speaks to us moment by moment because we've replaced His voice with the written word. Many churches, and organizations study the Bible and are right in their theology—but they're dead right because theirs is knowledge for knowledge's sake.

The New Testament was never intended to be an esoteric, intellectual, theological trip for people who like to fill notebooks, answer questions, and work on workbooks. That was never the intent of the New Testament writer. What was the intent? To provide a way believers could be confirmed or corrected in what they were already living out as a result of obeying the still, small voice of the Spirit.

The person who's really used by the Lord is one who simply says, 'You're going to tell me moment by moment what I should do, and, Lord, I will just say Yes to whatever You say.' A whole lot of people have made the New Testament writings the new Law. Like Pharisees searching for jots, tittles, and interesting insights, they fail to see that the Word was written to nudge them along in their walk and to confirm the voice of the Lord in their heart.

OCTOBER 29

But without faith it is impossible to please him: for he that cometh to God must believe that he is, and that he is a rewarder of them that diligently seek him.
Hebrews 11:6

Here are two keys to faith, the first being to believe that God is.

'Who do I say You are?' Moses asked God.
'*I AM THAT I AM*,' God answered (Exodus 3:14).

In other words, 'I am whatever you need.' Are you lonely tonight? God is the Friend who's closer than a brother. Are you confused about what to do? He is the Door. Are you feeling like you're walking in a haze? He's the Good Shepherd. Faith hopes for the unseen because it believes God Is.

Secondly, faith believes God is the One who will meet the needs deep within my heart. There are those who believe God is—but they don't really seek Him. Why must we diligently seek God? Why isn't it enough just to believe He is whatever we have need of? Because God knows if we diligently seek Him, the very things we were seeking

Him about will fade in importance as we realize it's *Him* we sought all along.

I believe most of us have no problem with the first of these two keys to faith. We believe God is. But because we don't believe He rewards those who seek Him, we seek Him haphazardly or half-heartedly, if at all.

'I don't have time,' you might be saying. Not true. We have time to golf; time to see the Blazers play; time to water-ski, fix the plumbing, and go to the dentist. Every single one of us has time. No exceptions. We do what we want and make time for what is of value to us.

Throughout history, the common denominator in the lives of those who have been blessed is they have all been those who realize God enjoys our company. And when we seek Him, we're rewarded not because we're going through some legal system, trying to earn brownie points—but just because hanging out with the Lord opens the door to fabulous blessing from Him.

OCTOBER 30

By faith Abraham, when he was called to go out into a place which he should after receive for an inheritance, obeyed; and he went out, not knowing whither he went.

Hebrews 11:8

Abraham didn't know where he was going—he just started moving. Most of us in his position would say, 'Father, I know You're calling me to leave Ur, and I'll be happy to go as soon as You give me a map of Mesopotamia.'

But the Lord doesn't work that way in the arena of faith. 'Start moving one step at a time,' He says. 'I'll direct you, but I will not give you directions for Step 2 until you first take Step 1.' A step of faith is the prerequisite for a man or woman to be used by God. He's looking for those who will come to the Jordan and get their feet wet (Joshua 3:15).

My tendency, however, is to say, 'Here I am, Lord. Right near the edge, just like You told me to be. Now, Lord, this ark is important cargo. You don't want to see it get dropped in the river and carried downstream, do You? That's not practical. So in order to help You protect Your good name, whenever you part the water, I'll be thrilled to go across. Here I am, Your man of faith, ready to serve You on the spot.'

But without faith, it's impossible to please God. 'Why?' you ask. 'Why does God take me to the edge of the Jordan, tell me to put my foot in, and risk me looking like a fool or the ark floating down the river? I don't get it.'

Guess what. You will—because faith is the lingua franca of eternity. God's not saying, 'I'm going to put you to the test for the fun of it. Let's see if you step in or not.' The Father has no joy in seeing His kids agonize at the edge of the Jordan. 'If this causes you agony,' He says, 'it's because you yet need to become a man of faith. After all, it's who you are in the arena of faith that will affect how I will use you in the next billion years to come.'

You see, gang, if you take eternity out of the equation, the whole thing seems like a bad joke. But once you understand that this whole deal on earth is to train and stretch, develop and mature you for heaven and the ages to come, then you start looking at everything in that way. 'OK, Father,' you'll say, 'this is a stretch for me. It's uncomfortable. It's not easy. But You told me to be like Abraham, so even if I don't know where I'm going, I trust You.'

OCTOBER 31

By faith he sojourned in the land of promise, as in a strange country, dwelling in tabernacles with Isaac and Jacob, the heirs with him of the same promise: For he looked for a city which hath foundations, whose builder and maker is God.

Hebrews 11:9-10

Why did Abraham embark on such a venture, such a journey? Because he was looking for a city which had foundations, whose builder and maker was God—all the while knowing that what he was looking for would never be found anywhere on the face of this earth.

Why is this so important? Because when I moved from San Jose to Applegate, for example, if I had been looking for a city on earth to satisfy me, I would have been paralyzed by fear. I would have said, 'What if I get there and discover Applegate's not it?' But since the longing of my heart was for a city without foundations, I already knew Applegate wouldn't be it!

'What if I go there, and it doesn't work out?'
Don't worry—it's not going to work out!

'What if I marry her, and she doesn't fully satisfy me?'
Don't worry—she won't!

'What if I take that job, and it's not what I hoped?'
Don't worry—it won't be!

You'll never be a man or woman of faith if you're looking for fulfillment here. No matter your ministry, your geographic location, your job, or your spouse—you'll not find it here. Like Abraham, don't look for a city that has foundations on earth. Look for eternity, and you'll experience heaven in your heart, you'll be blessed in your soul wherever you are.

Had Abraham looked for a city on earth, he would have been stuck in Ur forever. But at some point, God by His grace allowed Abraham to understand that everything on earth is in preparation for heaven. If you don't understand what the writer is saying about Abraham as a model of faith, you'll be perpetually paralyzed and completely frustrated. You must understand that God only leads you one step at a time. He doesn't tell you what lies around the bend. But even when you get around the bend, you must understand it's not going to be what you were hoping for, because what you really crave is heaven.

In spiritual life, the Lord will take you as far as you want to go—and not one step further. If you choose to take one baby step and stop, God will still love you because His love for you is not based on anything you do or don't do. But if you choose to walk by faith from Ur of the Chaldees all the way to the Land flowing with milk and honey—He'll be with you every step of the way.

People wonder why some folks are so spiritual, why others seem particularly blessed, why others are mightily used. It's not that God is playing favorites. It's just that those who seem to have a special relationship with God are simply those who chose to keep going. Whether it's in expression of praise, gifts of the Spirit, or aspects of ministry—however far you want to go in spiritual life, God will never say to you, 'You're going a little too far. You're getting a little too spiritual.' Never.

NOVEMBER 1

By faith the walls of Jericho fell down, after they were compassed about seven days.

Hebrews 11:30

To claim the Promised Land, God's strategy for His people was fairly simple: drive a wedge through the middle, dividing the north from the south. There was only one problem, however. To do this, they had to take Jericho—a city which seemed absolutely impenetrable because of the thick double walls surrounding it. Certainly as the Israelites marched around the walls once a day for six days, the people in Jericho must have looked down on them and laughed. *'That's their army?'* they must have scoffed. *'That's their strategy?'* On the seventh day, however, the heretofore impenetrable walls came down.

Listen, gang, the walls came down not brick by brick, but by *faith.*

'There's a wall between my 18-year-old daughter and me' cries the brokenhearted mother. 'We've gone to counseling; we follow the workbooks; we try all the techniques—and, although a brick or two might get chipped away, within a month there are three more in their place.'

'The walls between my son and I are keeping me out of the Promised Land of what I know a Christian family should be,' says the weary father. 'I try to reason with him, but there's a wall between us.'

Perhaps you are looking at a wall in your own family which seems impenetrable, a wall which appears as though it will never come down. The key? Not counseling, not dialoguing, not role-playing. The key is *faith.*

'But I've been marching around, working on, going through this situation for a long time,' you say.

Great—because the longer the wall has been up between you and your husband, or you and your father, or you and your daughter— the more you know it can't be brought down by your own effort. Walls come down when God moves in—but until God moves in, you'll just chip away, and frustration will fill your heart. Have faith in *God*, for when you finally realize that human skill or ability is insufficient, when you finally say, 'Lord, if anything's going to happen, it's going to be because of *You*,'—that's when the wall will fall.

Oh, it might take a week or a month, a year or a decade. But by faith in God, the wall *will* come down. How? In a way you would never have guessed, planned, or predicted. The older I get, the less impressed I am with people's abilities to solve problems, and the more amazed I am at God's faithfulness if we'll just believe Him. If you think that's a cop-out, join the jeerers of Jericho. But if you want to see a miracle, march with the Lord, and see what *He'll* do.

NOVEMBER 2

Wherefore seeing we also are compassed about with
so great a cloud of witnesses...

Hebrews 12:1

We are in a race, folks, observed and cheered on by a cloud of witnesses. Who are these spectators? They are the ones spoken of in Hebrews 11, the heroes of faith...

Shortly before He was to die outside Jerusalem on a hill called Calvary, Elijah and Moses appeared with Jesus on Mt. Hermon (Matthew 17). They had come, if you would, to cheer Him on.

So too, it is my firm conviction that right now, you and I are being cheered on by those in heaven. Furthermore, I believe the clouds spoken of in I Thessalonians 4:17, in which we will be caught up during the Rapture, are not of the cumulus or nimbus variety. Rather, they're clouds of those who have gone before us.

Next time you feel you're being 'wailed on,' think of Jonah. He's up there cheering you on.

Next time you feel like you're in a fiery trial, look for Shadrach, Meshach, and Abed-nego in the stands.

Next time you feel like you're up against a giant of a problem, remember David, the giant-slayer, and take heart.

NOVEMBER 3

See that ye refuse not him that speaketh. For if they escaped not who refused him that spake on earth, much more shall not we escape, if we turn away from him that speaketh from heaven: Whose voice then shook the earth: but now he hath promised, saying, Yet once more I shake not the earth only, but also heaven. And this word, Yet once more, signifieth the removing of those things that are shaken, as of things that are made, that those things which cannot be shaken may remain.

Hebrews 12:25-27

'In the year King Uzziah died, I saw the Lord,' wrote Isaiah (6:1). Under the reign of Uzziah—one of the greatest kings in the history of Judah—wealth flowed throughout the Jewish empire, and the borders of the nation were not only protected, but expanded. So powerful was he, it is said his name was on the lips of everyone from Babylon in the north to Egypt in the south. But when did Isaiah see the Lord? In the year Uzziah *died.*

So too, in each of our lives there are Uzziahs: good things, wonderful things—but things in which we trust and upon which we depend instead of trusting in and depending on God. And because He loves us and wants the best for us, our Father says, 'As good as Uzziah might be, he's not Me. As secure as you might feel because of his weaponry, it's not nearly as secure as you would be if you were looking to and leaning on Me.'

Because we are so prone to put our trust in things which cannot be proven trustworthy, God shakes our world as surely as He shook Mt. Sinai in order to knock away anything we are trusting in and living for. Gang, He loves you enough to say, 'If year after year, I let you trust in that, lean on him, or live for her, you will be a spiritual midget. I don't want that for you. You don't want that either. So, I've got to shake it to remove it, that you might again lean on Me, look to Me, and walk with Me—for then you'll be blessed, strengthened, and prepared for eternity.'

November 4

By him therefore let us offer the sacrifice of praise to God continually, that is, the fruit of our lips giving thanks to his name.

Hebrews 13:15

'I don't feel like praising the Lord,' some say. 'The traffic bugs me,' or, 'The dishes are getting to me.' Gang, those are the *best* times to praise Him—because then it's a sacrifice of praise as you worship the Lord in spite of your own fleshly inclinations.

You see, here's the deal: in my Christian walk, I find myself going through seasons...

There's springtime—when, with new understandings and fresh growth, I sense the Lord's presence in my heart. Springtime leads to summertime—those warm, wonderful days when the new growth bears fruit from which people glean. Summertime leads to fall—when the winds blow and shake the leaves off my tree. Fall leads to winter—when the fall winds give way to a cold, wintry silence. And I used to freak out in wintertime. Then I learned that if I am going to be a man who walks by faith and not by sight, I must not constantly monitor my feelings because feelings are fickle. The Lord allows you and me to go through regular seasons of wintertime, asking us, 'Are you going to walk by the state of your emotions—or by the promises of My Word?'

This has afforded me the privilege of being a minister of the Gospel regardless of any tragedy or heartache in my own life. Truly, if I hadn't learned the lessons of the winter season, I wouldn't be sitting here right now. But the good news is this: winter doesn't last forever. It gives way to spring.

Tonight during worship, some of you were elated, caught up in an overwhelming sense of the Lord's presence. And that's good. Others of you said, 'I'm here tonight. But I don't feel anything. However, I'm still going to lift my hands and my voice in a sacrifice of praise to the One who has done so much for me in the past, to the One whose touch I know I will feel again in the future.'

NOVEMBER 5

My brethren, count it all joy when ye fall into divers temptations.

James 1:2

Newer translations render this verse, 'Count it all joy when ye fall into various *trials*.' Why? Because the Greek word for both 'trial' and 'temptation' is one and the same.

You see, what God will send or allow as a trial to strengthen our faith, Satan will seek to exploit to get us to sin. Conversely, what Satan throws our way as a temptation, God allows to be a trial. Satan wants to use the event to tear us down and wipe us out; God wants to use the same event to show us how faithful He is and how real He can be.

Think of it this way: if Jerry, a master woodworker, invited me to sit in a chair he had made, I wouldn't do so wondering if it would hold me up, but rather marveling at how well it was crafted. If, on the other hand, our youth director, Tad, invited me to sit in a chair, I would be leery, knowing it would probably either be pulled out from or collapse underneath me.

So too, the chair that Satan seeks to pull out from under us is the very one God uses to show just how strong He can be.

In the Book of Job, we see Satan trying to wipe Job out by afflicting him physically, causing him to lose his family, and ruining him financially. But God was proving something else. God was showing how faithful He would be. As a result, all of history would marvel in studying how, in the midst of what Satan meant for evil, God used for good as He sustained Job all the way through, and rewarded him ultimately.

When a trial comes your way, Satan will be there the same day to try and get you to do what Mrs. Job suggested her husband do—curse God and die (Job 2:9). But God will be there as well, waiting to show you His strength in seeing you through.

NOVEMBER 6

...With whom is no variableness, neither shadow of turning. Of his own will begat he us with the word of truth, that we should be a kind of firstfruits of his creatures.

James 1:17-18

Not only is God good in the gifts He gives, but in who He is. In Him there is no variableness or shadow of turning. That is, He's not moody. He doesn't have bad days. He's not generous with me one day, but grouchy the next—as I can so often be.

We're variable. We go through ups and downs. God doesn't. He can be nothing but good. He doesn't react to me according to how I'm doing with Him. He is faithful when I am faithless (II Timothy 2:13). He is good when I am grumpy. He doesn't change. He's locked into His nature.

That's why I love the Lord so much. He's solid as a Rock. And I can just enjoy Him without worrying about Him being ticked with me or tired of me. He gives nothing but good gifts, for He is a good God.

NOVEMBER 7

And the scripture was fulfilled which saith, Abraham believed God, and it was imputed unto him for righteousness: and he was called the Friend of God. Ye see then how that by works a man is justified, and not by faith only. Likewise also was not Rahab the harlot justified by works, when she had received the messengers, and had sent them out another way? For as the body without the spirit is dead, so faith without works is dead also.

James 2:23-26

Arguing that faith without works is dead, the Book of James so incensed Martin Luther that the reformer called it 'a veritable straw epistle that should be thrown into the Rhine River.' Yet James proves that faith without works is dead by pointing to the example of Abraham. It's not that Abraham was saved by taking Isaac up the mountain to sacrifice him in obedience to God. No, James says the work which saved Abraham took place years before that when he simply believed in God (verse 23).

When was Abraham declared to be righteous? As James quotes Genesis 15:6, we understand that Abraham was declared to be righteous when he simply believed God would do what He said He would do when He told Abraham He would make his descendants more numerable than the sands on the seashore. Interestingly, Paul would also point to Abraham as proof that man is justified by faith apart from works (Romans 4:3).

James and Paul are in full agreement because they both maintain that the moment Abraham simply believed God was the moment God imputed righteousness unto him.

It is not faith *and* works which saves a man. It is not faith *or* works. It is faith *that* works. All Abraham was doing on Mt. Moriah was showing the reality of what had taken place in his life years earlier when he simply believed God.

If your faith is real, it will show itself. How? By obeying the Word of God and following the leading of the Lord even though you may not understand where it will lead. At the time, Abraham could not have understood the significance of what he had done on Mt. Moriah. But this side of Calvary, we see it was a perfect picture of what God the Father would do in sending His Son to that same mountain to die for the sins of the world.

You know you're truly born again when you find yourself obeying God. We're not saved by obedience. But our obedience proves we're saved, for true faith works.

NOVEMBER 8

My brethren, these things ought not so to be. Doth a fountain send forth at the same place sweet water and bitter? Can the fig tree, my brethren, bear olive berries? either a vine, figs? so can no fountain both yield salt water and fresh.

James 3:10-12

'We live in a pleasant area,' said the men of Jericho to the newly-anointed prophet. 'But our crops are dying because our water is poisoned.'

So what did Elisha do?

He poured salt into the water, and the water became sweet once again (II Kings 2).

Salt into polluted water? Yes, because Paul tells us our speech is always to be seasoned with salt, that is grace (Colossians 4:6).

What does this mean? It means that in any given moment, I can bring healing to an otherwise poisonous situation by speaking grace. If I keep talking about how gracious God has been to me, and how gracious He'll be towards others, the polluted puddles of put-downs and pettiness will become pools of purity and praise.

I want this in my life so badly I can taste it. Oh, I'm far from what I should be—but I see the wisdom of James, for I've known people who have refused to listen to gossip and who have instead learned to speak graciously. And there is a beauty about their lives and a refreshment from their lives I so desire. If you want to be the man or woman God uses, join me in praying that we will be those who add the salt of grace to everything we say.

November 9

Ye ask, and receive not, because ye ask amiss, that
ye may consume it upon your lusts.

James 4:3

'I do pray,' you may say. 'But I don't get what I ask for.'

That's because you're asking amiss. Prayer is not giving orders. It's reporting for duty. And once a person finally understands that prayer is not man saying, 'Bless the business; bring in the money; solve the problem,' and God saying, 'Aye, aye, captain,' his prayer life will be revolutionized.

Prayer is saying, 'Father, what do *You* want to do in my life? I want You to do what You see is best for me because I get mixed up so easily.'

I walked into his room during his nap to find one-year-old Peter John laying on his back, eagerly reaching for an object dangling just inches above his head. Living in a rustic cabin in the woods at that time, we were sometimes surprised by the visitors we would have. And this particular afternoon was no exception, for I was surprised indeed to see the object for which Peter was so intently reaching was a black widow spider.

We're just like Peter John. We lay on our beds or kneel beside them and, through prayer, grab for things we think would be so wonderful, failing to realize they are nothing but black widows. Therefore, every bit as exciting to me as prayers God does answer are those He doesn't answer because I know I'll see that what I thought was so intriguing and tantalizing will prove to be poisonous and deadly. Oh, may we learn not to give orders or grab spiders but to do what Jesus did in the Garden: to submit to whatever the Father has for us.

NOVEMBER 10

Draw nigh to God, and he will draw nigh to you.
James 4:8

One of my favorite verses in all of the Bible: Draw nigh to God, and He might draw nigh to you. No. Draw nigh to God, and He will sometimes draw nigh to you. No. Draw nigh to God, and He *will* draw nigh to you. That's a promise! Don't let anyone cast aspersions on God's goodness or nature by saying, 'I tried to get close to the Lord, but He is just so far from me.'

The Bible says He will draw nigh—always.

People say to me, 'I've tried, but I can't seem to connect with God.'

'I don't believe you,' I lovingly answer, 'because God's Word says He will always draw near to us if we draw near to Him, and I have found this promise to be true. Without fail, every time I have been serious about seeking God, He has made Himself known to me through a Scripture, in my heart, or through the Body.'

Sometimes, gang, we need to lovingly say to those who whine about feeling far from God even though they claim they have tried to draw near to Him, 'You're deceiving yourself, or you're trying to deceive me because God's Word says that if you take the time and expend the energy to draw near to Him, He *will* draw near to you.'

November 11

Cleanse your hands, ye sinners; and purify your hearts, ye double minded. Be afflicted, and mourn, and weep: let your laughter be turned to mourning, and your joy to heaviness. Humble yourselves in the sight of the Lord, and he shall lift you up.

James 4:8-10

Draw near to God, and He will draw near to you. When? When you're serious about seeking Him. The idea is to be serious about it, to turn off the TV, to take some time and make an effort. Why? Not because God is saying, 'Only when you mourn and are afflicted will I speak to you.' That's not it at all. The purpose of mourning and cleansing is not so that God will speak—but to get me tuned into the right frequency so I can hear Him already speaking. Think of it this way...

Right now, Channel 10 is broadcasting all sorts of words and images. But we aren't tuned into the frequency. To get the picture, we'd have to take some time, bring in a TV, and put up the antenna. Would we do that to impress Channel 10 to send pictures our way? No. They're already doing that constantly. We'd have to bring in a TV and put up an antenna simply to get us in the position to receive what's already being broadcast from Channel 10 continually.

If people don't read this passage right, they begin to say, 'If we afflict ourselves like the prophets of Baal on Mount Carmel, if we slash our bodies and dance in a frenzy, God will speak' (I Kings 18). That's not the heart of the Father. That's the heart of a false god.

The purpose of washing your hands and humbling your heart implies quitting your normal activities and taking some time to get tuned into the proper frequency. Go to the park. Get away. Do whatever it takes to change your setting and say, 'Lord, I've been tuned into work. I've been dialed into parenting. I've been positioned to pursue my hobbies. But now I'm taking time to hear from You because I know You're broadcasting 24 hours a day, and I want to hear what You say.'

NOVEMBER 12

Blessed be the God and Father of our Lord Jesus Christ, which according to his abundant mercy hath begotten us again unto a lively hope by the resurrection of Jesus Christ from the dead, To an inheritance incorruptible, and undefiled, and that fadeth not away...

I Peter 1:3-4

To these who are feeling discouraged, displaced, depressed, or in danger, Peter addresses the issue right away saying, 'We have a living hope based upon the resurrection of our Lord and Savior.'

Unlike living hope, human hope tends to get weaker and dimmer and finally dies altogether the further one goes down the road of life...

I was an awesome pitcher. As I stood in the street and pitched a tennis ball against my garage door, you wouldn't believe my split finger fastball, my curve, my sinker. I knew even Hank Aaron would strike out if he ever faced me at the plate. Oh, I might go to the full count, but I would always come through—every single time. In my imagination, I pitched perfect game after perfect game as a nine-year-old. But it finally hit me about two years ago that, in reality, I'll never pitch for the San Francisco Giants. Even if I practice *really* hard, I now know it's just not going to happen. My hope that once shone so brightly is now gone altogether.

The same is true for all of us, for as we go down the road of life, we check off more and more things we thought we would one day do or be. Regarding spiritual life, however, the opposite is true—for the further down the road we walk with Jesus, the more we realize our hope doesn't lie in this earth, but in heaven. We don't need to be a people who wrestle with mid-life crises because our hope is not to make the San Francisco Giants or to make ten million bucks. Our hope is in heaven. And heaven's getting closer every day.

NOVEMBER 13

...Through faith unto salvation ready to be revealed in the last time.

I Peter 1:5

A young man who was being hazed by a college fraternity was taken to a secluded spot where he was told to hold on to a knot at the end of a greased rope as his fraternity brothers lowered him into a dark well. Thinking they would pull him up after a few minutes, he was terrified to see them tie their end of the rope to the bar across the top of the well, leaving him suspended in mid-air.

'This can't be!' he thought as he called for help. But none came.

As he approached the 15-minute mark, his arms aching unbelievably and his shoulders feeling as though they were on fire, he started to cry.

Finally, after about 25 tortuous minutes, able to hang on no longer, he let go—and fell two inches—just as his fraternity brothers had calculated.

Isn't that just like us? 'Where are You, God? I don't know if I'm going to make it,' we cry. We fret and blubber and scream until finally we let go. And guess what we find? We discover that our Solid Rock, Jesus Christ, was there all along.

A bunch of us have burning shoulders and aching arms for absolutely no reason. We're trying to hang on through our own efforts, by our own spirituality. We get disgusted with ourselves and worried we're not going to make it. But if we would just let go of the rope and rest in what Jesus did on the Cross of Calvary, we would realize it's not our puny efforts which will see us through, but the power of God.

This is what Peter is telling the believers who no doubt were wondering whether, when the temperature rose and persecution came down, they would be able to hang in there.

'I want you to know something,' Peter said. 'You have an inheritance waiting for you which can't be taken from you. You are kept by the power of God who is committed to see you through. And all that remains for you to do is believe.'

November 14

> *...Being much more precious than of gold that perisheth, though it be tried with fire, might be found unto praise and honour and glory at the appearing of Jesus Christ.*
>
> I Peter 1:7

'I know you're going through exceedingly difficult days, with even tougher times coming your direction,' says Peter, 'but you can choose to rejoice.' Why? 'Because trials strengthen faith.'

In likening faith to gold tried by fire, Peter reaches back to a statement made by a man who knew uniquely what it meant to go through trials and difficulties...

> *But he knoweth the way that I take: when he hath tried me, I shall come forth as gold.*
>
> Job 23:10

In Bible times, when a man wanted to make something of fine gold, he would subject the golden ore to such intense heat that all of the impurities would be burned out. And the goldsmith would know that the work was done when he could see the reflection of his own face in the liquefied gold.

The same thing is true with us. The Lord says, 'I've got big plans for you, huge plans not just for this life, but for eternity. Therefore, I may need to turn up the heat a bit to work out the impurities. But My hand is on the thermostat. I know exactly what I'm doing. And, although at the present moment, it might not be easy, you'll thank Me for the next billion years to come because what I'm after is to see the reflection of My face in your life.'

Why? God doesn't want to see His reflection in our lives because He's on some sort of an ego trip, but because He knows that although we may not realize it, what we really want is to be like Him. But there are things in our lives which keep that from happening. So the way He deals with them is to turn up the heat a bit in order that we'll come out of the fire stronger in faith and more like the Lord.

> *...But we glory in tribulations also: knowing that tribulation worketh patience; And patience, experience; and experience, hope: And hope maketh not ashamed; because the love of God is shed abroad in our hearts by the Holy Ghost which is given unto us.*
>
> *Romans 5:3*

When you finally understand this, you'll rejoice in difficulty rather than rebel because you'll see it as a purifying process which will work wonderful things into your life. Tribulation works patience because when you're going through difficulty, there's not a lot you can do other than wait for the Master Goldsmith to finish the process. Patience in turn works experience as we learn that God truly knows what He's doing. And experience works hope—the absolute expectation of coming good.

NOVEMBER 15

Whom having not seen, ye love; in whom, though now ye see him not, yet believing, ye rejoice with joy unspeakable and full of glory.

I Peter 1:8

Not only do trials strengthen our faith *in* the Lord, but they deepen our love *for* the Lord. Although those to whom Peter was writing had never seen Jesus physically, such was not the case with Peter, for Peter had not only seen Him daily in His humanity, but had actually seen a sneak preview of His deity. Yet Peter's joy was not unspeakable on the Mount of Transfiguration, for he merely said, 'Lord, it's good for us to be here' (Matthew 17:4).

Therefore, I suggest that even though Peter had beheld Jesus physically, those to whom Peter was writing would experience an even deeper love and keener perspective due to the trials they faced.

Certainly Shadrach, Meshach, and Abed-nego found this to be true...

Inside a furnace heated seven times hotter than it had ever been previously, these guys were in a fiery trial indeed. Yet because a 'fourth Man'—the Son of God—was in the fire with them, they didn't come out of the furnace until they were commanded to do so (Daniel 3:26).

A lot of us are getting to the place where we say, 'Lord, keep me in the fire continually if that's what it takes for me to see You more clearly.'

'Your joy is unspeakable,' Peter says, 'because you've seen Jesus in ways that far transcend seeing Him physically—even when He was transfigured in glory.'

NOVEMBER 16

Receiving the end of your faith, even the salvation of your souls. Of which salvation the prophets have inquired and searched diligently, who prophesied of the grace that should come unto you: Searching what, or what manner of time the Spirit of Christ which was in them did signify, when it testified beforehand the sufferings of Christ, and the glory that should follow.

I Peter 1:9-11

'What you're experiencing,' Peter says, 'is something which the prophets were intrigued by, interested in, but couldn't get a handle on.' You see, the prophets wrote about things they just couldn't figure out, for they saw the glory of Psalm 2; but they also saw the suffering of Isaiah 53. They saw the triumph on the Mount of Olives where the returning Messiah will stand; but they also saw the blood on Mt. Calvary upon which Messiah died. 'How can it be,' they must have wondered, 'that He will be despised and rejected, smitten and suffering, yet also ruling and reigning? This doesn't make sense.'

They saw Mt. Calvary. They saw the Mount of Olives. But what they didn't see was the valley between the two—a valley of about 2,000 years. They didn't understand that they were writing of two comings—that Messiah would come as a Suffering Savior before returning as a Conquering King.

So too, some today might say, 'I hear all of the promises—but I don't see any glory.' That's because there's a valley between them which might last a week, a month, a decade, a lifetime. But God's plan is being unfolded nonetheless, for glory always follows suffering. Always.

NOVEMBER 17

Ye also, as lively stones, are built up a spiritual house...

I Peter 2:5

That we are living stones who are being built up, or fit together, as a spiritual house brings to mind a most interesting Scripture...

And the house, when it was in building, was built of stone made ready before it was brought thither: so that there was neither hammer nor axe nor any tool of iron heard in the house, while it was in building.

I Kings 6:7

When Solomon's Temple was being constructed, all of the chiseling, hammering, cutting, and chipping was done underneath the old city of Jerusalem so that when the stones were taken to the Temple Mount, they could be fit together in silence.

We're living stones being fit together for an eternal temple in heaven. This life is the quarry—which explains why we always feel like we're being chipped and chiseled. 'Why am I next to this blockhead?' you ask, or 'Why are they part of the family?'

Because as *living* stones, we constantly rub against each other, knocking rough edges off each other in the process. You see, God puts us right next to the very people He knows will smooth us down so He can build us up into a temple for His glory.

The problem is that I try to get away from the blockhead I'm rubbing up against. But because God puts us in fixes to fix us, He puts us with people and in situations He knows will shape us most effectively. So if I try to fix the fix God put me in, He will be faithful to put me in another fix to fix the fix He wanted to fix in the first place!

If we don't learn this, we'll go from fix to fix until finally we say, 'OK, Lord. I'm not going to try to fix this or wiggle out of that, but I'm going to embrace and accept where You have me because I know You're doing a work on me, shaping me for eternity.'

NOVEMBER 18

> *For even hereunto were ye called: because Christ also suffered for us, leaving us an example, that ye should follow his steps: Who did no sin, neither was guile found in his mouth: Who, when he was reviled, reviled not again; when he suffered, he threatened not; but committed himself to him that judgeth righteously: Who his own self bare our sins in his own body on the tree, that we, being dead to sins, should live unto righteousness: by whose strips ye were healed.*
>
> I Peter 2:21-24

Facing persecution, the early believers were not left on their own without a Model to follow, for 'Christ also suffered for us, leaving an example, that we should follow in his steps.'

When Peter John was about three-years-old, we were playing in the snow, and I said, 'Come on, PJ, follow in my footprints if you can.' But he couldn't. My stride was too big.

Folks, to be frank, I look at a verse like this and read that when He was being wrongly, cruelly, and terribly treated, Jesus didn't answer back—and that I am to follow His steps. Yet I know I can't do this because I want to fight back; I want to let my opinion be known; I want to make sure I'm heard. But here's the good news: Jesus not only is our Example, but He is our Enabler, not only the Lamb, but also the Shepherd of our souls.

Peter John did indeed follow in my steps that day—as I lifted him into the air and back down again and again so that he could put his feet in each one. He followed in my footsteps because I not only gave him steps to follow, but I enabled him to do so by lifting him up.

That's what our Lord does. He's the One who hoists me up and allows me, if I'll let Him, to follow in His footsteps when I never could in my own ability. And He'll do the same for you.

NOVEMBER 19

For the eyes of the Lord are over the righteous, and his ears are open unto their prayers: but the face of the Lord is against them that do evil.

I Peter 3:12

As one who knew the Word, Peter continues quoting another who experienced brutal days...

What man is he that desireth life, and loveth many days, that he may see good? Keep thy tongue from evil, and thy lips from speaking guile. Depart from evil, and do good; seek peace, and pursue it. The eyes of the LORD are upon the righteous, and his ears are open unto their cry. The face of the LORD is against them that do evil, to cut off the remembrance of them from the earth.

Psalm 34:12-16

With Saul out to kill him, David found himself seeking refuge in the Philistine city of Gath. But when he realized that he was recognized in the city as the one who had slain Goliath, David knew he was again in danger. So in order to make it out of Gath alive, he clawed at the gates of the city, ranting and raving like a lunatic as he feigned insanity. When the king heard there was a crazy man within his gates, David was allowed to go his way.

Psalm 34 was written while David was in Gath, running for his life, and yet what does he say? The Psalm begins, 'I will bless the LORD at all times: his praise shall continually be in my mouth, for I have tasted and seen in the midst of this difficulty that the LORD is good.'

Who will love life and see good days? Society says it's the one who can make his life problem-free, who insulates himself from difficulty, who escapes adversity. But David says just the opposite. He says it's when you're wondering how the next bill will be paid, or if the marriage will work out that the Lord makes Himself most real to you. He says it's when you're trapped in Gath that suddenly you see God.

Now, if we really embraced what Peter is saying, what David is declaring, and what James is saying when he declares, 'Count it all joy when you fall into various trials' (James 1:2), we would not try to make our life easier. Instead, we would be those who say, 'It's in the day of difficulty, in the years that are hard for me that I'm going to have the opportunity to taste and see that the Lord is good.'

We all know people who are insulated from problems, who don't have challenges, and who have succeeded in making their lives as easy as they possibly can. But the easier it gets for them, the less joy there is within them.

Peter says something which is absolutely shocking—at least in the ears of our culture—when he states, 'In the midst of sufferings, difficulties, and challenges, don't seek to fix the problems. Don't seek to make things easier. Choose instead to do good and to seek peace. Don't murmur, don't complain—and you'll find that you love life because God will meet you in the midst of your difficulties.'

NOVEMBER 20

Casting all your care upon him; for he careth for you.
I Peter 5:7

Epirrhipto, the Greek word translated 'cast,' is interesting because it means to roll something which will most likely roll back upon you. Have you found that after casting your care on the Lord, you feel OK for a day or two, but then the burden rolls right back on you once again? If so, know that's the way of the Lord. Why? Because He wants us to stay in close touch with Him, and if we cast our care upon Him never to feel the pressure, the anxiety, the tension, or the worry again, we would not be people who pray.

You see, the Father wants to do something bigger than merely taking our burdens from us so we can go on our merry way down the road of life without thinking about the things of eternity. He wants to develop a relationship with us.

Thus, the burdens and struggles which repeatedly roll upon us cause us to become linked to Him in continual prayer. And that's infinitely more important than the solution to the burden for which we were praying in the first place.

So cast your care upon Him—and keep doing it over and over and over again knowing how deeply He cares for you.

NOVEMBER 21

Grace and peace be multiplied unto you through the
knowledge of God, and of Jesus our Lord.
II Peter 1:2

The more knowledge you have of Jesus Christ, the greater understanding you'll have that our God is truly a God of grace.

At the outset of his ministry, Billy Graham was referred to as 'God's Machine Gun.' But as he went on in his knowledge of the Lord, he found himself becoming more and more oriented towards grace—so much so that many Christians today scratch their heads and wonder how he can be open to so many. '*That* denomination can't be Christian,' they scoff. Or, 'Surely, *those* people can't be saved.' But Billy has a way of being incredibly embracive without compromising. And in his own writings, he explains that as he grows older in the Lord, he's more and more amazed by the grace of the Lord.

The older you grow in the Lord, the more grace-oriented you'll be as you realize the Christian life is all about Jesus and the undeserved, unearned favor He lavishes upon us so freely due to the finished work of Calvary.

The result?

Unmistakable, undeniable, unshakable peace—for truly grace and peace walk hand in hand.

NOVEMBER 22

According as his divine power hath given unto us all things that pertain unto life and godliness...
II Peter 1:3

Notice that Peter is not telling us that everything we have need of pertaining to life and godliness *will be* given to us. No, he says everything we need to live an abundant, fulfilled life—and everything we need to live like Christ has *already been* given to us.

This is radical because many of us don't have this understanding. We think we're still pursuing some key, and if we can find it, then we'll be able to unlock the secret of life. We're looking for the combination on the padlock of godliness. But Peter says something wonderful when he says God has already given us all things—not most things, not a bunch of things—but *all* things that pertain to life and godliness.

When my son Benjamin was born, although he wasn't all that he will be one day, everything he needed was already packed in his little body. His job, then, was not to find additional body parts to add to himself. His job was simply to grow.

'That's obvious,' you say. But a whole bunch of Christians do what I did for some years in my walk—they read, search, and look for what's missing in their faith instead of simply taking God's Word at face value which says His divine power has given us everything we need for godliness and all we need for abundant life.

Knowing this can save us a bunch of time and a lot of money. For instead of searching bookstores and infomercials to find the seven secrets of effective people, or the way to 'awaken the giant within,' we can simply grow in the knowledge that we've already been given everything we need to live abundantly and godly.

NOVEMBER 23

Wherefore I will not be negligent to put you always in remembrance of these things, though ye know them, and be established in the present truth. Yea, I think it meet, as long as I am in this tabernacle, to stir you up by putting you in remembrance.

II Peter 1:12-13

Very likely in prison, even as he writes this letter, Peter knows he's about to die. And he uses whatever life he has left to say, 'I know you know this stuff. But I will not be negligent to put you in remembrance of it until you are established in it.'

If you are a Sunday school teacher, parent, elder, or anyone else who wants to be used in service, this is a huge point, for the key to ministry is putting people in remembrance of things they already know. You see, because our minds have been affected by sin, we forget the things we should remember and remember the things we should forget. Therefore, your job as a dad, my job as a pastor is to say the same things over and over and over until those in our charge are established in them.

It's not how much you know that counts, gang. It's how *well* you know what you know. What matters is how *well* you understand the basic truths and how deep they sink into the soil of your soul.

NOVEMBER 24

Looking for and hasting unto the coming of the day of God, wherein the heavens being on fire shall be dissolved, and the elements shall melt with fervent heat?

II Peter 3:12

Are you tired of death, disease, and depression? Have you had your fill of sadness and sickness and sin? If so, there are two ways you can hurry the day when righteousness will rule the earth.

First, the day of God is hastened *by our prayer*. In teaching us to pray, Jesus taught us to ask that His Kingdom come (Matthew 6: 10). This is precisely what one who heard Him teach that prayer did. At the end of the book of Revelation, Jesus said, 'Behold, I come quickly'—to which John responded in prayer, 'Even so, Lord, come quickly.' The same is still true. Prayer influences the timing of God—including the coming of the Kingdom.

Secondly, the day of God is hastened *as we share*. According to Acts 2:47, the Lord adds daily to the Church such as should be saved. Thus, there is someone who is the last one to be added to the Church to complete the Bride of Christ. And when that last one gets saved, the Body of Christ will be complete, and we'll go up.

Consequently, as we witness, share, and invite people to be a part of the family and make a decision for Jesus Christ—we actually bring closer the day of His return.

But the benefits of hastening the day are not limited to future times. Rather, this kind of living and thinking has benefits now, as it produces within us three important qualities...

Purity. I John 3:3 tells us that he who looks for Jesus' coming purifies himself. It's amazing how careful a person drives when he looks in his wallet and realizes his license has expired. So too, it's amazing how purity will characterize the life of one who believes this could be the day, this could be the hour of Christ's return.

Peace. The one who looks for the Lord's coming takes a whole lot more things a whole lot less seriously. In other words, the one who looks for the Lord's coming is not uptight about the scratch in his car, the bruise to his ego, or the slight at the office because he sees the bigger picture of eternity.

Purpose. The life of the one who looks for the Lord's coming, who is involved in the work of the Kingdom, is neither boring, predictable, nor routine. If you feel that your life is simply going in circles, it could be because you've lost sight of your purpose.

Hasten the day, gang, by your prayer and as you share. Live for eternity, and you'll find unparalleled purity, purpose, and peace.

NOVEMBER 25

This then is the message which we have heard of him,
and declare unto you, that God is light, and in him is
no darkness at all.

I John 1:5

People who are depressed in their spiritual lives because they think being a Christian is so hard don't match up with true Biblical Christianity because John says there's no dark side to God; there's nothing negative about Him; there's not a mean bone in His body. Therefore, a sour, dour, dark, and discouraged Christian is an oxymoron, a contradiction of terms.

'Wait a minute,' you say. 'Wasn't Jesus the Man of Sorrows?' (Isaiah 53:3).

Yes. Jesus wept over Jerusalem (Luke 19:41). He wept at the tomb of Lazarus (John 11:35). When Jesus wept, however, it was always for others.

What about when He wept in the Garden of Gethsemane?

The night before He would go to the Cross, Jesus sweat blood because He was terrified not by the pain of the Cross, the spittle that would run down His face, or the flagellum that would rip into His back. Jesus was almost literally scared to death by the thought of being temporarily separated from His Father when He would be made sin on our behalf.

'What if I can't pay the bills?' we wonder. 'What if the car doesn't work?' 'What if I lose a loved one?' 'What's next?' 'Who else?' These are the things which frighten us. But separation from the Father? We don't even give it a second thought. God have mercy on us. We're terrified of all the wrong things.

NOVEMBER 26

*He that saith he is in the light, and hateth his brother,
is in darkness even until now. He that loveth his
brother abideth in the light, and there is none occasion
of stumbling in him. But he that hateth his brother is
in darkness, and walketh in darkness, and knoweth
not whither he goeth, because that darkness hath
blinded his eyes.*

I John 2:9-11

The new commandment of which John speaks is the greatest
commandment of all: to love.

'What is the greatest commandment?' the young lawyer asked the
Master.
And Jesus said, 'How do you read it?'
'Love the Lord thy God with all thy heart and soul and mind and
strength,' the lawyer answered.
'That's it,' Jesus said. 'And the second is like unto it: Love thy
neighbor as thyself' (Matthew 22:36-39).

The fresh word for you and me is that we are to love, for if we say
we're walking with the Lord and are close to the Lord but have
hatred in our hearts towards our brother, then something is not
right.

It's a wonderful thing to be able to say, 'To the best of my knowledge,
I'm not bitter towards anyone, mad at anyone, or angry with anyone
because I know what a sinner *I* am. I know how much *I've* failed. I
know how gracious God has been to *me*.' When that's our heart, we
know things are right.

November 27

*Beloved, now are we the sons of God, and it doth not
yet appear what we shall be: but we know that, when
he shall appear, we shall be like him; for we shall see
him as he is.*

I John 3:2

We don't always act like sons of God or look likes sons of God, but John says when He shall appear, we shall be like Him. Do I like that? Yes, because I like Him! After all, Jesus Christ is the Man everyone desires to be like...

So gentle was He that little children flocked to Him (Matthew 19: 14).
Yet so commanding was He that a single look from Him parted the angry crowd intent to do Him in (Luke 4:29-30).

So authoritative was He that fierce storms would be quieted by His word (Mark 4:39).
Yet so tender was He that He stilled the storm of criticism which swirled around the adulterous woman (John 8:11).

So embracive was He that sinners called Him friend (Matthew 11: 19).
Yet so righteous was He that His blood could wash away the sin of the entire world (I John 2:2).

Jesus is indeed the Perfect Man. He's everything every one of us innately wants to be.

The more you read the Gospels carefully and thoughtfully, prayerfully and contemplatively, the more you will develop a profound appreciation of His personality, character, integrity, wisdom, and strength. When I didn't know as much about Jesus as I know now, I wasn't as impressed with Him as I am today. And this is amazing, because in every other case, the better you know someone, the more disillusioned you become as you begin to see their cracks and flaws.

Not so with Jesus. The longer you walk with Him and the more you learn about Him, the more you will be impressed by Him, and the more you will long to see Him. Even though now I only see Him through a glass darkly (I Corinthians 13:12), I like what I see!

NOVEMBER 28

Ye are of God, little children, and have overcome them: because greater is he that is in you, than he that is in the world.

I John 4:4

The walls of the submarines which descend two miles in the Mariana Trench of the Pacific Ocean are constructed of thick steel plates to withstand the tremendous pressure placed upon them. But guess what the pictures taken from such heavily protected submarines reveal? Fish swimming two miles below the surface of the water with scales no thicker than that of any other fish. How can this be? The answer is simple: the pressure on the inside of those fish is equal to the pressure of the water around them.

That's the beauty of Christianity. Some people erect massive walls to insulate themselves from the attacks of the enemy—only to find themselves filled with the frustration of isolation. The key is not to put up massive walls to protect you from the enemy—but to realize the One inside you is greater than whatever pressure threatens to attack you.

When we understand that He that is in us is greater than *any* temptation, problem, trauma, or difficulty which could come against us, we can move through life freely.

November 29

...Whom I love in the truth; and not I only, but also all
they that have known the truth; For the truth's sake,
which dwelleth in us, and shall be with us for ever.

II John 1-2

Although John talks about love more than any other writer in Scripture, he also emphasizes truth more than any other writer—using the word 'truth' 20 times in his Gospel, 9 times in I John, 5 times in these opening verses of II John, and 5 more times in III John.

I find it interesting that it was the apostle of love whom the Lord tapped on the shoulder to also be the one who stressed truth. When you talk about love, it's very easy to get mushy, to become sentimental, to begin to say, 'I'll just love that person rather than be honest with him.' Such is not the case with John.

And his example is a needful one in a day when the economy has eclipsed integrity as our nation's top priority, in an age where what is true for one person may or may not be true for another, in a culture which embraces Pilate's question, 'What is truth?' (John 18:38), rather than Jesus' declaration, 'I am the truth' (John 14:6).

While I don't want to be one who causes people to batten down the hatches whenever they see me coming, neither do I want to let the church or my kids walk in ways I know will be destructive.

Our relationships with our kids, our spouses, our sisters, and our brothers in the Lord cannot survive without truth. That's why Paul says we are to speak the truth in love (Ephesians 4:15), for you can't truly have one without the other.

NOVEMBER 30

Having many things to write unto you, I would not write with paper and ink: but I trust to come unto you, and speak face to face, that our joy may be full.

II John 12-13

We have a tendency to get tripped up by that which we don't understand. For example, we wonder what God will do with those who are seemingly and sincerely tricked by the cults or isolated in regions of the world where they never hear the Gospel.

In answer to such questions, the Lord says to you and me through the Apostle John, 'Hold on. I'm coming soon. Everything will make sense when you see Me face to face.'

In the meantime, we are to do what we do understand: we are to stay away from those who propagate heresy, and we are to preach Christ to people with a sense of urgency. We must do what the Word says and let God do what He wants to do rather than say, 'I don't have to witness to him. I don't have to share with my neighbor. They'll probably make it to heaven anyway. My kids are probably saved; I don't want to bother them.'

DECEMBER 1

For I rejoiced greatly, when the brethren came and testified of the truth that is in thee, even as thou walkest in the truth. I have no greater joy than to hear that my children walk in truth. Beloved, thou doest faithfully whatsoever thou doest to the brethren, and to strangers; Which have borne witness of thy charity before the church: whom if thou bring forward on their journey after a godly sort, thou shalt do well: Because that for his name's sake they went forth, taking nothing of the Gentiles.

III John 3-7

In the days before Motel 6, Gaius would not only house itinerant preachers, apostles, and prophets, but would provide for them financially so that, as they journeyed, they wouldn't have to take anything from the Gentiles. So too, for us to walk in truth and love means we assist people on their journey towards heaven by reminding them of God's faithfulness and heaven's nearness.

It is our privilege and our responsibility to say to people, 'God will do what He promised. He will never leave you. He will see you through here on earth.' And it is also our privilege and responsibility to direct their eyes to heaven. It was by immediately directing their hearts to heaven that Jesus could calm the disciples' troubled hearts on earth (John 14:1-2). If one takes heaven out of the equation, he's left with desperate, disturbed, depressed people. Heaven in the equation changes everything.

DECEMBER 2

I will therefore put you in remembrance, though ye once knew this...

Jude 5

The foundational theme of this wonderful epistle, as found in verse 21, is an exhortation to keep ourselves in the love of God. Underline this phrase because it is the hinge upon which the Book of Jude swings. Jude's heart is, 'Yes, there are heretics and deceivers, but you, beloved, keep yourselves in the love of God.'

Keeping yourself in the love of God does not mean earning God's love by being a 'good little boy or girl.' God's love is unconditional—so much so that in Romans 5:8, Paul declares that God demonstrated His love towards us in that while we were yet sinners, Christ died for us. When did God demonstrate His love for you and me? Not when we were trying to be good Christians, but when we were pagans, heathens, and rebels. When you couldn't have cared less about Him, God looked at you and said, 'I love you deeply.'

Never buy into the thinking that you earn God's love by being good. Many Christians look at God as being like Santa: He's making a list, checking it twice, and He's gonna find out who's naughty and who's nice. If you've been good, you'll get gifts; if not, you'll be lucky to get a lump of coal.

But nothing could be further from the nature of our Father. Making a list? Checking it twice? Paul says that the list of our failings was blotted *out* by blood of Christ (Colossians 2:14). The list of my sins was pinned to the Cross of Calvary and cleansed so thoroughly by the blood of the Lamb that the writing became completely illegible. God's love for us is not based upon anything we do or don't do—His love is unconditional.

What, then, does it mean to keep yourself in the love of God? It simply means to keep yourself in the place where you can receive

His blessings. In other words, God is constantly showering us with blessings, love, and grace. He's not saying, 'Hmm, you've been bad today, so I'm turning off the spigot.' No, God's blessings are *always* coming down (Lamentations 3:23).

'Then why am I not being blessed?' you ask. The answer is easy: you're not under the spout where the blessings come out. You have wandered away. God didn't close the spigot—because even when we are faithless, He is faithful still (II Timothy 2:13). God doesn't monitor the flow of blessings depending on how we're doing. No, the spigot is on full blast all the time. Therefore, the only thing we have to do is to make sure we're in the place where we enjoy God's blessings—that we're standing under the spout where the blessings come out.

DECEMBER 3

Who bare record of the word of God, and of the testimony of Jesus Christ, and of all things that he saw.

Revelation 1:2

Revelation was entrusted to John because he *bore record* of the testimony of Jesus and of all the things he saw. People who say, 'I just don't seem to be getting any revelation from the Lord; I don't seem to be growing,' must understand that when it comes to revelation, information, or inspiration, the Lord has a very definite prerequisite: are we going to personally receive it in our heart and freely release it to others?

After visiting with Abraham, the Lord said to His angels, 'I'm going to tell Abraham what is going to come down in Sodom because I know he will receive and share it' (Genesis 18:17-19).

Jesus put it this way: take heed how you hear, for the one who has shall be given more (Mark 4:24-25).

In other words, if you come to Bible study or your morning devotions saying, 'Entertain me,' or, 'I'm just kind of curious about prophecy,' you won't receive. But if you are hearing, studying, learning, praying, and reading for the purpose of embracing it personally and sharing it with others, then the Lord will give you continual revelation, continual inspiration.

DECEMBER 4

I was in the Spirit on the Lord's day, and heard behind me a great voice, as of a trumpet, Saying, I am Alpha and Omega, the first and the last...
Revelation 1:10-11

Why is this repeated? After all, John said the same thing just two verses earlier. I suggest it is because most people don't struggle with the Alpha or the Omega. They know God looked at creation and declared it good. And they know in the end, in heaven, things will be good. But where people have a hard time is in the middle. They question and struggle with the things going on presently. 'Why is this happening? Why didn't God do this? Where was God when that happened?' they cry.

So what does a pastor, a theologian, a poet do? He whispers in people's ears over and over again: God is in control. God is on the throne. The same God who did the good work in the beginning is here in the middle and will come through in the end.

And that's what we must do. We must whisper over and over in the ears of our teenagers, our friends, our neighbors, 'God is here, and He's going to see you through.'

DECEMBER 5

And I turned to see the voice that spake with me...
Revelation 1:12

The Christian experience is a journey if we choose to be like John on Patmos, who, when he heard something behind him didn't say, 'Oh well, I know the Bible. After all, I wrote a good part of it,' but instead, turned to see what this meant.

Jesus was One who lived His entire life 'turning to see.'

'What I see the Father do, that I do,' He declared in John 5:19— nothing more, nothing less, nothing else.

Wouldn't this be a radical way for us to live—to base all of our analyses, judgments, and evaluations solely on what we see of the Father?

'The judgment I make is right because I judge on the basis of what I hear from the Father,' Jesus said.

What if we did the same? What if, before I gave my two cents' worth about a person, I said, 'Wait. I'm going to make no evaluation, no judgment until I talk to the Father'? What would that do?

May we be a people who love the Lord and are led by the Spirit in a fuller, fresher measure—doing what He tells us to do, living as Jesus did.

December 6

I counsel thee to buy of me gold tried in the fire, that thou mayest be rich...

Revelation 3:18

In Bible days, smelters would take the gold brought in from the mines and heat it by fire until it liquefied. After stirring it until the impurities were burned out, they would know the process was complete when the smelter could look into the pot of liquid gold and see the reflection of his own face.

Because Jesus is the Master Smelter, He uses heat as well. So to these people who were impure, carnal, indecisive, and lukewarm, He says, 'Get into the fire. Get into the battle. Engage yourself like you once did in ministry.'

Before the Battle of Trafalgar, knowing this particular battle would determine the fate of Europe, Lord Nelson assembled his men and said, 'In the event you cannot see or read the signals in the heat of battle, know this: no captain in this fleet can do wrong if he places his ship alongside that of an enemy.'

I like that! 'Captains, if you can't read my signals and you don't know what to do, the answer is very simple: engage in battle the first enemy you can find.'

So too, when you feel yourself becoming complacent, get involved in serving, in sharing, in ministering. Determine in your heart to engage yourself once more in the fire of ministry—not because God wants to watch you burn, but because He wants to warm your heart and get you going again.

DECEMBER 7

...And anoint thine eyes with eyesalve, that thou mayest see.

Revelation 3:18

The same Jesus who says, 'Anoint your eyes with eyesalve,' is the One who put mud in the blind man's eyes in John 9. The way of the Great Physician is to allow irritation to produce illumination. 'You're seeing everything in a carnal way,' He says, 'and you need to humble yourself before Me and deal with the mud.'

'Ouch,' we say. 'That mud hurts.'

But in reality, there must be an awareness of the problems in our hearts and the troubles in our souls before we can see.

'Search me, O God,' cried David, 'and see if there be any wicked way in me' (Psalm 51). Listen, if you're feeling Laodicean, if you feel lukewarm, you need to ask the Great Physician to search you, for that will be the eyesalve which will allow you to see clearly.

How long has it been, dear saint, since you've been on your face before the Lord saying, 'Search me concerning the words on my lips, the bitterness in my heart, the thoughts on my mind'? Truly, confession precedes vision as surely as irritation precedes illumination.

DECEMBER 8

And the first beast was like a lion, and the second beast like a calf, and the third beast had a face as a man, and the fourth beast was like a flying eagle.

Revelation 4:7

In Chapters 1 and 2 of the Book of Numbers, God declares that His people were to camp in a certain order as they traveled through the wilderness.

He told the Levites to surround the Tabernacle on the north, south, east, and west sides. Why? Those serving the Lord—whether in their neighborhood, on their campus, or in their church always end up camping closest to where God's glory is. That's the beauty of serving the Lord: you get to camp out closest to His glory because when you're serving Him, sharing your faith, praying for others, or teaching Sunday school, you experience most fully the Chabod—the glory of God. That's why God lets us serve Him. He doesn't need us. Rather, He allows us the privilege to serve because in so doing, we find true fulfillment.

Numbers 2 goes on to say that on each of the four sides were to be three tribes. Judah, Issachar, and Zebulon, numbering 186,400, were to camp on the east side and were known as the Camp of Judah. What is the symbol, the ensign of Judah? The Lion. Why were they on the east side? Because when Jesus comes back, roaring with authority, He's going to come from the East.

Ephraim, Manasseh, and Benjamin, numbering 108,100, were to camp on the west side and were known as the Camp of Ephraim. Their symbol was an ox.

Reuben, Simeon, and Gad, numbering 151,400, were to camp on the south side and were known as the Camp of Reuben, whose symbol was a man.

Dan, Naphtali, and Asher, numbering 157,600, were to camp on the north side and were known as the Camp of Dan, signified by an eagle.

With the largest number of people camped on the east, the smallest number on the west, and an almost identical number of people on the north and south sides of the Tabernacle, the configuration is that of a Cross—which is as applicable practically as it is significant spiritually...

Fearing the approaching Israelites, Balak, king of Moab, hired a prophet named Balaam to curse them.

'No problem,' thought Balaam. 'These people have been idolatrous and rebellious, ungrateful and immoral. Surely God will curse them.'

But Balaam erred greatly in thinking God was angry with His people, for when he opened his mouth to utter a curse over them, all that came out of his mouth was a blessing (Numbers 23-24).

Why? Because as he looked over the camp of Israel from the high places of Baal, what did Balaam see?

A Cross.

So too, we think we deserve to be cursed because we rebel, murmur, and complain; we don't do what we should, and instead, do what we shouldn't. But God looks upon us and sees us in light of the Cross. Therefore, all He desires to do is bless us.

DECEMBER 9

...And they rest not day and night, saying, Holy, holy, holy, Lord God Almighty, which was, and is, and is to come.

Revelation 4:8

Why 'Holy, Holy, Holy'? Because God is Triune—Father, Son, and Spirit. The word 'holy' means 'whole'—not eroded by sin, not falling apart at the seams, not hypocritical or flawed in any way. And it is this holiness, this wholeness, which causes the cherubim to fall down in worship. Then, rising to go their way, they see Him again and bow again in ecstasy and awe, and on and on it goes perpetually—not because the cherubim are some kind of wind-up angels programmed to do this, but because they are totally overwhelmed by the beauty of holiness (Psalm 29:2).

Truly, there is nothing as lovely as holiness in a man or woman, in a church or family—for, without even being able to identify it, people are attracted to it. Oh, they might be enamored or seduced by evil or darkness for a season—but when judgment comes, people hate it. Holiness, on the other hand, never becomes disillusioning or disappointing. The more holy a person, family, or congregation is—the more satisfying they are.

Full of vision and insight, the cherubim understand this. And that's why they can't take their eyes off this One who is holy.

DECEMBER 10

*...For thou hast created all things, and for thy pleasure
they are and were created.*

Revelation 4:11

Why is worship so important?

First, worship is the program in heaven. If you want heaven in your heart tonight or heaven in your home—if you feel as if you're trapped in a hellish situation at work or in a terrible situation in a relationship—you can bring heaven into it by worshipping.

Secondly, worship is the purpose of creation. You see, everything exists for one reason: to please God. Therefore, to the extent you please Him is the extent to which you will experience fulfillment in the deepest part of your soul.

How do we worship? The word itself tells us. *Proskuneo* in Greek, means 'to turn and kiss.' Thus, true worship is any sincere expression intended for the Lord's pleasure. Worship is the program in heaven, the purpose of creation on earth. May His will be done in our lives, as it is in heaven.

DECEMBER 11

*And one of the elders saith unto me, Weep not: behold,
the Lion of the tribe of Judah...*

Revelation 5:5

The 'Lion of the tribe of Judah' takes us back to Genesis 49, where Jacob calls his 12 sons together to pronounce a blessing upon them. As he comes to Judah, Jacob likens him to a lion's whelp and then says that power and authority would be his until the coming of Messiah...

The year is A.D. 12. In the springtime, the Romans issue a decree declaring that the Jewish people would no longer be able to carry out capital punishment. The rabbis' response to the decree was immediate because they believed capital punishment was the cornerstone of government as defined in the Noahic Covenant. When they were denied this fundamental aspect of government, and thereby rendered powerless as a nation, the rabbis rushed into the streets of Jerusalem, rending their clothes and smiting their breasts.

In fact, we are told the whole city was filled with the wailing of rabbis who understood that something terrible was happening. The scepter had departed; the authority was gone; and Messiah had not come—or so they thought. For on that very day, guess who was sitting in the temple in Jerusalem as a 12-year-old young Man, confounding the scribes and thinkers on the scene? The Lion of the Tribe of Judah—Jesus Christ.

So too, how often we throw dirt in the air and wail and moan, ripping our clothes and crying, 'Where are You, Lord?'—when He's right in our midst, working everything out perfectly.

DECEMBER 12

And I beheld, and, lo, in the midst of the throne and of the four beasts, and in the midst of the elders, stood a Lamb as it had been slain...

Revelation 5:6

According to Isaiah 52, Jesus' visage is marred more than that of any other man. Marred more than a man in a train wreck, a plane crash, Hiroshima? Yes. You see, it's not only that Jesus' beard was plucked out, that His back was beaten, that His side was pierced, that His wrists were nailed. It's the psychological and spiritual stress He experienced in the Garden of Gethsemane which caused the blood vessels in His face to burst. Jesus experienced marring and scarring in ways we'll never understand until we see Him.

But here is the interesting thing: the terror which would mar Him psychologically and physiologically was neither due to the physical suffering He would endure nor to the blood He would shed. The one thing which terrorized our Hero was that He knew He would, for a time, lose contact with His Father as He who knew no sin became sin for us.

We shudder at the thought of hearing our boss say, 'You're through,' or of our girlfriend saying, 'Goodbye.' But if someone were to say, 'You're going to lose fellowship with the Father for a day,' we wouldn't care. Why is it that we are nonchalant about that which terrified Jesus—and we are fearful about that which He said 'Let not your hearts be troubled'?

Jesus was close *to* His Father,
Drew His life *from* His Father,
Was in love *with* His Father.

That's why He bled from His face at the thought of being out of fellowship with His Father for even a short period of time. That's why He asked that this particular cup be taken from Him. That's why He was marred more than any other man in history. Truly, when we see Jesus, we'll be awed, amazed, and broken by what He did to get us to heaven.

DECEMBER 13

And the shapes of the locusts were like unto horses prepared unto battle; and on their heads were as it were crowns like gold, and their faces were as the faces of men. And they had hair as the hair of women, and their teeth were as the teeth of lions. And they had breastplates, as it were breastplates of iron; and the sound of their wings was as the sound of chariots of many horses running to battle. And they had tails like unto scorpions, and there were stings in their tails: and their power was to hurt men five months.

Revelation 9:7-10

Even this description of bizarre and horrific demons would remind John's congregation of God's promise. You see, in Joel 2, we find a parallel passage to Revelation 9...

Historically, the prophecy of Joel 2 was fulfilled in Joel's day when Israel was besieged with locusts.

Symbolically, the prophecy was fulfilled in 722 B.C. when the Assyrians marched south and carried the ten northern tribes into captivity.

Prophetically, the locusts speak of the demons which will be released from the *abussos* (bottomless pit) in Revelation 9.

But nestled among the dire warnings of this terrible invasion is a wonderful promise...

And I will restore to you the years that the locust hath eaten, the cankerworm, and the caterpillar, and the palmerworm, my great army which I sent among you. And ye shall eat in plenty, and be satisfied, and praise the name of the LORD your God, that hath dealt wondrously with you: and my people shall never be ashamed.

Joel 2:25-26

Gang, whenever we obey Scripture—when we listen to the trumpet, repent, and seek the Lord with sincerity—the Lord not only forgives us, but makes up to us what was lost. Amazing! I would have thought it would be enough for God to forgive us. But He says, 'No, I'm going to do more than that. I will restore to you what the locusts ate.'

You might be 50-years-old—or 60, 70, or 80—and you might be saying, 'There's a big chunk of my life eaten away by grasshoppers.' Good news for you: whenever you choose to humble yourself and call out to the Lord, He'll make up for lost time.

DECEMBER 14

And he said unto me, thou must prophesy again before
many peoples, and nations, and tongues, and kings.
Revelation 10:11

The idea of 'must' here is not a command, but a statement of what will inevitably happen when one takes in the Word. How do you know you've really heard the Word? When you have compassion for the sinner and/or conviction of your sin.

'Then why go to Bible study?' you ask. 'Who wants a bitter belly? I want sweetness.' And I understand this...

I'm watching CNN on TV when a commercial for Compassion International suddenly appears: Sally Struthers showing starving kids in Africa or Southeast Asia.

'Oh, no,' I say to myself. 'I don't want to deal with this now.' Click. Sally disappears. So do the kids.

That's what people do with church and devotions and witnessing. 'I don't want to go anymore,' they say. 'It makes my belly hurt.' Click,

Wednesday night Bible study—gone. Click, Thursday morning worship—gone. Click, devotions—gone. 'I don't want to deal with this sin, these attitudes, that cynicism. Just give me the sweet stuff.'

But you know what happens to those people? Their lives begin to unravel because staying in the Word is the only way to experience prosperity and success (Joshua 1:8). Yes, it will trouble you. No doubt it may upset you. But as time goes on, you will begin to see that your life is centered and grounded, fruitful and prosperous because the Word always does its work.

My prayer is that we will be those who, like John, devour and digest Scripture—the bitter portions as well as the sweet—in order that we, like John, would impact our world for the Kingdom.

DECEMBER 15

And after three days and an half the Spirit of life from God entered into them, and they stood upon their feet; and great fear fell upon them which saw them. And they heard a great voice from heaven saying unto them, Come up hither. And they ascended up to heaven in a cloud; and their enemies beheld them.
Revelation 11:11-12

These witnesses are examples of what you can be in the last days in which we live. You're to share the Gospel with people. Yes, you'll be beat up emotionally and verbally, ostracized, left out, not invited to the party. But you know what will happen? Three and a half days later, you'll rise. There will be a spring in your step and joy in your heart as you find yourself soaring emotionally. Truly, gang, there is nothing, nothing, nothing like sharing your faith. Even if you're put down, beat up, left out, you'll find yourself revived.

If you feel your relationship with the Lord is stagnant or tedious—witness. I guarantee, like the two witnesses in Revelation 11, you'll be caught up into heavenly places. Witnessing is the single most important way I have found to see my own faith revived and renewed.

Jesus didn't tell us to preach the Gospel because He wants us to be miserable. On the contrary, He said, 'Give, and it shall be given unto you; good measure, pressed down, and shaken together, and running over, shall men give into your bosom. For with the same measure that ye mete withal it shall be measured to you again' (Luke 6:38).

DECEMBER 16

And to the woman were given two wings of a great eagle, that she might fly into the wilderness, into her place, where she is nourished for a time, and times, and half a time, from the face of the serpent.
Revelation 12:14

After choosing a site on a rocky cliff sometimes thousands of feet above the ground, a mother eagle constructs her nest. For protection, she arranges sharp sticks along the perimeter, but inside, the nest is soft and comfortable for the eggs. So, when Ernie Eaglet pops out of his shell, he find his accommodations quite to his liking. 'Wow! What a view!'

And with Mama Eagle dropping breakfast, lunch, dinner, and an after-dinner mint into his beak every day, he's a happy eaglet indeed—until his girth increases and he begins to bump into the sharp sticks Mama purposefully placed around the nest. Suddenly, the once-cozy abode becomes a little uncomfortable.

The same goes for us. When what was once so cozy—that group you were in, those people you were linked to, the job you had—gets a little irritating, you may have a tendency to grumble. But you must realize God does this intentionally because He will not allow you to perpetually nest in a place of fatness and flightlessness.

Then, just when Ernie thinks he can't stand one more poke, Mama Eagle comes and, with her powerful wings, bumps the nest—sending Ernie tumbling out. Flapping his little wings frantically yet futilely, he falls hundreds of feet and is about to crash when Mama Eagle scoops him up on her wings and takes him back to the nest.

'Whew! What was *that* about?' Ernie wonders.

And for a couple of days, he's happy again, being served breakfast, brunch, lunch, and dinner. But then the pesky sticks begin to bother him again, and after a couple of days—bump goes the nest, and out he falls. Once more, right when he thinks his life is over, there's Mom bearing him on her wings, returning him to the nest. Now Ernie's really wondering. 'Every time I get comfortable, every time I settle back in, Mama comes and turns my nest over. What kind of parent is she, anyway?' Yet the process is repeated five or six times, until one day—Ernie soars. And as he does, he understands the pokes, the overturned nest, the perilous plummeting were all about spurring him to do what he never would have done on his own. They were all about teaching him to fly.

Precious saint, if you've been flapping or squawking or crying, this word is for you: God says, 'I found you in a wasteland. You are the apple of My eye. I've got nothing but the best in My heart for you. You're not going to crash. I'll always be there to catch you. But I'm going to continue working with you that you might fly.'

As a result, I am slowly learning not to be quite as squawky, quite as angry, quite as fearful—but to remember the plan of the Father to bear me on eagle's wings. The pokey sticks are preparatory for the overturning of the nest. And the overturned nest is absolutely essential to teach me to fly.

DECEMBER 17

Here is the patience and the faith of the saints.
Revelation 13:10

Do you realize how blessed we are tonight because we know the end of the story? You may be in a difficult marriage, persecuted on the job, fighting illness, undergoing severe pressures financially, or weary of your flesh which rears its ugly head constantly. But we know one day it will all be solved. That's what John told his people. And that's what the Spirit would say to us tonight. We who have been saved awhile take this for granted—but what if this was the first time you understood that all which plagues you presently will be gone in a heartbeat; that you're going to heaven where everything will be wonderful forever and ever?

'If any man have an ear, let him hear. Listen up,' says Pastor John. 'I don't care if you miss everything else, get this: the forces against you are soon going to be done away with: the beast, persecution, problems, will undo themselves.'

That's why I need to read the Book of Revelation over and over again. It's not about getting the mark of the Beast rap down. It's not written to help us figure out who the false prophet or antichrist is. It's written to give us hope and to bring us back constantly to the fact that life is short, and we'll be in heaven soon. The person who doesn't understand the Book of Revelation will go through life in his own personal Tribulation. The person who grabs hold of Revelation, on the other hand, will live in a state of anticipation and celebration. Every one of us will either go through this week in tribulation or celebration.

Life is short.
The Lord is in control.
We're going to heaven.
That's what this Book is about.

DECEMBER 18

And I heard a voice from heaven, as the voice of many waters, and as the voice of a great thunder: and I heard the voice of harpers harping with their harps: And they sung as it were a new song before the throne, and before the four beasts, and the elders: and no man could learn that song but the hundred and forty and four thousand, which were redeemed from the earth.

Revelation 14:2-3

Why could no one else sing the song of the 144,000? Because they alone went through testing and Tribulation, yet maintained their integrity. Thus, they alone could sing of what they were able to observe the Father do on their behalf in the time of Tribulation. Every one of us goes through times of tribulation. God's intention is that they might produce in us 'as it were, a new song'—a symphony...

There they were—in a damp, dark dungeon—without even a crust of bread to eat or the ACLU to plead their case. Yet what were they doing? They were singing. At midnight—in the darkest hour—Paul and Silas sang. They weren't singing to try and get God to do something. They sang simply because the Lord was with them, and they were happy (Acts 16:25).

'Well, that hasn't been my experience,' you might be saying. 'My marriage,' or 'my job,' or 'my health is a dungeon to me, and I'm not happy.'

Precious brother, dear sister—God's intent is to give you a new song. But there's one thing which will stand in the way: sympathy.

You see, I can either go through challenges and hard times with a symphony in my heart because the Lord has promised not only to strengthen me in them (Isaiah 41:10), but to walk with me through them (Matthew 28:20)—or I can choose to get sympathy from people.

If I choose to tap into sympathy, it will always be at God's expense because the underlying though unspoken implication is that what is happening in my life is out of God's control.

God is totally, absolutely, completely faithful to meet us in every trial, in every difficulty. Don't let His plan get short-circuited by those who say, 'I feel sorry for you.' Instead say, 'God is good. Sure, what I'm dealing with right now is a challenge—but I am discovering the Father is exactly who He claimed to be—a God who comforts me completely.'

It's tempting to let people feel sorry for us, but we mustn't because it puts God in a bad light. Don't settle for sympathy, gang. Go for the symphony.

DECEMBER 19

> *...And he shall be tormented with fire and brimstone in the presence of the holy angels, and in the presence of the Lamb: And the smoke of their torment ascendeth up for ever and ever: and they have no rest day nor night, who worship the beast and his image, and whosoever receiveth the mark of his name.*
>
> *Revelation 14:10-11*

Those who suggest either that hell is not a literal place or that it won't last for eternity haven't read the Bible. In fact, Jesus taught more on hell than He did on heaven. That is why this angel cries with a loud voice, warning people to reject the mark of the beast.

Hell is real. It's not a game. I think of the 20th chapter of Isaiah, where a most amazing thing happens...

Although the Assyrians were headed in their direction, the people of Israel didn't take the threat seriously. 'Oh, come on,' they thought. 'Certainly we won't be wiped out by the Assyrians.'

So God said to Isaiah—the eloquent orator, the educated, articulate prophet—'The stakes are high. But the people aren't listening. So I want you to take off your sandals, take off your clothes, and walk naked throughout this region for three years.'

Now, whether this was three years continually, or three years sporadically, Bible scholars disagree. But the fact remains that stately Isaiah did in fact obey. Why was he told to do this? Because the people had grown so callused to the prophets' words, they weren't heeding the message. So God used this bold move to get their attention and to illustrate the fact that, as captives of the Assyrians, the Israelites would be led naked across the desert into captivity.

Like Isaiah, we too live in crucial times, gang. You have relatives; I have friends; we have co-workers who are going to hell because, like the Israelites, they have become callused to the threat of hell. But the stakes are too high for us just to say, 'Well, whatever.' No, we must share the naked truth with them—not baring our bodies, but baring our souls.

'But they'll laugh at me,' you say.
What do you think they did to Isaiah?

Here in Revelation, the angels preach with a loud voice, 'Don't take the mark. You'll be tormented forever.'

People are in tribulation even today. Share the everlasting Gospel with them, and, like the angels, you'll soar in heavenly places.

I guarantee it!

DECEMBER 20

...And in his hand a sharp sickle. And another angel came out of the temple, crying with a loud voice to him that sat on the cloud, Thrust in thy sickle, and reap: for the time is come for thee to reap; for the harvest of the earth is ripe. And he that sat on the cloud thrust in his sickle on the earth; and the earth was reaped.

Revelation 14:14-16

According to this passage, it would seem that there comes a point in the Tribulation when salvation is no longer possible. The 144,000 have been called to heaven; the angels have made their proclamation; and now there will be a separation between those who become Christians in the Tribulation and those who don't.

So too, in your own tribulation you need to understand there comes a time when your own heart—even as a believer—can become hardened.

The Bible speaks of a root of bitterness which can take hold in the soil of a man's soul (Hebrews 12:15). I've seen believers go through tribulation and, rather than allow the Lord's work of grace to take place in their hearts, choose instead to be bitter and unforgiving.

Don't let that happen. Don't be unforgiving. Don't be cynical. Don't be bitter. Don't play that game because if you let bitterness and unforgiveness continue, there will come a point in your own tribulation when it will become an irreversible part of who you are.

DECEMBER 21

...And them that had gotten the victory over the beast, and over his image, and over his mark, and over the number of his name, stand on the sea of glass, having the harps of God.

Revelation 15:2

It is intriguing to me that those who lose their lives in the Tribulation because they choose to listen to the message of the 144,000 and believe God rather than take the mark of the beast or bow before the image are seen not *around*, but *on* the sea of glass.

Why does this intrigue me? Because it reminds me of another tribulation...

Out on the sea with the wind blowing and the waves rolling, the disciples were understandably terrified. Seeing the Lord walking towards them, Peter cries, 'Lord, if that's really You, bid me come.'

Jesus said, 'Come,' and Peter did just that (Matthew 14:28).

So too, in our text, these guys are walking on water. On earth they didn't.

Having been persecuted and destroyed by antichrist, on earth they would have been seen as losers. Not so in heaven. In heaven, they're water-walkers.

If you don't factor in heaven, none of Biblical Christianity works. Without heaven, folks, you're going to go down the wrong path in your experience of spiritual life. You've got to factor heaven into every single equation.

If you get nothing else out of the Book of Revelation, my prayer would be that you would first of all see Jesus Christ on the throne in control, and secondly, that you'd understand it's all about *heaven*.

DECEMBER 22

And one of the four beasts gave unto the seven angels seven golden vials full of the wrath of God, who liveth for ever and ever. And the temple was filled with smoke from the glory of God, and from his power; and no man was able to enter into the temple, till the seven plagues of the seven angels were fulfilled.

Revelation 15:7-8

Knowing that sin bites, burns, brutalizes, and butchers His children (Romans 6:23), God sends His surgical team of angels with vials of the bitter medicine of judgment in their hands in order to deal with the sin that destroys humanity.

In a parallel passage, we see David dealing with the repercussions of his own sin following his adulterous relationship with Bathsheba, and the subsequent murder of her husband, Uriah...

Purge me with hyssop, and I shall be clean: wash me, and I shall be whiter than snow. Make me to hear joy and gladness; that the bones which thou hast broken may rejoice.

Psalm 51:7-8

When a lamb repeatedly jeopardized his own safety by continually wandering away from the flock, the shepherd would break its leg. Then, throughout the healing process, the shepherd would carry the heretofore straying lamb on his shoulder, during which time something amazing transpired in the lamb.

You see, when after five or six weeks, his bone could again support his weight, the lamb remained close to the shepherd, never to wander again—not because he feared another broken bone, but because he had become attached to the shepherd. So it is as a shepherd that David cries, 'Lord, I know that the bones which Thou hast broken shall rejoice again.'

Precious people, if we wander away and continue in sin, the Good Shepherd will do what He did with David, and what David did with his own sheep: He'll break the bone of our self-sufficiency in order to force us to draw close to Him in ways we never would have otherwise.

But lest you think the vials of judgment about to be poured out in the Tribulation are still unfair, take another look at our Shepherd, and you'll realize that the Good Shepherd is also the Lamb of God, who suffered not a broken bone, but a broken body and a broken heart as He died for our sin.

December 23

And I heard another out of the altar say, Even so, Lord
God Almighty, true and righteous are thy judgments.
Revelation 16:7

The phrase 'another out of' does not appear in the original Greek text. Thus, newer translations correctly render this verse: 'And I heard the altar say, Even so, Lord God Almighty, true and righteous are thy judgments.' Now whether this voice be figurative or literal, I cannot say. But this much is sure: the voice which cries, 'True and righteous are thy judgments, O Lord,' originates at the altar.

In our own times of trial and tribulation, there can be a tendency within us to question the fairness of the Father.

But the altar, the place of sacrifice—the Cross—speaks just the opposite.

If you don't see this, you'll go through life one day blessing the Lord in the amphitheater and the next day cursing Him because of your troubles at work.

God demonstrated His love for us in that while we were yet sinners, Christ died for us (Romans 5:8). Therefore, I must look at every trial I face, every hard time I endure through the lens of God's love as shown on the altar of Calvary.

'What shall we say then...He that spared not his own Son, but delivered him up for us all, how shall he not with him also freely give us all things?' (Romans 8:31-32). Because God loved me enough to hang on the Cross in my place, to pay for my sin, to die for me, I know everything He does in my life—whether or not I understand it at the time—is *right*.

If I complain about my job, boss, paycheck, kids, singleness, employees—it only means I am not listening to the cry of the altar, that I have forgotten Calvary. Allow the Cross to 'altar' your view, precious people, as you look at everything in the light of Calvary.

DECEMBER 24

...And glory, and honour, and power, unto the Lord our God: For true and righteous are his judgments: for he hath judged the great whore, which did corrupt the earth with her fornication, and hath avenged the blood of his servants at her hand.

Revelation 19:1-2

The people on earth wail following the destruction of Babylon. But heaven rejoices. Why? Because, although the natural tendency of people is to say, 'Wasn't that a bit brutal, Lord? Did You really have to drop 100-pound hailstones? Wouldn't 30-pounders have done the job? What are You doing, Lord? Why do You allow such difficulty, tragedy, pain?'—Chapter 19 shows us there is no such questioning in heaven. It's not because there's a 'No Questioning Allowed' sign in heaven—but rather in heaven, the full picture becomes clear. And what seemed to be so terrible, painful, and unnecessary on earth will seem brilliant and perfect and righteous from the vantage of heaven.

The same is true regarding trials in our lives presently. Why doesn't the Lord just show us the whole story now? Because He is teaching you, forcing me to learn to walk by faith and not by sight. Why? Because He knows that developing faith in you and me is absolutely necessary in light of what we will be doing throughout eternity.

DECEMBER 25

> *...And behold a white horse; and he that sat upon him was called Faithful and True, and in righteousness he doth judge and make war. His eyes were as a flame of fire...*
>
> *Revelation 19:11-12*

Based on I Corinthians 3:12-13, I used to think there would be a great big oven in heaven, a kiln of some sort into which all my works would be shoveled. The wood and hay and stubble would burn, while the gold and silver and precious stones would remain.

But in light of our text, I no longer expect an oven. Instead, I expect Jesus will just look at me, and everything in my life that is worthless will ignite and disappear. I've got *cords* of wood, *bales* of hay, *truckloads* of stubble—and I'm so thankful that with one look from my Lord, they will all go up in smoke.

'Take your only son to Mount Moriah,' God commanded Abraham (Genesis 22:2). God didn't even acknowledge Ishmael as Abraham's son because Ishmael was a product of Abraham's flesh, while Isaac was the product of God's faithfulness.

I love this because most of us have a bunch of Ishmaels running around—things we've done in our flesh while trying to help God. But God doesn't even acknowledge them. Glorious will be the day when He'll look at me with His eyes of fire, warming my heart and melting the junk.

DECEMBER 26

...And shall be tormented day and night for ever and ever.

Revelation 20:10

The cartoons are wrong, and Hollywood is terribly mistaken when they present hell as a hot place where people play poker and talk to each other amidst flickering flames and an occasional jab by Satan's pitchfork. You see, in addition to being called a lake of fire, hell is called a place of outer darkness (Matthew 8:12). Consequently, the torment in a place so dark even the flames of the lake of fire don't shed any light is exceeded only by the inner torment people feel throughout eternity as they recall the sermons they heard and the invitations to salvation they ignored.

Jesus said specifically that hell was not created for people but for the devil and his angels (Matthew 25:41). Peter said God is not willing that *any* should perish (II Peter 3:9)—but—

God, being Light, if man says, 'I don't want God,' he will be consigned to darkness;

God, being health, if man says, 'I don't want God,' he will be relinquished to a place of pain;

God, being a Father, if man says, 'I don't want God,' he will spend eternity in isolation.

God, on the other hand, says, 'I would rather die than live without you.' And He did just that when He died on the Cross in order that, forgiven of our sins, we might live with Him forever.

December 27

...And the books were opened: and another book was opened, which is the book of life: and the dead were judged out of those things which were written in the books, according to their works. And the sea gave up the dead which were in it; and death and hell delivered up the dead which were in them: and they were judged every man according to their works.

Revelation 20:12-13

If you're a Christian, your name is written in the Book of Life. The names of those who said, 'I didn't buy into that Christian stuff they were always trying to cram down my throat,' or 'I needed my space,' or 'I had to explore various aspects of spirituality,' aren't.

'But I lived a pretty good life,' they'll protest.
Yet the books wherein are recorded the reasons for everything they ever did will prove otherwise...

'I was an outstanding member of Rotary.'
Yes—but the books indicate it was to make some business contacts.

'Oh, but I gave blood.'
Perhaps—but the books indicate you were paid $25 in return.

'But I saved the whales, marched for peace, built homes for the homeless.'
All well and good—but you did so to hear the applause of men.

You see, God made us in such a way that we are spared from remembering the sins we have committed. He let us remember enough sin to make us aware of our need for salvation—but not every motive, every word of gossip, every cutting comment, every angry feeling. When the books are opened, the utter weight of all one's sin will come to light. God sends no one to hell. By the time Volume 167 of one's sins is opened, it's as if he cries, 'Depart from me for I am a sinful man,' and sends himself to the lake of fire.

That's why I am so glad I'm saved. The Bible says the 'handwriting of ordinances that was against us'—all of our mistakes, sins, and failures—were blotted out by the blood of Jesus Christ (Colossians 2:14). In other words, the pages and pages containing my sin are all illegible because they're covered with the red blood of Jesus.

DECEMBER 28

He that overcometh shall inherit all things...
Revelation 21:7

Secondly, we see responsibility. The inheritance here is that of a father who's sharing the family business with his son. Thus, the inheritance spoken of incorporates not only acquisition, but administration. That is, in eternity, there will not only be stuff to acquire, but things to do. In Luke 19, Jesus says if we're faithful in our responsibilities here on earth, we'll be given cities to rule over in the ages to come eternally.

'I'm not really into ruling,' you might be thinking.

Listen, the things you really wish you could do here but can't will, I believe, be your area of rule, your responsibility in heaven. Some of you are master mechanics and find total satisfaction in tearing down and rebuilding an engine. Others are authors, artists, or athletes who never seem to have enough time to do what you love because of your responsibilities here on earth. I believe those are the very areas with which you will be involved eternally—or else why would God have given you those desires and gifts in the first place?

Those of you who feel life has passed you by without your ever being able to do what you really loved—take heart! I believe the time is coming when you will be ruling in heaven in the very arena which intrigues you here on earth.

DECEMBER 29

And I John saw these things, and heard them. And when I had heard and seen, I fell down to worship before the feet of the angel which shewed me these things. Then saith he unto me, See thou do it not: for I am thy fellowservant, and of thy brethren the prophets, and of them which keep the sayings of this book: worship God.

Revelation 22:8-9

The interesting thing to me about this is that the same thing happened just a couple pages earlier in Chapter 19, where, after he fell down and worshipped an angel, the angel said to John, 'See thou do it not.'

So how could John worship an angel *again*? The same way we make the same mistakes, commit the same sins over and over and over again.

But the good news is that the Lord taught us to forgive so many times that we lose count (Matthew 18:22). And if He taught us to forgive to that degree, how much more will He!

'Oh, Lord, I blew it again,' I cry.

'Again?' He says, 'What are you talking about? I don't remember you blowing it before' (Hebrews 8:12).

If a man suddenly charged up these steps and punched me in the nose, that I could forgive him is within the realm of possibility. But I would never, ever forget it. I don't have that capability. Only God can say, 'I'll not only forgive you, but I won't remember your sin.'

You see, so precious, so powerful is the blood of Jesus to the Father, that it obliterates every trace and memory of sin. I love that! It's what gives me such boldness to come before the throne of grace, that I may obtain mercy, and find grace to help in time of need (Hebrews 4:16).

DECEMBER 30

And the Spirit and the bride say, Come. And let him that heareth say, Come. And let him that is athirst come. And whosoever will, let him take the water of life freely.

Revelation 22:17

The invitation to 'Come' is not given to the Lord, but rather to a world which is lost and dying, doomed and damned. It is the Spirit who woos people to Jesus; but we, as the Bride, have the privilege of issuing the invitation.

Throughout Scripture, 'Come' has always been the invitation...

'*Come* now, and let us reason together, saith the Lord...' (Isaiah 1: 18, emphasis mine).

'Ho everyone that thirsteth, *come* ye to the waters...' (Isaiah 55:1, emphasis mine).

'*Come* unto Me, all ye that labour and are heavy laden...' (Matthew 11:28, emphasis mine).

'Suffer the little children to *come* unto Me...' (Mark 10:14, emphasis mine).

'*Come* and see...' (John 1:39, emphasis mine).

DECEMBER 31

And if any man shall take away from the words of the book of this prophecy, God shall take away his part out of the book of life, and out of the holy city, and from the things which are written in this book. He which testifieth these things saith, Surely I come quickly. Amen. Even so, come, Lord Jesus. The grace of our Lord Jesus Christ be with you all. Amen.

Revelation 22:19-21

The last phrase in the Old Testament is, 'Lest I come and smite thee with a curse' (Malachi 4:6). That's the Law. 'God is upset. You should be doing more. What's wrong with you?'

But the New Testament ends this way: 'The grace of our Lord Jesus Christ be with you all.' *Grace* is the final word of the New Testament. 'Grace be with you ALL.'

Seek first the Kingdom, gang.
Set your heart on things above.
His coming is nigh.

And I can't wait!